SOMETHING NEW IN THE AIR

McGILL-QUEEN'S NATIVE AND NORTHERN SERIES
Bruce G. Trigger, Editor

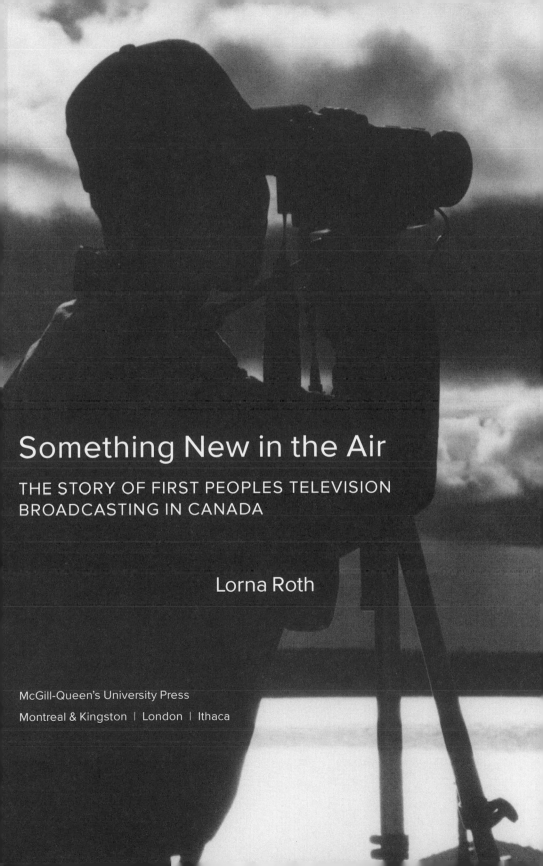

Something New in the Air

THE STORY OF FIRST PEOPLES TELEVISION
BROADCASTING IN CANADA

Lorna Roth

McGill-Queen's University Press

Montreal & Kingston | London | Ithaca

© McGill-Queen's University Press 2005
ISBN 0-7735-2824-5 (cloth)
ISBN 0-7735-2856-3 (paper)

Legal deposit second quarter 2005
Bibliothèque nationale du Québec

Printed in Canada on acid-free paper that is 100% ancient forest free (100% post-consumer recycled), processed chlorine free

This book has been published with the help of a grant from the Canadian Federation for the Humanities and Social Sciences, through the Aid to Scholarly Publications Programme, using funds provided by the Social Sciences and Humanities Research Council of Canada. Funding has also been received from the Dean's Office, Concordia University.

McGill-Queen's University Press acknowledges the support of the Canada Council for the Arts for our publishing program. We also acknowledge the financial support of the Government of Canada through the Book Publishing Industry Development Program (BPIDP) for our publishing activities.

Title page: Kevin Gargan photographed by Kelly Reinhardt. Used with permission of the Native Communications Society of the Western NWT.

CANADIAN CATALOGUING IN PUBLICATION

Roth, Lorna Frances, 1947–
Something new in the air : the story of First Peoples television broadcasting in Canada / Lorna Roth.
(McGill-Queen's native and northern series ; 43)
Includes bibliographical references and index.
ISBN 0-7735-2824-5 (bound). – ISBN 0-7735-2856-3 (pbk.)
1. Aboriginal television broadcasting – Canada – History.   2. Television broadcasting – Canada – History.   3. Television broadcasting policy – Canada – History.   4. Television broadcasting – Canada, Northern – History.   5. Television broadcasting policy – Canada, Northern – History.   6. Native peoples – Canada.   7. Intercultural communication – Canada.   8. Television Northern Canada.   9. Aboriginal Peoples Television Network. I. Title. II. Series.
PN1992.3.C3R68 2005   388.55'089'97071   C2005-900808-3

Set in 10.5/13 .5 Adobe Minion Pro with Mark Simonson's Proxima Sans
Book design and typesetting by zijn digital

DEDICATION

I would like to dedicate this book to the memory of my parents —

To SYLVIA KOTOFSKY ROTH (1915–91),
whose respect for and belief in crosscultural communications
was an inspiration to my life and work;

To MORRIS ROTH (1906–94),
who never quite understood why I didn't go to Florida instead;

and

To the diverse First Peoples of the North and South
without whose passionate interest, cooperation, and generous
hospitality this research could never have been completed.

This book's for you ...

Contents

Tables and Maps

Illustrations

Acknowledgments

As I sat down to write these acknowledgments, even I was surprised at how many people and institutions have been involved in the process of my researching and writing this book over the last twenty years. Many apologies if I've left someone out. I would first like to thank the following institutions for their significant financial contributions to this project: The Association for Canadian Studies Writing Assistance Program, the Social Sciences and Humanities Research Council of Canada; the Division of Graduate Studies, Concordia University, for their J.W. McConnell Memorial Fellowship; Concordia University's Faculty of Arts and Science – in particular, Dr Martin Singer for his support of this writing project; and the Northern Scientific Training Program of the Department of Indian and Northern Affairs.

On a more personal level, I particularly want to acknowledge the dedicated support of Gail Valaskakis, friend and colleague, for her engaging and enriching intellectual discussions about Northern communications over many years. My sincere thanks also to my dear friends and extended family members – Lon Dubinsky, Philip Szporer, Marc Raboy, Bill Gilsdorf, Nina Gregg, Kathryn Harvey, Valerie Alia, Heather Menzies, Didier Giovannangeli, Warren Palmer, Tom Wilson, Tom Axtell, Sean St. George, George Hargrave, Irene Halikas, Nicole Montpetit, Fo Niemi, Faye Ginsburg, Ron Blumer (who initially turned my interests Northward in the mid-1970s), and Ron Sloan for their ongoing conversations with me about this work. Jamasie Teemotie, Jimmy Naumealuk, and Joanasie Salomonie, all of whom are no longer with us, inspired me to move forward to explore the Northern media imaginary. To them, I am grateful for their timely friendship and interest in my research.

To my sister Rella Roth Caplan, my nieces, Sarah, Debbie, and my brother-in-law Fred Caplan, with whom I have not had much time to spend over the last years, I welcome the opportunity to experience unclouded moments with you again.

At Northern Native Broadcasting, Yukon, I am especially indebted to George Henry, whose lengthy discussions with me were invaluable to my thinking about this material. I would also like to thank Ken Kane, Joanne Henry, Bob Charlie, Jan Staples, Lantry Vaughn, and Frank Fry. Outside of NNBY, but still in the Yukon, many thanks to Carol Geddes and Shirley Adamson. Also much appreciated was the friendship and hospitality of the late Sarah Gaunt during my field research in the Yukon.

At TVNC, a heartfelt thanks to Lorraine Thomas, Jerry Giberson (also at APTN), and Ken Todd; at IBC, Rosemarie Kuptana (former president) and Debbie Brisebois have been most generous with their information over the years. I really enjoyed all of the time spent with members of the staff at Northern Native Broadcast Access Program, particularly Florence Woolner (former chief of the program), Art King (present chief), and Terry Rudden (former regional coordinator), whose cheerful responses to my numerous questions were always appreciated.

At APTN, my interviews with Abe Tagalik, Dan David, Jennifer David, Pat Tourigny, Jerry Giberson, and Jim Compton were informative and useful. Many thanks for your generous donations of time, energy, historical materials, and support for this work.

For technical assistance, I want to thank Linnet Fawcett for her excellent editorial work, Robert de Leskie for his early contributions to the transformation of this manuscript from a thesis to a book, and Emily Moody, Christiana Abraham, Natalie Kallio, Naomi Angel, Ricardo Andres Garza, and Genevieve Lycke for their administrative assistance. Also many thanks to Aurèle Parisien and Joan McGilvray at McGill-Queens for their determination and good humour while working with me on the preparation of this manuscript, and to Claude Lalumière for his excellent editing.

Lastly, to Thierry Le Brun, whose encouragement and stimulating intellectual companionship nourished my romancing of this book, I want to say … the flowers worked.

Acronyms

ACP	Accelerated Coverage Plan
AFN	Assembly of First Nations
ANCS	Alberta Native Communications Society
APTN	Aboriginal Peoples Television Network
Cancom	Canadian Satellite Communications Incorporated
CBC	Canadian Broadcasting Corporation
CRC	Communication Research Centre
CRTC	Canadian Radio-Television and Telecommunications Commission, known until 1976 as the Canadian Radio and Television Commission
DBS	Direct Broadcast Satellite
DIAND	Department of Indian Affairs and Northern Development
DIANA	Department of Indian and Northern Affairs
DOC	Department of Communications
DSOS	Department of the Secretary of State
FCP	Frontier Coverage Package
GHz	GigaHertz
HF	High Frequency
IBC	Inuit Broadcasting Corporation

ICC	Inuit Circumpolar Conference
ITC	Inuit Tapirisat of Canada
NABET	National Association of Broadcasting Engineers and Technicians
NACS	National Aboriginal Communications Society
NBP	Northern Broadcasting Policy
NCP	Native Communications Program
NCS	Native Communications Society
NFB	National Film Board of Canada
NNBAP	Northern Native Broadcast Access Program
NNBY	Northern Native Broadcasting, Yukon
NPP	Northern Pilot Project
NQIA	Northern Quebec Inuit Association
NWT	Northwest Territories
PIC-TV	Pond Inlet Community Television
SOS	Secretary of State
TNI	Taqramiut Nipingat Inc.
TVNC	Television Northern Canada
VTR	Videotape recorder

SOMETHING NEW IN THE AIR

Prologue

It's 10 February 1975, and I am in Frobisher Bay, Baffin Island   a former American/Canadian military base town in the Canadian Arctic set up as an administrative centre and service reference point for the Distant Early Warning (DEW) line workers.[1] The temperature outside is about -40 Fahrenheit.

I am working for the National Film Board of Canada (NFB) in one of their two film workshops designed to prepare the Inuit to produce their own television programming. It is three years after CBC television service has been parachuted into the North and there is only one fifteen-minute interview program on the air that directly relates to Inuit interests and is broadcast in Inuktitut.[2]

It is 12:20 on a Tuesday afternoon. I am with a young Inuit man – Jamasie Teemotie, a fourteen-year-old student who studies and hangs out at the workshop. We are on our way to visit his sixty-five-year-old grandfather. I am honoured to have been invited to his home, though I feel more than a little nervous about my ignorance of the appropriate protocol. It is my first visit to the home of a local elderly resident.

We arrive at Mr Teemotie's house at a significant hour – the hour of each day that steals the attention of 98 percent of the residents of Frobisher Bay. It is during this hour – from 12:30 to 1:30 p.m. – that the community stands still. The paths and walkways are abandoned. No vehicles move along the ice-packed roads. The wind blows as usual across the flat terrain, uninterrupted for this one short hour by those quick moving silhouettes of bodies that habitually dot the endless horizon. For it is during this hour, on each and every weekday, that people can be found either sitting in or wandering around their overheated homes: their ears and eyes attentive as *The Edge of Night* – at the time, the most popular soap opera in the North – unfolds on the TV screen before them.

I follow Jamasie into Mr Teemotie's home and look around with curiosity. It is constructed of skidoo-crate wood and patched with snow that fills the cracks and acts as wind proofing. The porch, where we enter, is cold – not much different from the outside temperature, but at least it offers some protection from the howling Arctic winds. Antlers and tools are strewn here and there across the snow floor – these are used for carving, eating, and scraping animal furs. In one corner, there is the carcass of a frozen seal, one third of which has been eaten. In another, there are frozen fur skins, stiffened into a variety of shapes. There is a bench nearby – I imagine that this is where Jamasie's grandfather sits while carving stone or antler, or while cutting meat. The door that leads from the porch into Mr Teemotie's one-room dwelling is slightly ajar. We enter quietly, so as not to disturb him.

Central to the room is a rusted oil barrel with a makeshift pipe chimney cutting through the roof. This provides the home with a source of heat. There is a large, Arborite kitchen table in one corner of the room. Adjacent to this is a wooden platform on top of which three mattresses are piled. This is where Mr Teemotie is seated. Directly facing Mr Teemotie is a chest of drawers; his eyes are fixed on the twenty-one-inch colour Sony television set that sits atop it. As we stand there waiting for Mr Teemotie to acknowledge our arrival, not once do his eyes stray from *The Edge of Night*.

I have never been a fan of soaps, my lifestyle being unsuited to the kind of steady and stable scheduling that they demand. However, I am curious about what attracts others to them, and as I watch Mr Teemotie watching TV I cannot help but wonder what he makes of the program's text and images. He does not understand English, so it cannot be through language that he is creating meaning. Not yet familiar with formal audience reception theories or methods, and still fairly new to the whole realm of field research, I am naively curious: what sense, I wonder, is Mr Teemotie deriving from this cross-cultural source?

After the program is over, Jamasie introduces me to his grandfather. We shyly greet each other and then sit in silence until Jamasie and I depart. I leave with many unanswered questions. What, for instance, does all this mean to Mr Teemotie? And how can I begin to find out to what end he is using television programming? Over time, Jamasie asks his grandfather some of my questions. And with the aid of Mr Teemotie's responses, I begin the long process of assessing and coming to understand some of television's impact upon him.

If Mr Teemotie's access to *The Edge of Night* and other Southern programs was the result of an administrative decision made in Ottawa in 1969 to unify, via domestic satellite, the vast and separated geographical areas of Canada, what I eventually came to understand about Mr Teemotie's actual viewing is this: he was using television as an anthropological field site; he was drawing upon the lifelike texts of the soaps to learn about "qallunaat" or "white people."[3] The drama was appealing, the sex scenes were enticing, and the conflicts were of interest to him. One might say that, through the mediated text of television, he was *looking back* at the anthropology of an *elsewhere* life. He was examining its relationships and its social fabric in order to inform himself about the newest residents in his world about whom he now needed to know more if he was to get on with them, not to mention make life choices *without* their interference.

My first foray into this Northern television environment piqued my interest in finding out more about the cross-cultural impacts and uses of television, about how television can both mediate and be mediated by cultures, and about whether television programming could be indigenized by communities that have not been involved in its original technical creation. Since that initial 1975 visit to Frobisher Bay (later renamed Iqaluit),[4] I have personally been interested and involved in observing, documenting, and analyzing the development of First Peoples[5] communications.

Three years after the launching of the Anik-1 satellite (1972) and two years after it had become operational (1973), there was very little aboriginal-oriented programming on CBC Northern Service television. Radio was a different matter. It had easily adopted Inuktitut (the language of the Inuit) as a second broadcasting language (the other being English) and did not present nearly as much of an outside intrusion into aboriginal cultures and audiences. If, however, CBC Northern Service radio had set the attitudinal context for the arrival of television by its inclusion of native languages as an integral part of its programming schedule, CBC Northern Television turned out to be somewhat of a cultural disappointment. True, there were those who saw it as a linguistic gift in that it helped their English and French speaking skills evolve to a more sophisticated level. But it was certainly not introduced into the North in the convivial manner that radio had been.

I arrived at a significant transitional time with a wide-open mandate from the NFB's Media Research department as well as its *Challenge for Change* program – a federally sponsored interdepartmental program designed to experiment with the use of media as a tool for community participation and development. My project was to research and assess television's impact on the Inuit and to identify future media needs in the North that the NFB might address. This was one year after the CBC had begun to implement its Accelerated Coverage Plan, designed to bring telecommunications services, live television, and radio broadcasting to all communities in the North with a population of five hundred or more. Around this critical moment of joining the North to the South, there had begun a proliferation of academic research projects in and about the North, designed to document the projected and actual changes due to the arrival of systematic outside media influences (among others: Mayes 1972; O'Connell 1977; Valaskakis 1979; Coldevin 1977a, b; Dicks 1977). Most of these were historical research projects undertaken to assess the pre- and post-satellite media environments and the impacts of satellite communications on Inuit and Cree populations. Researchers tended to concentrate on the impact of television rather than radio, because it had become clear to them, from existing Northern experiences and international communications and development research, that television had much more of a cultural displacement effect than did radio.

Within the wider context of ethnographic and anthropological research studies, scholars saw this historical period of transition as a golden moment in which to map out the implications of switching from a media-isolated to a media-connected environment; from a state of "media naïveté" to a state of exposure to the "civilizing influences" of modern television programming.

Historically, several waves of social change agents had already intruded into the North "to act upon mandates and motives of outside institutions" (Valaskakis 1981, 210). These included the explorers, whalers, missionaries, traders, and government personnel, beginning with the Royal Canadian Mounted Police (originally the North-West Mounted Police) and enlarging to include various specialized personnel of contemporary settlements. As the pioneering work of Valaskakis so well documents, electronic media was seen to be the last colonizing force to expand its mandate into the North and to strongly influence the further erosion of native authority and control. At this point in the 1970s, there emerged a complex "North" – suitable as an object of scholarly study and particularly interesting to communications researchers.

Having been in and out of the North over the past three decades, I have had the opportunity to closely survey significant developments from personal, political, and analytical perspectives as they were anticipated, as they occurred, and in retrospect. Although other First Peoples were involved in the experiments and projects I am about to describe and analyze, Inuit and Yukon Indian participants were the most organized in terms of how they used the data generated from the outcomes. It is for this reason that I mostly focus on their cases. It is important to note, however, that as these two nations were developing and arguing their policy strategies with federal bureaucrats, other Native Communications Societies were undertaking parallel efforts and working in convergence with them. I often allude to the Inuit and Yukon Indian corpus of materials because I was personally involved with *their* efforts, thereby having the actual onsite experience of working with the people, the materials, the policy proposals, and their outcomes.

I have had the time to do more than a cursory study of the sociocultural and political developments surrounding their communications' histories, having undertaken my work well before it became "trendy" in the 1980s to study minority broadcasting as an emerging niche. In other words, the fact that I have been immersed in Northern broadcasting developments over the last three decades enables me to recognize and place significant events at both the cultural and administrative levels within a longitudinal context. Over the years, I have been able to collect firsthand observations of aspects of a number of other First Peoples' experiences (the Cree, Algonquin, Dene, among others) and have attained a sense of what Raymond Williams refers to as a "structure of feeling" (Williams 1977, 128–35) – that is, the dominant affective impact that relates to each of the critical transitional periods being investigated.

A number of years have passed since my last significant engagement in the field, during which time I have been keeping track of the events, interviewing key players, teaching about First Peoples communications and development, and studying others' research on the subject, although the amount of scholarship seems to be very limited.[6] This has enabled me to rethink my own experiences in relation to the more recent changes in media practices, policy shifts, and analytical conceptions of ethnographic and scholarly research related to human subjects.

The emergence of self-reflexive fieldwork accounts elaborated in the work of Clifford and Marcus (1986), for example, has pointed to helpful models of reconceptualizing and writing cultural analyses. As "culture" is always relational and inscribed within communicative processes that exist, "historically, *between* subjects in relations of power" (Clifford in Clifford and Marcus 1986, 14–15), I find it important to both contextualize these communicative processes within their social fields and to represent a variety of viewpoints on the same issue. The acknowledgement of and focus on subjectivity in social research, elaborated in feminist and other poststructuralist and post-colonial research methodologies, such as studies of "otherness," has further lent support to the way in which I am attempting to weave together multi-perspectival empirical evidence, scholarly research, and some of my personal experience in the field. Writing from a qualitative and anticolonial perspective – making, so to speak, the familiar strange – I have not been hesitant to critically draw on my own experiences to fill in some speculative gaps. This technique of looking at one's familiar research corpus from "the perspective of a Martian" has been analytically useful. My personal accumulation of experience and research over three decades of close observation and interaction has been invaluable in giving me a richer set of historical accounts than could any positivist "objective" tool or method of research.

As a non-native, Jewish, "White" woman, I am by no means claiming to speak in this book on behalf of First Peoples. Nor am I promoting their specific interests. What I am trying to do is weave together the historical, the theoretical, and the empirical, starting with a focus on Northern broadcasting history and integrating the Southern experience *only* when Television Northern Canada transformed into the Aboriginal Peoples Television Network in 1999 and began to work with Southern production and administrative staff.

In writing about First Peoples broadcasting issues, I feel a sense of responsibility and accountability to those Northerners (aboriginals and others) with whom I have talked and worked over the years. I have tried to focus on their identified preoccupations and to do so from both an insider's and outsider's perspective, having been privy to knowledges and experiences to which few non-native peoples have had access. I am aware of the importance of sensitively placing this knowledge into the existing communications history corpus and of the potential impact of its circulation within and outside of First Peoples' communities.

As a cross-cultural outsider, a witness, and a communication rights activist, I hope that the material in this book will trigger public discussions about the positive value of cultural and racial inclusiveness in the practices and production of knowledges related to Canadian media history and development.

Introduction

Stated in its broadest sense, this book is about the roles and rules that broad casting practices and policies play in both inhibiting and promoting indigenous national self-development in contemporary, multicultural, postindustrial Canada.

The evolution of Canadian indigenous media policies, discourses, and practices is an important subject to examine at the beginning of the twenty-first century as aboriginal self-government comes closer to a negotiated consensus than ever before. First, as a direct result of the development of indigenous media over the last three decades, there has been a restructuring of the Canadian broadcasting system to include aboriginal broadcasting as an integral element. Second, First Peoples broadcasting lobbies have also had an impact on the formation of new mediating structures in Canada, such as policy frameworks, a new broadcasting channel (Aboriginal Peoples Television Network – APTN), more open access arrangements with existing channels, funding programs, and technological infrastructures. Third, First Peoples broadcasters have used television as an emancipatory tool. Their use of television in this way sets up grounding and motivating assumptions and beliefs about its relationship to other institutional and political realities – to change, to learning, to the struggle for national identity, and to a particular notion of empowerment and rationality vis-à-vis social action. The aim of First Peoples media – locally, regionally, nationally, and culturally – tends to be political development and community empowerment.

Rooted as their media have been in sociocultural movements focused on broadcasting rights, First Peoples have turned outwards from the invisible networks of people organizing the media towards building an alignment with diverse and visible audience communities. Among First Peoples practitioners and audiences, technology is viewed strategically as a tool to facilitate larger social or cultural projects. These include language and/or cultural reinforcement, education, self-development, and cross-cultural political influence-building (personal interview with George Henry: 7 August 1990). Finally, First Peoples media initiatives, such as those described in this history, can provide insights into the ways in which other Fourth World[1] communities might chart the courses of their broadcasting development. Canada's aboriginal broadcasting system is, to date, the most advanced such system in the world. Holding such a status has led potential and actual indigenous broadcasters from other circumpolar regions and from countries with indigenous populations (Alaska, Greenland, Australia, New Zealand, Finland, Sweden, Norway, the United States, countries in South America and Latin America) to seek advice from Canada's Northern and indigenous broadcasting networks on how to access and control their own media services.

Historically, the demand by Canadian indigenous and minority constituencies for state support of local, regional, and national identity-building tools such as sustained media access, regional control over programming and distribution of broadcasting signals, and fairer portrayal and employment practices, has resulted in new configurations of democratic power. These have become central to the process of "constructing" the indigenous nation and the Canadian state. In increasing the inclusion of indigenous and ethnic voices in public media representations, Canada has bolstered its international reputation as a state that supports multicultural and multiracial services. At the same time, minority group media have played a significant role in defining just what it means to be Canadian. Marc Raboy, a prominent Canadian policy scholar, suggests why this might be so important: "In Canada, a multiplicity of less-than-national, less empowered identity groups have struggled for recognition of their interests against the dominance of a one-dimensional Canada, and it is in fact their efforts that have maintained the Canadian difference against the overwhelming forces of continental integration in North America" (1990b, 8).

The federal government's cultural development strategy – three key components of which are multiculturalism, ethnic broadcasting, and aboriginal broadcasting – inscribes cultural pluralism as a prime characteristic of the democratic state, making it appear as if it were an unproblematic issue. This is not so, as we see when we unpack the assumptions of the policies and practices related to diversity and as we focus on the complexity of the power and social relations among the variety of "distinct" national and constituency groups living within the Canadian state.[2] These latter include the aboriginal or pre-Canadian communities (those aboriginal peoples whose territorial residence on this continent preceded that of the Europeans); the Canadians who claim their citizenship rights as national communities; and the immigrant populations who search for ways in which to "preserve some of their non-Canadian ways, as befits the Canadian commitment to a cultural mosaic" (di Norcia 1984, 148–9).

Focusing mainly on First Peoples' perspectives, this book examines some of the critical sites where they and other constituency groups have discursively and practically worked out the parameters of their social, political, cultural, economic, and institutional relationships. To move effectively towards this accomplishment, it has been necessary for First Peoples to develop an ongoing strategy of interpersonal and mediated communications. Given the range of critical cultural differences among First Peoples themselves as well as with other populations, their communications approach has had to be sensitive to the cross-cultural: recognizing complicated and unpredictable responses, a range of interpretive frameworks, and dialogical variations. As Karim H. Karim (1993) has noted:

The increasing recognition of the many cultures existing within the borders of Canada requires the development of polyvalent theoretical and analytical models that can aid in the understanding of the multicultural country. Post-modernist conceptions of decentred societies in which a diversity of discourses is continually competing for the attention of audiences seem particularly suited to studying contemporary socio-cultural developments. Polyvalent approaches can also avoid the encapsulation of major issues into the exclusive dichotomies of "English and French Canada," "aboriginals and non-aboriginals," and "visible minorities and non-visible minorities." (214)

I am interested in the history of these diverse discursive spaces and the mass-mediated public spheres presently occupied and managed by First Peoples in Canada. Through broadcasting, First Peoples are combining the forces of postmodernity with their own particular cultures, to synthesize their heritage with the project of undertaking their own development. The process has taken three decades and dedicated commitment by First Peoples broadcasters and lobbyists. The result of their work has been the legal recognition and acceptance of aboriginal voices within the Canadian public and private broadcasting spheres, as integral participants in the developing fabric of a pluralistic community of communities.

CULTURAL PLURALISM, BROADCASTING, AND BORDER CROSSINGS:
SELF-ORGANIZED DEVELOPMENT AND FIRST PEOPLES

The inherited discourse on Canadian cultural pluralism, as exemplified in Lord Acton's celebrated 1862 essay on "the national question," characterizes the management of cultural coexistence as one of the dominant tests of the liberal state: "The coexistence of several nations under the same state is a test, as well as the best security of its freedom. It is also one of the chief instruments of civilization; and as such, it is in the natural and providential order, and indicates a state of greater advancement than the national unity which is the ideal of modern liberalism" (Acton 1862, 160).

In much of the early writing about cultural and racial diversity, the assumption would seem to be that "diversity" consists of the peaceful co-existence of cultural and racial *communities* – and not of self-identified and distinct nations occupying and challenging the legitimacy of neighbouring territorial, resource-based, or symbolic universes (among others: Condon and Yousef 1975; Dodd, ed., 1982; UNESCO 1983; Young Yun Kim, ed. 1986; Ting-Toomey and Korzenny 1991). I argue that, in Canada at the beginning of the twenty-first century, the latter is more the case as regards indigenous communities who see themselves as nations of "special status" and expect financial and other resource allocations commensurate with their political position.

As Acton implies, policies and empirical issues involved in broadcasting aimed to promote cultural and racial diversity are complicated and periodically challenge the stability of the Canadian state. They are problematic because they involve an implicit commitment to a form of unidirectional cross-cultural communications (from the centre to the periphery of a given territory), the aim of which is to improve levels of tolerance in social relations between majority and minority populations (CRTC 1985). Furthermore, from a majority perspective, existing policies and practices are characterized by simplistic thinking embedded in implications that multicultural (which includes Anglophones and Francophones) and aboriginal audiences will magically become tolerant when exposed to liberal ideas, assumptions, production values, and culturally specific genres and formats. The challenge for Canadian policy-makers and media practitioners has been to figure out how to go beyond the paradigms of ethno-exhibitionism and folkloric salvaging to create a range of meaningful alternative representations that can empower both their producers and their audiences.

To complicate matters, there has been much disagreement about which of the constituency groups are in fact being addressed in Canadian multicultural policies. First Peoples clearly differentiate themselves from multicultural communities given that Canada is their only ancestral land. They argue that though they appear to represent just "another" cultural/racial constituency group, they in fact merit a special status because of their exceptional positioning within Canada's history as a subjugated people in a settler society. Consequently, they do not consider themselves to be subsumed under the rubric of "multiculturalism" or any of the existing policies related to it.

If we track First Peoples' initiatives in broadcasting over time, we see that – consistent with this – what they have demanded is not just better representation in mainstream broadcasting but the transfer of power and control over broadcasting to their own communities. They have sought full national media citizenship,[3] comparable to that of French and English cultural communities, and not just a broadcasting status as "special" cultural producers and distributors. Theirs has been a struggle to get on track, to be included without question as players on the electronic channel grid, and to participate in a co-development process – their part of which is recognized as "special."

While the federal government has acknowledged their unique position by its attribution of a special legislative status to aboriginal peoples (Government of Canada, *Indian Act* 1876 and subsequent revisions; *Northern Broadcasting Policy*, 1983; *Broadcasting Act*, 1991), the discourses on both First Peoples and multicultural/multiracial communications have continued to show traces of ideas appropriated from each other because of their overlapping and confusing constituent elements.

With this in mind, I should state here that though I periodically borrow a useful argument or concept from multicultural discourses, the main corpus of materials from which I have drawn pertains to First Peoples public service television broadcasters in the international communications/development context. Because my primary focus is on the mediating structures, institutions, interests, blind spots, and stakes of First Peoples *public* service broadcasting interests in Canada, I do not deal with those independent indigenous (multi)media production sectors whose current expansion can be attributed to an increase in television and other digital venues on which to exhibit their productions.

In examining the social field of Canadian cross-cultural relations through the organizational lens of aboriginal television broadcasting services, I argue that First Peoples self-development involves not only control over production and distribution of their own messages to their own communities but also the seeking of cross-cultural links and coalitions through program content considerations and through diffusion to populations outside of their immediate regional territories. Self-development of Fourth World nations contained within First World states is about having the power to frame, finance, and implement their own national agenda and priorities without the state's appropriation and control of the parameters of that evolution. This power is based on the possibility of building a consensus among the constituency groups living within a democratic society. Given that direct, interpersonal contact between indigenous and non-native peoples is often limited, what role can the aboriginal electronic media play in shaping the general public's attitudes about First Peoples issues?

To answer this and other questions, I focus on the ways in which First Peoples communities in Canada have been mobilized by others and are using media politics and promotional processes to negotiate media spaces for their self-representational and varied cross-cultural purposes. In the past, First Peoples were positioned outside of the Canadian national project and rendered invisible at many levels – the territorial, the social, the political, the economic, and the cultural. With few exceptions, the way they have been represented in the media reflects this "outsider" positioning. Given that mainstream media portrayals are one of the more powerful factors in the formation of our cultural identities, this symbolic erasure has been troubling. If, as Robert Stam (1993) contends, we live within language and representational practices without direct access to the "real" and if, as he also suggests, media representations act to constitute us within an "already textualized and discursivized socio-ideological world" (15), then it follows that we live out our lives as "representations to ourselves" (Tomlinson 1991, 61). In other words, it matters deeply what media representations of ourselves we see reflected back to us.

From within this perspective, and through the use of a number of illustrative case histories, I demonstrate that as problematic and complicated as discourses, policies and images of cultural and racial "differences" in broadcasting might be, they *have* influenced the emergence of a series of culturally distinct, if parallel, participatory development processes in Canada. These could not have been anticipated by governmental policies involving multiculturalism and aboriginal development planning (1971; 1988). In Canada, culturally and racially distinct communities and their media might best be described as being in a state of co-development, with each following its own historical trajectory and timeline, and the one not necessarily coordinating with the other. My use here of the term "co-development" differs from the way it has recently been used in France to refer to collaborative cultural cooperation and subsidization of economic development in postcolonial states with which France has historical connections (www.france.diplomatic.fr/cooperation/dgcid/rapport_01_gb/page, 27 October 2003). Nor am I using it in the way some have utilized the term to simply mean international "partnerships" (www.codev.org/codev/, 27 October 2003). For me, the term encapsulates the complex and non-static ways in which multiple constituency groups simultaneously negotiate their national places and spaces in relation to one another inside a given state.

Indigenous media discourses have been generated in conjunction with important participatory development processes taking place both in and around spatially remote Canadian television and radio broadcasting sites. These processes and experiments represent significant and distinct "innovations at the margins." Consequently, one of my assertions is that new foundations for media policies and innovations are being constructed in these territorial and social margins by First Peoples media producers. This focus on what is going on in the media margins provides new empirical material through which to broaden our understanding of the relationship in Canada between media access, cross-cultural/social/political/economic debates and power relations among constituency groups.

Even in its earlier incarnations, relatively few academics have written about the overall development of First Peoples broadcasting in Canada.[4] There has been almost nothing that directly focuses on its cross-cultural implications,[5] except for my own work on Radio Kahnawake during the 1990 crisis (1992), the research of Armitage (1992a,b), Jhappan (1990; 1992), and some comparative research on indigenous communication among Australia, the South Pacific, and Canada (Molnar and Meadows 2001). To date, no comprehensive overview of the history of First Peoples broadcasting – one that accurately maps its historical evolution up to the present – has been undertaken. Texts that do exist are in the form of reports, evaluation documents, policy interventions and position papers (Seaton and Valaskakis 1984; Roth 1990); Masters or doctoral theses (Mayes 1972; O'Connell 1977; Valaskakis 1979; Roth 1983, 1994; Wilson 1981, 1987); the odd article in a periodical or chapter in a book; a couple of books on media representation and journalism among aboriginal peoples (Alia 1999; Molnar and Meadows 2001); and several anthropological works that more often than not only touch on

Canadian indigenous media developments (Ginsburg 1992, 1993; Mander 1991; Brody 1975, 1987; Coates and Morrison 1989; Browne 1996). In short, this book represents the first broad and integrated overview of the history of First Peoples television broadcasting, up to and including the operations of the Aboriginal Peoples Television Network (APTN), which commenced in 1999.

That Canadian aboriginal broadcasters have taken some unanticipated steps in establishing both new and more representative broadcasting systems, making Canada internationally distinctive and a prototype for other Fourth World nations living within First World multicultural and plurilinguistic states, is noteworthy.[6] As cultural workers and theorists, we should be paying attention to these accomplishments, for they stand out in the larger scheme of things as pioneering and innovative templates that contribute to a more inclusive international communications (re)order.

THE NOTION OF "CULTURAL PERSISTENCE": FROM "CULTURAL SUBJECT" TO "MEDIA CITIZEN"

Having not had access to their own means of social definition and authority in the past, First Peoples initially slipped into becoming objects, as opposed to subjects, of history. Treated as "objects," their presence in historical analyses of broadcasting has been seen as insignificant. When they *have* been made evident in literary and visual media, it has been in the context of "cultural subject": that is, as culturally or racially *Other* – as peoples who are different from the norm of the dominant Euro-Canadian. Positioned as "special subjects" rather than as fully enfranchised citizens within the political sphere, their visual and discursive descriptions have been subjected to centuries of distortions and misrepresentations by others' writings and imagery.

Northern First Peoples' active participation as media producers systematically began after the Anik satellite commenced service in 1973. Importantly, this time was also convergent with their recognition that the federal government's attempt to assimilate their cultures into mainstream Eurocentric society (as outlined in the White Paper of 1969) would not be an answer to their cultural and political objectives of having a special status in Canada. It was around this same time, as the Telesat debates on the Canadian domestic satellite were taking place, that First Peoples leaders realized how important an ally public media would be to them in the future.

The world brought to them via television in 1973 was one in which they rapidly became aware of their apparent public non-existence. The recognition of this absence by Northern First Peoples television viewers further politicized them, and they began to demand a presence in all aspects of media production and distribution. It was, therefore, only after the intrusion of Southern media into the North that their exclusion as active agents from traditional social and historical narratives became a loudly contested issue.

At this time, First Peoples began to demand new kinds of research and approaches from historians to unsettle the distortions deriving from their fixed positions in history. They called for compensatory histories and anthropologies: ones that would empower them as activists, fill in the gaps and highlight a range of experiences from multiple indigenous perspectives, and transform them from being positioned as "just part of the scenery" to active political, social, and cultural agents. It soon became apparent that no one but they themselves could take on this challenge, as only they had the necessary knowledge and passion to make it effective.

Through discussions between myself and pioneering Northern communications scholar Gail Valaskakis, it has become clear to both of us that what First Peoples have demonstrated more than anything in their broadcasting initiatives has been a *cultural persistence*. This differs from the notion of *cultural resistance*, as currently popularized in Cultural Studies, in that it is not just a reaction *against* the unpopular or distasteful. In fact, as I have pondered the concept over the years, I have realized how important it is as a strategic recognition that all cultures *count* and *matter* in the general scheme of things: making it worth the effort for First Peoples to develop cultural promotion strategies; making it evident that this is indeed what has guided the development of First Peoples television over the years.

It follows that the meaning of "culture" shifts over time, and as a result of cross-cultural contact. First Peoples cultures are not exotic or fixed – *frozen* in time. Rather, they are cultures whose priorities have persisted and yet whose continuing and engaged dialogue with others – both insiders and outsiders – and whose constant process of re-evaluation have seen their political and organizational media status shift from that of "cultural subject" to that of national "media citizens."

In order to demonstrate how this transformation has taken place, as well as highlight the distinct (and shockingly underexamined) history of aboriginal television broadcasting in Canada, I have devised a six-phase framework that commences with the lengthy period prior to the introduction of broadcasting into the North and then traces out the significant landmarks in native-produced information flow and audience expansion up until the year 2002.

Demarcation points separating clusters of native broadcasting events into periods have been determined on the basis of shifts that have occurred in the technical environment, in policy discourse, or in representational practices. It is notable that within each period, there is also an evolutionary shift from a narrower to a wider audience, based on a larger range of access tools.

In building an understanding of each of these periods, and elaborating upon them, I have used Raymond Williams's dynamic model of dominant, residual, and emergent social processes. These refer not only to separate stages but to ones that may vary and overlap in their internal dynamic processes (Williams 1977, 121). Thus, although each of these periods appears to be distinct, they are in fact stitched to, and mediated by, both previous *and* emergent time periods. As Williams (1977) suggests:

We have certainly still to speak of the "dominant" and the "effective," and in these senses of the hegemonic. But we find that we have also to speak, and indeed with further differentiation of each, of the "residual" and the "emergent," which in any real process, and at any moment in the process, are significant both in themselves and in what they reveal of the characteristics of the "dominant." (121–2)

Several of the time periods in First Peoples broadcasting history typically overlap or interconnect – and many concurrent events fit into more than one frame of analysis. Moreover, not all Native Communications Societies across Canada have progressed at the same rate of development or had the same public impact. Nor can we ignore the influences that each might have had on others. Did, for example, the Inuit Broadcasting Corporation – because it was the first Native Communications Society to produce television programming – set a pan-Northern standard for aboriginal television? It is also necessary to consider the impact that access to similar technology forms had upon First Peoples engaged in different stages of their organizational and national development.

One must equally keep in mind that "The North" does not exist in a vacuum. The First Peoples' and the various Canadian governments' positions on international communications rights, for instance, have had an influence on broadcasting developments in the North and vice versa. Furthermore, it is important to take into account what was simultaneously happening in the realm of general aboriginal policies throughout Canada in order to have a comparative basis from which to evaluate the state of Northern indigenous broadcasting during any given time period.

Finally, I should mention that the actual *process* of periodizing First Peoples television broadcasting history – though potentially problematic due to the danger of slipping into reductionism – has enabled me to effectively organize the vast quantity of material required to undertake as broad-ranging a study as this. That said, readers should bear in mind that the demarcation lines I have drawn are somewhat porous in places.

HISTORICAL PERIODIZATION: SIX PHASES OF FIRST PEOPLES TELEVISION HISTORY

For the purposes of quick and easy reference, and in order to give an overall picture of these six phases and their timeframes (phases that roughly correspond to the chapter layout of the book), a table is provided. There follows a short description of each period's core contribution to First Peoples broadcasting development.

Phases I and II – Pre-Northern TV Context and (De)Romancing the First Peoples and Their Territories: The Policy-Makers' Imaginaries (Early 1900s to 1970s)

Phase I represents the period in which Southern-produced imagery of First Peoples was characterized by stereotypical misrepresentations, when and if they were present at all in the visual domain. It was into this distorted visual environment that television was parachuted onto the North and had the preliminary impact of reinforcing the already-existing absence of First Peoples and their lands from media texts.

This is followed by phase II, in which First Peoples became aware of the potential of televisual media to record themselves and their concerns. This period began in the late 1960s, when debates concerning the introduction of the first domestic satellite in the world were taking place in the Canadian Parliament. Concurrent with these debates and the passing of the Telesat Act (1969), there occurred a series of discussions revolving around Northern aboriginal television. Coupled with a federal policy initiative advocating assimilation (Government of Canada 1969), First Peoples began to realize the media's potential to either erode their cultural strength or, alternatively, act as a tool for self-development/empowerment in their struggles against pressures to conform to mainstream values of Canadian society. They saw it, also, as a vehicle for mediating social and race relations.

TABLE 1
PHASES OF FIRST PEOPLES TELEVISION HISTORY

Phase I (Early 1900s to 1970s)
Pre-Northern TV Context
• Absences, misrepresentations, and stereotypes in film and print
• Southern-Produced Media from South to North

Phase II (1968–81)
(De)Romancing First Peoples and Their Territories
• Satellite debates precipitate discussions around Northern media priorities
• Representation of First Peoples by First Peoples themselves
• Intra-regional, experimental media projects from North to North

Phase III (1978–91)
Policy-ing the North
• Surveying the field, data collection, policy principles established for the enshrining of aboriginal broadcasting in legislation
• Broadcasting Act of 1991 passed into legislation

Phase IV (1983–92)
Consolidation and Expansion of Broadcasting Infrastructure
• Inter-regional media from North to North
• Individual Native Communications Societies sell programs to Southern public broadcasters
• Television Northern Canada established

Phase V (1986–99)
Crossing Cultural, Racial, and Territorial Borderlines
• Multidirectional indigenous media
• Aboriginal Peoples Television Network (APTN) licensed on 22 February 1999

Phase VI (1992–)
An International Turn
• Building Fourth World media constituency groups through multidirectional media exchange and collaborative projects
• Aboriginal Peoples' Television Network launched on 1 September 1999; includes programming produced by non-Canadian indigenous peoples
• Possibilities for an international indigenous broadcasting undertaking equivalent to channels such as CNN or BBC World Service

Over the next few years, television was launched in the North. By 1975, most communities had receiver dishes. Between 1976 and 1981, several pilot projects were established in the North. From First Peoples' perspectives, the main activity of this period was using television as an experimental medium through which to explore interactive communications and community development practices. At the same time, the federal government wanted First Peoples to "modernize" and to become familiar with new technologies as a possible substitution for travel (expenses were prohibitively high), especially in relation to education and health matters. They also wanted First Peoples' feedback on alternative uses of satellite technology for community development purposes and on viable forms of intercommunity communications. In other words, there emerged a convergence of common interests and objectives that made it worthwhile for the government to invest money in field tests and for First Peoples to undertake the project work.

A number of project successes led to other more permanent initiatives such as the establishment of the Inuit Broadcasting Corporation (1981). By this time, lobby efforts for more complete and inclusive Northern television package services were well under way. It was at this point that the CRTC decided to license Cancom (Canadian Satellite Telecommunications Company) to deliver a range of Southern programming into Northern and remote communities as well as to provide carriage for Northern-produced broadcasts. The Commission also "expected" CBC Northern Service to carry native-language programming as one of the "social costs" of their public service broadcasting license.

Phase III – Policy-ing the North (1978–91)

This phase covers the critical period when the current Broadcasting Act was introduced, debated, and finally passed in 1991. At this historical conjuncture, policy always mattered and was recognized as being an essential framing tool for establishing a new technical infrastructure and legal discourse.

What was empirically happening in the field at this time was carefully monitored and documented as "data," which was then shaped into "evidence" to support constituency group broadcasting-access rights, as well as fairer and more equitable distribution services in the North. Lobbyists from the North and the South began to carefully survey each other, with First Peoples and their allies searching for openings in the 1968 broadcasting legislation (the previous Broadcasting Act) in which to inscribe their own constituency groups with a special status and the accompanying rights to both receive and transmit broadcasting materials. Academics and historians witnessing the process often used data from field experiments and pilot projects to mediate relations between First Peoples and federal government representatives.

Phase IV – Consolidation and Expansion of Broadcasting Infrastructures (1983–92)

By the time phase IV began around 1983, thirteen regional Native Communications Societies had developed north of the fifty-fifth parallel and had organized a lobby campaign aimed at establishing an explicit Native Broadcasting Policy. They considered this to be a critical step towards the enshrining of their communication rights in legislation.

In 1983, this policy was actualized and an accompanying program and funding vehicle called the *Northern Native Broadcast Access Program* was established, which earmarked $40.3 million for the long-term production goal of twenty hours of native-language radio programming and five hours of native-perspective television per week. This initial funding was for four years, but the program has continued to exist under considerable financial strain. It was originally administered by the Secretary of State's Native Citizens Directorate and is currently under the authority of the Department of Canadian Heritage.

After several years of initial functioning, two key problems emerged, neither of which had been anticipated in the original policy/program plans: namely, funding for training and distribution. One of the results was that employee and administrative training were handed over to Manpower Services. Though this solution was not without its problems, those people who did not have access to the private education system did pick up training from these resources.

On 4 June 1991, a new Broadcasting Act was passed. It enshrined multicultural, multiracial, and aboriginal broadcasting. Emergent from the Act, which supported the establishment of a First Peoples infrastructure, and following a public hearing in Hull on 28 October 1991, the CRTC approved the Television Northern Canada (TVNC) application for a native television network license to serve Northern Canada "for the purpose of broadcasting cultural, social, political and educational programming for the primary benefit of aboriginal people in the North" (CRTC 1991). By granting the license to TVNC, the Commission recognized the importance of Northern-based control over the distribution of native and Northern programming. TVNC was to become the vehicle through which First Peoples would represent themselves and their concerns to the entire North. In this sense, TVNC constituted a de facto recognition of the communication rights of the First Peoples in the North. TVNC began broadcasting on 21 January 1992.

Phase V – Crossing Cultural, Racial, and Territorial Borderlines (1986–99)

Phase V is characterized by expansion of aboriginal programming into the South. It is during this period that Northern Native Broadcasting, Yukon (NNBY) negotiated an arrangement for CBC Newsworld to carry its program "Nedaa – Your Eye on the Yukon," and the Inuit Broadcasting Corporation began producing cross-cultural programming on a contract basis. In response to federal budgetary cutbacks, others also got involved – selling their program services to raise money.

In light of TVNC's successful distribution of their programs across the North in the early 1990s, their administration began to contemplate shifting their programs Southwards in order to establish a more integrated national service. Having convinced its board of directors and its staff to pursue the establishment of a nationwide network, a vote was taken in June 1997, after which steps were initiated to make this dream into a reality (Explore North 1999). With the Commission's formal recognition of the importance of a national aboriginal channel, TVNC submitted an application to the CRTC for a broadcast license for the Aboriginal Peoples Television Network in June 1998. On 22 February 1999, the CRTC approved TVNC's application and granted mandatory carriage on basic cable and satellite services throughout Canada with a $0.15 fee per subscriber per month in the South. In the North, residents of the ninety-six communities would continue to receive the service free of charge (TVNC March 1999, 1). To provide continuity of service to Northerners, a separate Northern feed was to be established. APTN began broadcasting across the country – North and South – on 1 September 1999.

Phase VI – An International Turn (1992–)

When TVNC began operations, it was the only television network dedicated to aboriginal broadcasting in the world. APTN has expanded upon TVNC's original international content to include broadcasts from Greenland, Alaska, Finland, and Siberia, as well as from Australia, New Zealand, Brazil, and Bolivia. That this emphasis on international content is organized on a systematic – and not a casual – basis suggests that APTN looks to a future in which an international perspective is favoured, and a wide optic on aboriginal issues around the world is taken.

OVERVIEW OF CHAPTERS

Before delving into the nitty-gritty details of Canadian aboriginal broadcasting history, I think it is useful to examine how and where Canada fits alongside other countries' experiences of television infrastructural development for minorities. In expanding our scope to patterns of broadcasting evolution elsewhere, and in placing particular emphasis on how cultural differences have been handled historically, we can begin to see how the Canadian case is outstanding both for its uniqueness and for its contribution to international debates about media and development in neocolonial states. To this end, chapter 1 lays out a broad, theoretical framework that situates First Peoples media in Canada within an international context.

Chapters 2–7 detail the historical phases of Northern, and more recently, Canadian, indigenous broadcasting. In chapters 2 and 3, I examine the inherited legacy of distorted and stereotypical images of First Peoples as they moved into the twentieth century. In chapter 4, I look at the establishment of a telecommunications infrastructure in the North in the early 1970s, and the subsequent intrusion of live television into what were formerly small and isolated communities. Reflecting upon television's initial impact on First Peoples' cultures and daily life practices, I show how their early responses to television – far from being *passive* – became the basis through which a small group of Northern media activists recognized television's potential to help organize their cultural constituency group. In this regard, federally sponsored demonstration media projects were useful in helping to reposition First Peoples in the eyes of the government's telecommunications bureaucracy.

In chapter 5, we get to the crux of policy-making and media administration processes – with both described and analyzed in careful detail. The Northern Broadcasting Policy and the Northern Native Broadcast Access Program are outlined and problematized. The notion of "policy-ing" is central here, in that it conjures up the active process of policy surveillance: that is, the policing of the airwaves and of broadcasting legislation in order to find openings into which First Peoples' interests around access rights and fair portrayal practices could be inserted. This chapter ends with the successful enshrining of aboriginal broadcasting within the 1991 Broadcasting Act, guaranteeing both reception and transmission broadcasting rights. I also question the tenuousness of the initial funding for the thirteen regional Native Communications Societies.

Chapter 6 focuses on the opening up of new possibilities for aboriginal broadcasters. In particular, I examine the implications of the decision taken by several Native Communications Societies in the 1980s to target non-aboriginal audiences. In this chapter, I also explore the cross-cultural as it relates to, and expands upon, the work of Rod Chiasson – a CRTC bureaucrat who, in the 1970s, had a vision of circumpolar short-wave radio broadcasting in the Inuktitut languages to all of the Northern countries with Inuit populations. This leads to chapter 7, in which the formation of Television Northern Canada – the First Peoples' and the federal government's solution to distribution problems inherent in its prior policies and practices – is examined. TVNC, the pan-Northern distribution system that operated between 1992 and 1999, was the precursor of the Aboriginal Peoples Television Network (APTN) – the latter being the central subject of chapter 8.

Finally, in the conclusion, I reflect upon three important questions to emerge from this indigenous media case history. What role might indigenous broadcasting play in mediating social and race relations between First Peoples and non-natives who have never had direct contact with one another? What can the First Peoples' broadcasting case tell us about the policy-making process in Canada? How can indigenous media be understood in light of the existing crisis in development theory/practice, and what can it contribute to its revision?

With these questions in mind, let us now move on to chapter 1 with its focus on how the relationships between broadcasting, culture, and notions of progressive development as measured by the United Nations and other agencies of (inter)national stature have been theorized in the West. For it is within this wider, comparative optic of media, broadcasting, and development studies that I consider, and narrate, the story of First Peoples television history in Canada.

1 | Culture, Media, and Development

The rule in both personal development and social life is reproduction, and any sub-stantial change in course requires an exceptional convergence of numerous favorable conditions such that, looking backward, change looks overdetermined when, in actual fact, every one of these conditions was indispensable for it to occur.

Albert O. Hirschman (*Shifting Involvements: Private Interest and Public Action*, 72)

My purpose in this chapter is to lay out the dominant paradigms of media, culture, and development[1] as they have been deployed and critiqued in rela-tion to each other over the last half century. I am particularly interested in the way the term "culture" and its complex processes have been defined, promoted, and questioned within models of broadcasting.

At what point did recognition of cultural diversity in broadcasting become critical to national development both in Canada and elsewhere? When did local and regional cultures stop being an obstacle to the modernization process? When did other First and Second World states begin to recognize their Third and Fourth World populations by giving them access to their own media resources? Are Fourth World (aboriginal) development patterns distinct? What kind of relationship – generated through either personal con-tact (i.e., at international meetings) or collaborative projects – do Fourth World peoples in Canada have with indigenous communities elsewhere? How have satellite-mediated broadcasts into and out of Fourth World regions changed the national boundaries by which development has been tradition-ally defined and imagined?

The case of First Peoples' television broadcasting first in the North and then in all of Canada can contribute original insights into those notions of devel-opment that take into account the unstable and erratic global flows and move-ments of indigenous peoples, capital, media, technology, and ideas at the turn of the twenty-first century. Given its peripheral location on the northernmost rim of North America, and tied as it is to the Circumpolar Arctic through its extension into the North Pole along with seven other states (Denmark/Greenland, Finland, Iceland, Norway, Russia, Sweden, and the United States), the Canadian North represents a "culture area" in which, as Anthony D. Smith (1990) suggests, indigenous "families of cultures" are attempting to form a political constituency group on the basis of a common agenda and comparable cultural distance from the federal government (185–6). Communications among peoples within this Northern culture area criss-cross territorial and provincial boundaries on a daily basis as they re-establish what Orin Young (1992) describes as the "diverse and rather fluid patterns of interaction that prevailed in the Far North prior to the systematic imposition of state sovereignty in the region from about the 1930s onward" (11). The sophistication of the transportation facilities and transnational[2] projects (like APTN and international "culture family" initiatives such as TV-5) that enable these renewed ties and cross-cultural networks remind us of just how tentative and fragile the dominant discursive constructions of Third and Fourth Worlds as "underdeveloped" are.

As for the practical ramifications of such discursive constructions, what cannot be overstressed is the extent to which *each* phase of Northern broadcasting has reflected how "development" was being intellectually conceived of at the international level during any given time period: a point that only reinforces my belief that an awareness of how development has been theorized outside of Canada is essential to understanding what has happened within Canada. To this end, I provide here a brief overview of some of the fundamental theoretical shifts that have taken place in the realms of culture,[3] mass media, and development from the 1950s onwards. In particular, I identify, analyze, and critique implicit and explicit notions of culture and its relationship to the mass media within three major discourses: diffusionism, dependency/underdependency approaches, and communitarianism.

My approach to these discourses is representative, not exhaustive. Furthermore, there are definite evolutions within, as well as overlaps between, the three discourses. For instance, the original premises of the diffusionist paradigm have been clearly articulated in the literature and are easy to describe. However, as time has passed, and as "pure" attempts to match development theory to the empirical world have increasingly come under attack for being methodologically problematic and practically untenable (not to mention the product of political, social, economic, and/or cultural imperialism), a definite blurring of the diffusionist paradigm has taken place. Nonetheless – and in spite of being vigorously critiqued by theoreticians and practitioners from both the West and the developing nations (especially Latin America) since the mid-1970s – this school of thinking has continued to influence Western planners' institutional and political relationships with "Lesser Developed Countries" (LDCs) and with regions of their own countries.

As for the "dependency/underdependency" and "communitarian" models, both can be described as complex, multilayered, and sensitive to the specific conditions of a given nation's self-perception. These paradigms have not necessarily followed the same historical or neocolonial trajectory,[4] but they do share some common cultural premises[5] – suggesting not only that they are related to each other but that elements or fragments of various paradigms can coexist.

A SNAPSHOT OF THE CONCEPTUALIZATIONS OF CULTURE AND MASS MEDIA IN THREE DEVELOPMENT DISCOURSES

The Diffusionist Paradigm[6]

The development paradigm of *diffusionism* was first explicitly described in a speech by US President Harry Truman in 1949 in terms of a "'bold new program' of United States technical assistance and financial aid to poor countries around the world" (Schiller 1989, 138). Diffusionism was particularly significant to Canada at the time, in that it had an important bearing on how the federal government formulated its approach to First Peoples media services during the 1950s, 60s, and 70s.

Clearly delineated notions of what local, regional, or national cultures consist of in "developing nations" are intrinsically embedded within the diffusionist paradigm. Its key premise is that there are two distinct kinds of culture: "giving" cultures, which are the dominant, "developed," urbanized, mediatized, and privileged cultures of the West[7]; and "receiving" cultures, which are characterized as passive, rural, traditional, ahistorical, submissive, and one-dimensional.

In its initial formulation, minor attention was paid to non-economic factors of development. Culture as "a whole way of life" of the LDC was relegated to the realm of "background material" and was generally treated as an *obstacle* against which Western development agents and agencies had to struggle. Constructed as primitive and "backward," the belief was that lesser-developed areas evolved in a mechanistic manner. Based on the assumption that *all* national development patterns and stages should conform to those that had taken place in the West, cultural modernity was measured using a prototype continuum along which traditional/modern and poor/rich societies could be identified and rated. Indicators included the level of urbanization, the availability of education, the literacy rate, the capacity to empathize, and the degree of media exposure. "Development" meant moving from a low rating on the scale towards that of a wealthy and modernized society.[8]

The existence and utilization of mass-media resources to promote economic and other Western-authorized notions about development were identified as preconditions for the acceptance of modernization. According to Daniel Lerner (1958), who constructed the core premises of this theory after working in the Middle East in the mid-1950s, the move from a traditional to a modern society involved psychically preparing "underdeveloped" populations for integration into a North American-style consumer society, assumed to represent the model of a progressive state. Lerner's notion of "empathy" – when a "mobile personality" can see himself [sic] "in the other fellow's situation," and have "a high capacity to identify with new aspects of his environment" – was key to his assumption that "psychic mobility," and the mobility-multiplying effects of modern media, would psychologically prepare populations to accept innovations.

Also operationalized within this paradigm was Katz and Lazarsfeld's (1955) theory of the two-step flow of communications, which maintained that opinion leaders could influence the eliciting of a positive response to novel ideas and consumer items in what was perceived as a generally passive population, and Everett Rogers's (1969) work on how "peasants" could more easily be prepared for the acceptance and adoption of technological innovations. In addition, Wilbur Schramm's (1964) development process plan became an important prototype for the transformation and mediatization of underdeveloped nations. His recommendation to establish inventories of existing and future mass-media requirements as a first step towards modernization reinforced a quantitative perspective on development. In 1972, Robert G. Mayes, then a graduate student at McGill University, applied Schramm's approach in his MA thesis research on mass-media development in Northern Canada. In his work, he systematically enumerated each component of the mass communication system of the Canadian Arctic in an attempt to clarify both its structure and its function in the process of "Eskimo" adaptation to Western society. Showing that the spatial distribution system of available channels was biased, making many of them inaccessible to residents of the region, Mayes called for a more culturally relevant system of communications to ease the adaptation of "Eskimos" to Western society. In all of this research and theory, little effort was made to gather empirical data about native primordial attachments based around language, kinship, religion, custom, race, or ethnicity – except, that is, when such information was deemed necessary to hastening along the society's modernization process.

The framing of lived culture and tradition as a "nuisance factor" (as something that had to be successfully circumvented in order to get on with the important business of modernization) predominated in this approach and played itself out on many fronts. Blame for "being backward" was assigned to the developing nation itself. No financial, social, or cultural support was put towards the development of indigenous institutions and participatory infrastructures by so-called "aiding" nations. And precolonial history was, for the most part, either ignored or defamed. Not only were all underdeveloped areas and the people living within them perceived as one large unitary block, "culture" itself became identified with North American and Western European cultural industries and products.

The diffusionist paradigm represented a deterministic, limited approach. By the early 1970s, it was becoming clear that neither technology nor economic factors were the driving forces behind development. For one, experience had shown that the application of technology alone did not solve all of the problems of the lesser-developed nations. Likewise, the economic rationale upon which diffusionism was based – the assumption (known as the trickle-down theory) that, through capital-intensive investment, leading sectors would eventually spread their advantage to the lagging sectors – was found to be sadly lacking in that it produced an unequal distribution of economic benefits. Slowly, development theorists began to recognize that other factors, such as sociopsychological attitude, literacy, the existence of democratic social and political institutions, and peoples' basic quality of life, were equally important factors in a nation's development.[9]

In short, the diffusionist paradigm began to be seen as ahistorical, static, and structurally naive. Not only did it fail to acknowledge the synergistic interaction of a number of elements as productive of an overall effect, as a highly ethnocentric theory and practice based on a Western value system, it also failed to take into account variations in local, regional, or national development processes, cultural products, and historical circumstances. Most importantly, it created a discourse and a practice that, under the guise of assisting underdeveloped nations or regions to become equal partners, in fact imposed a technical and normative infrastructure of Western dominance, hierarchy, and imperialistic extension of empire.[10] This was the paradigm that guided the early development of satellite policies for the Northern and remote regions of Canada.

The Dependency/Underdependency Paradigm

Central to the dependency/underdependency paradigm – as typified in the works of Paul Baran (1957), André Gunder Frank (1970), Immanual Wallerstein (1975), Herbert Schiller (1969; 1978; 1989), Ariel Dorfman and Armand Mattelart (1975), Armand Mattelart (1983; 1984), Cees Hamelink (1984), and Dallas Smythe (1981) – are the issue of Western media imperialism and the question of how to contest it. Foregrounding "national culture" as a force through which to combat this particular form of imperialism, the key debates here have tended to revolve around notions of dependency, dissociation, and sovereignty.

Arguing from a Marxist macro-perspective, both Baran and Frank consider development and underdevelopment to be an "interrelated and continuous process, two aspects of a single global process, rather than an original state of existence" (Servaes 1986, 3). Blaming media and economic underdevelopment on factors and nations *outside* of a developing country itself, they have posited that Western superpowers, through manipulating mass-media infrastructures and content in order to *assure* a state of dependency, have succeeded in preventing autonomous development and have fostered cultural and electronic colonialism.

In identifying these particular factors and nations as the main causes of *under*development, this paradigm tends to see "development as an automatic outcome of liberation from imperialism" (Shinar 1987, 169). It follows that some form of cultural protectionism (be it of national values or of a particular way of life), dissociation, or sovereignty becomes the tactical method through which each nation can be assumed to be building its respective (inter)national identity. It is significant that, within this paradigm, the local and the regional (i.e., how culture is actually "lived" on a day-to-day basis) matter less than the overarching national image that a country projects to the outside world. This means that the reference point for any given country's cultural (re)construction is in fact located outside, rather than inside, the nation itself.

Here, as in the diffusionist paradigm, the trend to quantitatively measure cultural activities and products continues. However, the aims are quite different, in that such measurements are now used "to assess the degree of imbalance between the centre and periphery nations, as well as disparities within regions and countries" (Servaes 1986, 4). In other words, data is gathered in order to strengthen, rather than weaken, the argument for cultural sovereignty.

To operationalize the concept, Armand Mattelart (1983) argues that "information" or "cultural" industries could be transformed with an eye to restructuring international capitalism and formulating national strategies of resistance. Mattelart's position is that Western media should not be considered as mere instruments of power and imperialism but as *sites* in which power is constituted (17–67). In his perspective, it is only through appropriating these individual sites – each of which carries its own set of social contradictions and processes of mediation – that developing nation-states might first take control of the media and then use the media for their own development goals.

In a similar vein, Herbert Schiller's (1976) case against the Western ideological orientation of "foreign"-produced media products and technologies raises questions about the long-term effects of media on culture, ideology, and behavioural patterns in Third and Fourth World nations. If, for instance, the media are indeed able to influence social and cultural changes, then what strategies might be adopted by developing nations to best curtail Western media imperialism? Insistent that technology is not deterministic – an independent autonomous force that cannot be contested – yet ready to concede that Western technology and its products are to some extent responsible for Third and Fourth World cultural dependence on the United States and Europe, the argument here is that the use of nationally controlled and more "appropriate" technologies might be a better choice for developing nations. I would suggest, in fact, that this is a better choice for minorities the world over, who might harness those same technologies to foster their own cultural autonomy or sovereignty.

In Canada, Dallas Smythe (1981) contributed to the debate by calling for "cultural screens" as a means of protectionism. Consisting of "language, religious and mythical beliefs and customs, together with border control of the movement of people and things," Smythe defined "cultural screens" as those "aspects of a national culture or ideological system which serve to protect its cultural realism against disruptive intrusion." By cultural realism, he meant the "central values of the system as expressed in its artifacts, practices, and institutional policies. Collectively, they are the rationalizations that provide coherence to the people, things, and institutional policies of a country or ideological system" (232). An example of such a "cultural screen" would be The Northern Broadcasting Policy of 1983 with its protection of aboriginal languages and cultures. The Canadian Radio-Television and Telecommunications Commission's Broadcasting Regulations and its establishment and application of Canadian Content requirements would be another.

(Under)dependency theories, in summary, were more globally oriented than their predecessors and served to open up discussions about cultural autonomy and about possibilities for the *interin*dependence of developing nations. They did, however, tend to overlook local knowledge and regional disparities – in other words, the primordial aspects of cultural development – in their adoption of a macro-view that advocated the establishment of national production industries to counterbalance the influx of foreign cultural products and capital.

In the worldwide context, arguments for cultural autonomy within this model succeeded in furthering the objectives of the non-aligned nations, which, in the late 1970s and early 80s, had become well organized and had shifted the terms of UNESCO debates from "transnational" and "vertical" free flows of culturally biased information to the notion of a free and balanced information flow. UNESCO debates around the universal right to be freely informed, to communicate, and to enjoy cultural privacy culminated in the MacBride Commission study (1980), outlining the range of world communication problems and possible solutions. The resulting report – *Many Voices, One World* – laid the intellectual groundwork and set the strategic agenda for the democratization of communications and culture within the developing nations' territories. In addition to elaborating upon notions of cultural protectionism and autonomy, *Many Voices, One World* detailed a number of communication rights: the right to information reflecting one's own perspectives and voices through access to the mass media at the local, regional, and national levels; the right to cultural privacy, as well as to interact with, and give feedback to, the media; the right to one's own cultural heritage and the means via the media to preserve and reinforce it; and, finally, the right to determine national communication policies.

As might have been predicted, international responses to the document were mixed, with the various "sides" rushing to protect either their expansionist cultural and material interests, or their desire to gain cultural autonomy through the establishment of interindependent communication infrastructures. In Canada, the UN's explicit delineation of cultural and communication rights in the early 1980s served to mobilize federal government and public support for the development of aboriginal broadcasting. The MacBride Commission's work also heralded in a communitarian approach to issues involving culture and the media. This helped to persuade the Canadian Government of *Many Voices, One World*'s value as a guiding document in the protection and promotion of native languages and cultures in spite of the radical critique of First World imperialism that it equally contained.

The Communitarian Paradigm

The communitarian paradigm within development discourses can best be described as a flexible, syncretic model working to integrate old with new; interpersonal channels of communications with mass-media structures. It recognizes the coexistence of internal and external cultural factors when a new medium is introduced into a developing region and privileges neither the foreign influence nor the internal constraints and limitations of the receiving nation. Furthermore, it legitimizes the proposals of the MacBride Commission in its promotion of indigenous communications systems based on intracultural needs. In sum, as Dov Shinar – picking up on Clifford Geertz's seminal work in this area – explains:

Instead of seeing modernization and nation building as dependent on a society's ability to utilize available innovations or to escape from the grip of the superpowers, this approach views change and development as the interplay between institutional change and cultural reconstruction. There are no mythically predetermined paths, requirements, or results ... Rather, this convergence of social dynamics involves a series of simultaneous, multidimensional interactions between internal and external forces. It considers essentialism, the set of indigenous traditions and symbols, anchored in an inherited course, and epochalism the present course of things, as forces at work in relation to ideological, technological, economic, and other influences. A variety of functional and dysfunctional results – and thus different rates and patterns of change – may emerge out of these interactions, all depending on the ability and the willingness of a society to develop mechanisms for dealing with the symbolic and structural implications of these processes. The means and ends of change are not predetermined, as in the orthodox approaches, nor do they depend on one factor, as in the radical theories. (Shinar 1987, 170)

The communitarian paradigm acknowledges that modernization and development are two separate processes. Modernization, on the one hand, is of a mechanical, automatic, and manipulative nature, with decisions regarding change made outside the area undergoing transformation. Development, on the other hand, enables the subjects of transformation to make their own decisions (Freire 1973, 129–30).

An emphasis on the relevance of local, regional, and national cultures and channels of communications is integral to this latter process. The maintenance and continuity of a community of identity and tradition is also fundamentally important in achieving the self-defined goals of development. In the work of Freire (1973), Beltran (1976; 1980) Teheranian (1982), Shinar (1987; 1990), Innis (1951a,b), Valaskakis (from 1971 onwards), Servaes (1986; 1990), and Verhelst (1992), among others, we find communitarian development arguments that call for the reconstruction of cultural heritage and tradition, for the preservation of historically relevant ways of life and patterns of interaction, and for financially supported indigenous communication infrastructures.[11]

Democratic and participatory control over media content and the use of technologies, as well as a strong emphasis on indigenous information needs, patterns, and channels, are central to this approach. Freire (1973) and Beltran (1980), after critiquing the alienating premises of Western models of communication, have each proposed a model for democratizing the development process. Their prototypes revolve around horizontal and dialogical interpersonal small-group communications. Both of their models are characterized by: face-to-face communication procedures; combined mass media and interpersonal communications techniques; active use of local languages to produce cultural content for discussions, as well as for "produced" messages; the implicit recognition that everyone has the need and right to communicate satisfactorily with available and appropriate resources; the principle that democratic communication is a horizontally structured dialogical process, and not a vertical process in which one or several persons dictate and dominate the agenda; and the promotion of an active critical political consciousness.

Implicit in these kinds of models is a critique of Western agencies and organizations for having largely ignored indigenous cultures of Third World nations, or for having treated them as obstacles to modernization and development.[12] It follows that, if indigenous cultural values (including native spirituality) are to be at the heart of any development process, a balanced approach based on what Verhelst (1992) describes as a combination of intra-cultural and acculturative forces is necessary. Access to one's own cultural heritage resources is invaluable in this regard. The right to be different, to validate one's grassroots cultural communities and indigenous communications practices – these rights, as Verhelst insists, are key to any self-development process:

[development is] ... an all-inclusive process that is, in the final analysis, cultural. For it is the idea of culture that gives both meaning and direction to economic activity, political decisions, community life, social conflict, technology, and so on. It is in fact culture that gives development its raison d'être and its goal. It is each people's own culture that must decide what, for them, is a "good life." It is culture that instils [sic] its rhythm on the life of a community and gives it its direction. It is clearly better, therefore, not to speak of "the cultural aspects of development," as though culture were a more or less decorative accessory, or of "cultural development," as though it was only a question of culture as artistic creation. Culture is ... properly speaking, the basis of "development." (159–60)

This conception of development was popularized by the Dag Hammerskjold Foundation, which, in its Development Dialogue journal, outlined the "Anotherness in One World" model. This approach characterizes development as need-oriented, endogenous, self-reliant, ecologically sound, based on structural transformations, and involving some form of participatory democracy (Servaes 1986, 7). Advocating a user-oriented communications model, the emphasis here is on the need for what Dennis McQuail describes as "horizontalization, deprofessionalisation, decentralisation, access, symmetrical exchange, [and] active social participation" (Servaes 1986, 7). Similar to the prototype communitarian paradigm in terms of how it conceptualizes culture, the "Anotherness in One World" approach is multidimensional and multi-interpretive: emphasizing the internal cultural development of men and women; drawing on historical memory and the values of the developing society to provide cultural continuity.

In general terms, then, the communitarian paradigm – unlike the (under)-dependency paradigm examined earlier – does not assess development from a macrotheoretical perspective. For this reason, it has limited theoretical value when it comes to explaining power relationships among those communities involved in the process of planning and implementing development strategies. That said, this paradigm is to be commended for its privileging of the actual lived experiences of nations struggling for ways and means to accomplish the goals of local and regional self-development within the broader context of state relations.

DECOLONIZING THE WEST: THE INTERNAL COLONIAL CONCEPT

In recent years, there has been a turn towards self-reflection in Eurocentric societies within the so-called First and Second Worlds. As their populations become increasingly multicultural and multiracial, the critical discourses pertaining to development communications have begun to focus on the West itself as a site of internal colonialism.[13] Theories of development can no longer be exclusively tied to Third World countries "out there." Differences in development patterns between so-called First, Second, Third, and Fourth Worlds are now seen more in terms of volume and degree than actual substance (Shinar 1990, 3).

Theorists such as Clifford Geertz, John and Jean Comaroff, Stuart Hall, Cornel West, Homi Bhabha, Arturo Escobar, and bell hooks have significantly contributed to this refocused approach by showing us the relevance of problematizing our own development processes in the First and Second Worlds.[14] Their cultural writings – which both draw upon and bring together the realms of cultural studies, ethnography, development communications, and postcolonial discourse – fully engage in the debates on cultural and racial stereotyping, the decolonization process, the diaspora of the formerly colonized to the West, and the impact of settler societies on indigenous communities whose ancestral lands are those upon which arbitrary political boundaries, systems, and structures have been imposed.

Regarding this latter point, these theorists share the view that the migration of peoples to the West has not only necessitated a re-evaluation and retheorization of notions such as "the nation," "the state," "power," and "the citizen" but also highlights the importance of legally recognizing the ideology/policy of cultural and racial diversity as that which is best suited to the specific conditions of the late twentieth and early twenty-first centuries. Most importantly – and here they echo the groundbreaking writings of Edward Said (1979), whose analysis of the discourses of Orientalism has become a prototype for examining the production, management, and domination of the Western monopoly of knowledge and power – their writings take a self-conscious discursive turn, focusing in on the ways in which struggles over discursive powers themselves enable and constrain the democratic development of a range of cultural and communication rights. Among these rights are the right to be different from the dominant, the right to resist the hegemonic, the right to equal access to resources such as public media-spaces, and the political right to authoritatively define the parameters of one's own community development and self-determination goals. ˙

Each of these more elaborated rights has generated numerous transnational discussions, not to mention a host of conflicting strategies for intervention. With the help of the World Wide Web, civil society groups and social movements have joined forces to form international partnerships and set up collaborative projects. As a consequence, conventional notions and practices of development as contained within a single territory are being challenged and troubled.

REFRAMING THE DEBATE: INDIGENOUS BROADCASTING AS A SITE OF DEVELOPMENT COMMUNICATIONS IN A MULTICULTURAL SOCIETY

Canadians have always lived within a plurality of communities and cultures. In this regard, Canada is not unique. Most societies are, to some degree, pluralist. Since the Second World War, in particular, international population migration has increased, and challenges to the dominance of Eurocentric thought by liberation movements have created political and legal dilemmas that have rendered orthodox approaches to issues of tolerance and equality rights outdated. At the very least, the emergence of vocal and strong local, regional, racial, ethnocultural, gender, and economic communities has created cleavages in social, political, and cultural institutions.

In Canada, three constituency groups, to meet their cultural communities' information and entertainment needs, have each advocated for "special recognition" in policy and for "adjusted" special communications services. These groups are pre-Canadians (First Peoples), French and English Canadians, and immigrant populations (di Norcia 1984, 148–9). In response, the Canadian state has designed some basic communications policies and tools to facilitate coexistence. These include the Multiculturalism Policy (1971), the Multiculturalism Act (1988), A Broadcasting Policy Reflecting Canada's Linguistic and Cultural Diversity (1985), the Northern Broadcasting Policy (1983), and the Broadcasting Act (1991). Other relevant legislation includes the Canadian Charter of Rights and Freedoms, Sections 15 (Equality Rights) and 27 (Multiculturalism) (1982); the Official Languages Act (1977); the Canadian Citizenship Act (1977); the Canadian Human Rights Act (1976); and the Employment Equity Act (1986). These supportive policies and pieces of legislation, along with their accompanying programs, have placed Canadians in a particularly strong position as regards the ability to organize constituency group resistance to homogenization via the media.

Since the passing of the last Broadcasting Act in June 1991, which both materially recognized and legislatively acknowledged Canada's distinct need for a decentralized and deprofessionalized communications system as a strategy for coping with its unique geography and its culturally and racially diverse populations, Canada has become an exemplar of a fairly complex national development case unfolding *outside* of the Third World.

Most case studies and theoretical accounts in the realm of media and development have repeatedly focused on colonial, neocolonial, and postcolonial relationships in their national contexts, with the colonizer invariably placed in a position of dominance and control. And as documented in the works of Harold Innis and Gail Valaskakis, the extension of influence and authority in Canada (like elsewhere) tends to move from the centre to the periphery, and not vice versa. Though marginalized peoples elsewhere can and do learn to speak back to those in power, the cases I present in this book demonstrate that few have attempted such bold and culturally persistent initiatives as have the First Peoples of Canada. True, like many other media-based constituency groups, one of the aims of First Peoples broadcasters has been to achieve self-empowerment through producing programming *about* themselves for others *like* themselves. However, as we shall see in chapters 6–8, Canadian First Peoples broadcasters have not limited themselves to these aims, but have opened mediaspaces and administrative debates about (cross)cultural development processes in Canada and beyond.[15] What do these kinds of initiatives signify within the broader context of development studies? How would development theorists distinguish the special status of Canadian First Peoples broadcasting history, given its location in an officially multicultural society? And from which theoretical sources can we draw conceptual categories that would most appropriately explain First Peoples' role in the national development process?

As an international prototype for indigenous media development, the Canadian case points to the need for a more complex and inclusive theory of (trans)national and multicultural/multiracial development in a settler society. This theory should reflect upon and account for technological refinements, broadcasting policy bypasses, and for the kind of (inter)national crosscultural linkages that will force governments to rethink conventional development and policy strategies as well as international media/power relationships. As we follow the story of First Peoples television, we can begin to identify concrete data that can be used as evidence to support the construction of such a theoretical analysis.

The next chapter examines a wide range of powerful, stereotypical discourses and images of colonialism inherited from previous generations that First Peoples have struggled to correct. These are the very same images that policy makers have had to confront and work towards revising in order to create a fair and non-discriminatory broadcasting framework for Canadian society.

2 Towards the (De)Romancing of First Peoples and Their Territories: The Policy-Maker's Imaginary

Policy is formed by preconceptions, by long implanted biases. When information is relayed to policy-makers, they respond in terms of what is already inside their heads and consequently make policy less to fit the facts than to fit the notions and intentions formed out of the mental baggage that has accumulated in their minds since childhood.

Barbara W. Tuchman (*Practicing History: Selected Essays*, 289)

In his foreword to Raymond Stedman's *Shadows of the Indian* (1982), Rennard Strickland suggests that understanding the popular image is important not only for the view it provides of the Indian, but also for what it reveals about the society that created the image. Each new White generation has reinvented the Indian in the image of its own era and these images, Strickland insists, continue to dominate Indian policy. History and policy are opposite sides of the same coin, and one cannot begin to understand the realities of modern Indian life and what the prospects are for the next generations without understanding the popular images of the past and the present. In the case of the American Indian, Strickland maintains, the "facts" of how life has been lived are dramatically at odds with those "notions" of Indianness as perpetuated in dime novels and Saturday matinée movies (ix–xi).

Focusing on some of the inaccurate portrayals of First Peoples and their territories, this chapter provides a sense of just how hard the struggle for fair imagery and equitable representation has been for First Peoples primarily, but also for those policy-makers and administrators who have been mandated to provide equitable resources for all Canadian constituency groups. For these latter, too, have not only inherited this same legacy of racist images and histories but have had to contend with opinions formed in the sociocultural and political contexts of racism and distorted communications.

This chapter begins with a brief overview of how the North and First Peoples have been positioned both in and through a variety of mediated representations over time. These representations, I argue, have reinforced how the North and its peoples have been seen in the popular imagination and consequently treated in the political realm. Building on this notion of how groups become defined, I also look at how officials linguistically demarcated "Indians" from "Eskimos" for the purposes of financial administration. Following this, I turn to some of the typical media stereotypes that have circulated with regard to Indians and Inuit. Differentiating between Hollywood-style feature films and ethnographic documentaries, I show how the National Film Board of Canada's gradual incorporation of "the salvage paradigm" – an anthropological paradigm, particularly popular in the 1950s, promoting the documentation and preservation of activities that would rescue traditional cultural practices from obsolescence[1] – into film in the 1950s and 60s led to its series on Netsilik Eskimos in which the "real" lives of the Inuit were documented in order to "be preserved." The chapter closes with some reflections on how this negative media legacy, in combination with other forces, motivated First Peoples to take control of their own cultural images, languages and histories. When Canada passed the Telesat Act in 1969, making it possible for those in the North to receive improved telecommunications services, such as live television, First Peoples saw an opening. As it happens, this was the same year in which the then Minister of Indian and Northern Affairs, Jean Chrétien, proposed a First Peoples assimilationist policy in a government White Paper. This convergence of events played into the hands of First Peoples' politicians, who saw in it an opportunity to use the powerful medium of television to challenge the government's assimilationist policy. In other words, rather than merely contesting this legacy of distorted imagery, First Peoples began to think about strategies for attaining access to telecommunications services (especially television) due to be phased into Northern communities in 1973 and 1974 after the launching of the Anik satellite.

THE NORTH

Geographer Louis-Edmond Hamelin (1979) has defined "The North" as the area that exists above the tree line that – depending on where you are in the country – lies between the fifty-fifth and sixtieth parallels. It conforms with widely accepted geographic indicators of "Nordicity" based on latitude,

Map of Canada. Used with permission of Derek Parent, 2004.

annual temperatures below zero, types of ice, accessibility, regional population density, and levels of economic activity. Measures such as these are useful
in distinguishing geographical characteristics, but innumerable sources over
the centuries indicate that it is not, and never has been, science that has articulated the idea of the North in the North American public imaginary. Rather,
it is our own mythical notions of "The North" that circumscribe our views.

In his essay "The True North Strong and Free" from his book *Places on
the Margin* (1991), cultural geographer Rob Shields speaks of three Cana-

The Circumpolar North. Used with permission of Natural Resources, Canada.

dian "Norths": the administrative or geographical "North" as defined by the federal government, which usually includes the Northwest Territories (now divided into NWT and Nunavut) and Yukon; the imaginary "North" – "a frontier, a wilderness, and empty 'space' which, seen from southern Canada is white, blank"; and the ideological "True North" – an "empty page onto which can be projected images of the essence of 'Canadian-ness' and also images to define one's urban existence against" (165). Defined predominantly in terms of Southern interests, the "symbolic North" has been fabricated by non-natives who have talked about it, analyzed it, made statements

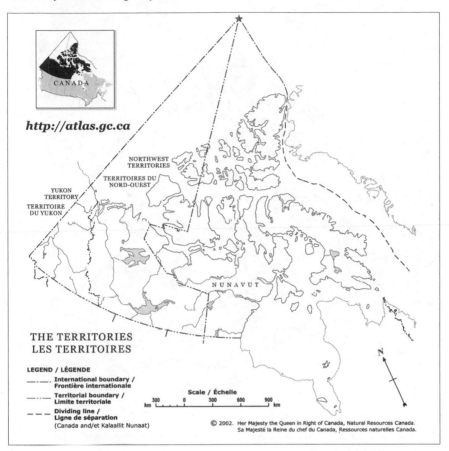

http://atlas.gc.ca

CANADA

NORTHWEST
TERRITORIES
TERRITOIRES DU
NORD-OUEST

YUKON
TERRITORY
TERRITOIRE
DU YUKON

NUNAVUT

THE TERRITORIES
LES TERRITOIRES

LEGEND / LÉGENDE

International boundary /
Frontière internationale

Territorial boundary /
Limite territoriale

Dividing line /
Ligne de séparation
(Canada and/et Kalaallit Nunaat)

Scale / Échelle

300   0   300   600   900
km   km

© 2002. Her Majesty the Queen in Right of Canada, Natural Resources Canada.
Sa Majesté la Reine du chef du Canada, Ressources naturelles Canada.

N

Canada's Territories. Used with permission of Natural Resources, Canada.

about it, settled it, ruled it, authorized certain views of it, managed it, photo-graphed it, and ultimately produced it as an "exotic" commodity for Southern consumption.

Ideas and fictions about the North have shifted over time as various Southern-based institutions have set up outpost organizations there to enact mandates originating outside of the North and representing Southern inter-ests. Historically, it has been these outsiders who have controlled the ima-gery, descriptions, and development imaginary of the North. Those involved in this production of "The North" have included the early explorers, the

"The Northern Zones of Canada." Adapted from the work of Hamelin and used with permission of Derek Parent.

missionaries, the whalers, the traders, the North West Mounted Police, the Royal Canadian Mounted Police, the military, Southern-based and, only recently, Northern-based media.

Distorted images of a fragmented and localized North permeate Canadian cultural texts, historical documents, and news reports. Characterized by inadequate information and often by out-and-out racism, most of these present a confusing and inaccurate view of the North to a generally uninformed Southern public. In this light, it is not altogether surprising to learn that, "To mark the occasion of the Olympic Games in Montreal in 1976, Canada issued a $5.00 coin displaying a map of the country ... [in which] part of the High Arctic does not appear" (McClymont 1988, 8).

FIRST PEOPLES' POPULATION IN CANADA'S NORTH

According to recent *Indian and Northern Affairs Canada* population statistics (December 2002, but based on the 1996 Canada Census), the Canadian Artic, Mander's (1991) so-called "unpopulated icy wasteland" (99), and, of course, the regions surrounding it, which make up one third of Canada's land mass, have a very low population density. As of July 2003, Canada's aboriginal populations comprised approximately three percent of the total Canadian population of 31,629,677. That said, the North is not empty, as the following figures from the 1996 Census indicate. Please note that in 1996, Nunavut had not yet separated from the NWT and so its figures are aggregated with those of the NWT. There are currently approximately 17,500 Inuit residing in Nunavut.

FIRST PEOPLES/CANADIAN POPULATIONS – 1996 CENSUS

	NWT	Yukon
Amerindians	11,400	5,530
Métis	3,895	565
Inuit	24,600	110
Total Aboriginal Population	39,895	6,205

Given the low population figures for First Peoples in these areas and the negative stereotypes against which they have to struggle, it is not surprising that one of their major challenges has been to figure out how to command equity of resources, services, and representation within Southern corridors of power and governance.

Then there is the case of the Russian nuclear satellite that, back in 1978, began falling out of orbit to Earth. As Jerry Mander (1991) explains: "To the relief of most people, the thing finally crashed to Earth in hundreds of bits along a 300-mile swath through what was termed an 'unpopulated icy wasteland' near the Arctic Circle. Actually, the disintegrating satellite flew over a region containing some twenty-six communities of Dene and Inuit, whose people have lived there for 20,000 years" (99).

The North, itself, has been alternatively described as a "despoiled paradise" and an "inhospitable landscape," and one finds endless examples of this dichotomy in the literature and imagery circulating about the North. Even more important, however, is how the peoples of the North have been framed over the years – and hence have come to be defined – by the so-called "ethno-graphic" data collected about them by outsiders and subsequently circulated in *non-indigenous* media. Until the latter part of the twentieth century, the Southern public's perception of the First Peoples of the North was based almost exclusively on what could be gleaned from Southern-produced films, photographs, books, and magazines like *National Geographic* and *MacLean's*. The resulting representations were problematic at the time of their production and, despite severe criticism, continue to be circulated on television, which recycles old films and imagery as "fill" programming.

Diverse nations have been characterized as one monolithic community and invariably portrayed as an "exotic," "primitive," and "uncivilized" people living in a timeframe outside of the author's (or reader's) own society. In other words, those documenting the lives and knowledges of First Peoples in North America tended to fall into the age-old anthropological pattern of assuming that hunters, trappers, and others living within traditional tribal communities were exemplary of an ancient world that was living out a history that the researchers' own ancestors had left behind centuries before. Through negatively circumscribing First Peoples images in discourses and media, hierarchical social and political relations could more easily be maintained and reproduced in Canada; moreover, this could be done with the silent consent of Euro-Canadians.

The fact that Euro-Canadians were the "classifiers" and First Peoples the "classified" in the various taxonomies that documented the diverse populations of Canada tells us more about the intellectual premises and conceptual categories of Euro-Canadian mainstream society and its anthropologists, politicians, and media makers than it does about First Peoples. It speaks to the inequality in power relations among the constituency groups and it demonstrates "the exercise of 'intensive surveillance' over the population to be governed through the acquisition of particular kinds of knowledge about its constituent members" (Smith, D. 1990, 42). Furthermore, the symbolic violence done to First Peoples through the stereotypical and racist reproduction of their lives in art, literature, cinema, television, and journalism has made it more difficult for them to disrupt the continuum of distorted representations. In other words, the cognitive effects of the proliferation and circulation of racist discourse – in manipulating First Peoples psychologically – presented almost insurmountable obstacles for them to bypass and organize against.

IMAGES OF FIRST PEOPLES AND THEIR REFLECTION IN POLICY

Not surprisingly, Canadian administrators fared no better in their treatment and social relations with members of First Peoples than did the media. Peter Kulchyski's (1993) work confirms this: "By the early 1900s, the Canadian state had established an array of structures that served to define, confine, and ultimately remove what it had constructed as its 'Native problem'" (24). These structures were built into the legislative framework of the Indian Act of 1876, which gave the state unusual coercive powers to dictate the terms by which Indians could conduct their lives. Consider the parallel restrictions on the self-development of First Peoples in the media and in various policies circumscribing their life choices.

In fact, it was the development of a whole series of strategies of containment – strategies that included the objectification of First Peoples through framing them as objects of anthropological study – that became the dominant feature of successive Canadian governments' relationship to aboriginal peoples in those early years. By the late 1930s, the failure of anthropologists to recognize the diversity of native peoples, combined with Parliament's desire to reduce costs and commitments towards the well-being of residents in the North, precipitated a jurisdictional conflict over financial responsibility for the Inuit. As Canada moved towards establishing its sovereignty over the Arctic Islands, a question arose as to whether or not the Inuit (or "Esquimaux sauvages" as they were called at the time) – particularly those living within Quebec – were in fact "savage *Indians*" and consequently, the responsibility of the federal government under Section 91 of the 1867 Constitution Act. The question was important because many Inuit had by that time become dependent for their welfare on the Hudson's Bay Company or on both federal and provincial governments – all of which had been inconsistent in carrying out their obligations to the Inuit. Furthermore, questions about the Inuit use of alcohol and their access to medical services could not be resolved until the legal status of the Inuit had been determined.

The Supreme Court of Canada took up the issue in 1939, stepping into a dispute that had raged between Ottawa and Quebec for years. In the end – and after ignoring anthropological and ethnological testimony from some of North America's most noted authorities – the consensus of the judges was that, indeed, "Eskimos were Indians." They justified their decision on the basis that in the spoken and written reports of missionaries, explorers, cartographers, and geographers, the two words were conflated into one meaning. As the judge presiding over the decision explained:

"THE FACE OF THE NORTH"

A typical example of distorted representation can be found in the cover story "Reports on the North" from a 1954 issue of *MacLean's* magazine. On an inside page, under the heading "The Face of the North," photographs of a cross-section of the North's population are shown.

The Face of the North

NURSE
Hazel Sproule in Yellowknife hospital. Because of isolation northerners often get better facilities than small Outside communities.

SURVEYOR
Cam Dubord works near Uranium City. North is alive with surveyors. Plumb bobs and transits are just as familiar as dog teams.

POSTMISTRESS
Sara Newsam weighs out the regular mail at Fort McMurray. Northerners now get frequent letter service except in eastern Arctic.

TRAPPER
George Lush, an old-time trapper on the barrens, wears homemade clothes tailored from skins of caribou. He shoots, tans and sews.

PRIEST
Father Vandevelde, Oblate missionary, lives in stone hut at remotest mission of all: Pelly Bay on Boothia Peninsula in Arctic sea.

DEACON
Jim Edwards, an Indian minister, preaches in three tongues—English, Loucheaux and Eskimo at All Saints Anglican Cathedral, Aklavik.

PROSPECTOR
Bill Johnson has taken part in all northern stampedes of past 50 years. He lost hands in a dynamite blast during rush to Yellowknife.

MINER
Al Boucher is one of a handful of men taking out preliminary ore at Pine Point, which is likely to be the scene of a future boom town.

ESKIMO
Jim Koiakak, fiercely independent, wears hair in old style. Once he started his own religion. At 80, he lives in a skin tent at Coppermine.

Pierre Berton – "The Faces of the North," in "The Mysterious North," *MacLean's Magazine*, 15 November 1954, 16. Courtesy of Pierre Berton and *MacLean's* Magazine.

[I]t appears that, through all the territories of British North America in which there were Eskimo, the term "Indian" was employed by well established usage as including these as well as the other aborigines; and I repeat the *British North America Act*, in so far as it deals with the subject of Indians, must, in my opinion, be taken to contemplate the Indians of British North America as a whole. (Canada Law Reports 1939, 104)

It goes without saying that those responsible for the decision were well aware that, if Eskimos could be positioned as Indians for administrative purposes, it would be all that much easier for the state to establish assimilationist policies at the federal level. The predictable shift in government policy from a coercive to a more ideological/assimilationist approach began in 1951. It escalated until the announcement of the Liberal Government's White Paper in 1969. Delivered by Jean Chrétien, then Minister of Indian and Northern Affairs, this controversial document called for the repeal of the Indian Act, the dismantling of the Indian Affairs bureaucracy, the transfer of responsibility for Indians to the provinces, and the loss of special status.

The aboriginal response was one of outrage. The Trudeau government had not consulted with native leaders over the drafting of this document and this made First Peoples' distrustful of the Cabinet – not only leading to an intensification of their political activity but marking the beginning of a new era in which aboriginal peoples became a highly visible and audible political presence within Canadian society. More than anything, this document catalyzed First Peoples' recognition that, while living within a circuit of mediated stereotypes, political manipulations and misrepresentations, they would have to seize control of the means of media production and distribution so that they could circulate information to the Canadian public from *their* multiple perspectives. It was as if this White Paper represented their "last straw," a push over the line that would shift not only their cognitive approach to the reception of information and imagery from outside of their cultural norms but also motivate a set of strategic media tactics to promote their interests across the sociocultural and political borderlines to the non-native population in Canada. How First Peoples began to represent themselves from this time onwards was in direct opposition to the stereotypical images they had inherited from the media. To get a better grasp of the distance First Peoples have travelled in this regard, it is important to lay out not in an exhaustive fashion but rather in a representative manner some of the actual images circulating at the time.

Front cover of Deborah Doxtator's *Fluffs and Feathers: An Exhibit on the Symbols of Indianness*, a resource guide, revised edition. Brantford: Woodland Cultural Center, 1992. Courtesy of the Woodland Cultural Centre.

EARLY VISUAL REPRESENTATIONS OF FIRST PEOPLES IN CANADA

Until the latter part of the twentieth century, outsiders tended to treat Indians and Inuit as if they were geographical features within the immense, empty, and hostile landscape of the Canadian North (Mayes 1972; Shields 1991). To American filmmakers in particular, "The North" did not consist of the region located above the sixtieth parallel, but rather comprised all of Canada – in other words, "Hollywood's North."

As a result, it is hard to distinguish early films about Canadian Indians in "Hollywood's North" from those supposedly depicting life North of 60°. Though a limited number of films – most of them ethnographic – were produced in Canada and presented a somewhat fairer and more representative "take" on the diverse lifestyles and practices of First Peoples, the majority of films were produced in the USA and presented a *simulated* North in which Canadian natives were depicted as mere carbon copies of their "Holly-woodized" American counterparts. Only a handful of feature films were made about Inuit life exclusively – among them *Nanook of the North* (Robert Flaherty 1922), *Land of the Long Day* (Doug Wilkinson 1952), *The White Dawn* (Philip Kaufman 1974), and *The Savage Innocents* (Nicholas Ray 1959) – and these, because they unfolded in a terrain that could not be simulated in the United States, managed to escape the kind of generic stereotyping derived from Wild West shows, dime novels, and the Indian Princess tradition that characterized the bulk of these so-called "representations" of Native life. More than anything, what these latter ended up creating were opportunities for Whites to play First Peoples' roles. As Mohawk author Deborah Doxtator (1988) comments in her book, *Fluffs and Feathers: An Exhibit on the Symbols of Indianness*: "Most of the 'big name' actors of the 1950s and early 1960s have played Indian ... Any actor could play an Indian in the movies. All that was required was a wig, make-up and a headband" (38–40). Likewise, films about the Inuit produced their own "noble savage" stereotype.

Though Hollywood producers often employed native costume and cultural advisers, much of their counsel was ignored.[2] Relying, instead, on what Ralph and Natasha Friar (1972) – cataloguers of literally thousands of films made about Indians – have referred to as "The Instant Indian Kit," filmmakers preferred to continue the production of the expected. This "kit" – consisting of "wig, war bonnet or headband (beaded or otherwise), vest or shirt, breech-clout ...[buckskin] leggings or fringed pants, and moccasins" (223) – contributed to a homogenized view of what constituted "Indian Dress" among non-Native moviegoers; and Natives, too, were influenced by Hollywood's framing of their so-called "traditional" garb. The headband, for example, was a non-native invention, but it became so frequently utilized as a symbol of Indianness that, as Pierre Berton (1975) has pointed out, some Indians still consider it to be part of their traditional heritage (101).

Pierre Berton, in fact, has written extensively on Hollywood's stereotyping of Canadian First Peoples, and his work highlights the narrow range of roles with which Indians, Métis (or "half-breeds"), and the Inuit were to become identified. In his analysis of more than sixty films made before 1975, Berton found four in which the half-breed character, for instance, might be called "good." All other representations depicted half-breed characters as "villains of the deepest dye – sneaky, untrustworthy degenerates who coveted defenseless White women, sold base whisky to the Indians, and let others take the rap for their crimes" (87). As a stock Hollywood character, the stereotype of the half-breed in American-made films about Canada was always a mix of Indian and French (the Métis). In his study, Berton was unable to identify a single Indian-English half-breed character.

Half-breed women fared no better. Reinforcing all the stereotypical myths associated with degenerate, flamboyant women, they were portrayed as jealous and coquettish, with a penchant for treachery. In short, they were: "[S]neaky spitfires who would do anything to get and hold their lovers, usually White men. They wore standard Hollywood Female Half-Breed Costumes: long black hair in braids, often to the waist, long necklaces of beads or animal teeth, buckskin or leather skirts, and high boots" (97).

How Indians differed from Métis in these Hollywood depictions, according to Berton, is that they tended to have more justification for their savagery. Among the stock reasons underlying their violent actions were the need to protect their hunting grounds, alcoholism (a condition introduced by the White man), and obeying the wise elders (103). Indian maidens, on the other hand, were generally portrayed as *almost* White, as sad-eyed and seductive, and as victims of unrequited love. This early Hollywood stereotype would go on to be immortalized in the "Indian princess" paintings: becoming an emblem of, and calendar girl for, all that was considered beautiful in the White Indian "Brooke Shields" cliché.[3]

Ward Churchill's (1992) more recent analysis of the stereotyping of *American* Indians in film identifies three subgenres within the larger genre: those films in which Indians are "creatures of another time"; films in which native cultures are defined by Eurocentric values; and films that adopt the attitude of "seen one Indian, seen 'em all" (232–6). Churchill suggests that it is upon the members and daily life of the Plains Nations, circa 1825–80, that the generic American Indian of cinema is based: "The essential idea of Native America instilled cinematically is that of a quite uniform aggregation of peoples (in dress, custom and actions) which flourished with the arrival of Whites upon their land and then vanished somewhat mysteriously, along with the bison and the open prairie. There is no 'before' to this story, and there is no 'after'" (232).

Noting that, in the majority of these films, "indigenous people are defined exclusively in terms of certain (conflict and demise) interactions with Euroamericans" and that "[t]here is no cinematic recognition whatsoever of a white-free and autonomous native past" (233), Churchill goes on to suggest that there are very few films that attempt to deal with contemporary Indian realities. One of the early exceptions is a film called *Journey through Rosebud*

(1972), which was a commercial failure. Criticized in the popular press for depicting Indians as "wooden," Native Americans judged it to be an accurate and convincing portrayal of themselves. Soon after it was released, it was withdrawn from circulation "as an embarrassment" (233). Pitted against the weighty image of the hybrid Hollywood "Indian," this film's less stereotypical portrayal just didn't stand a chance.

Film representations of First Peoples can be read as signs of popular views and discourses. They clearly indicate to us messages about contemporary sociocultural beliefs and practices. It is easier for a non-aboriginal filmmaker to tap into the pool of "shorthand" Indian stereotypes, with the goal of quickly assembling a popular film based on fantasies of violence and confrontation, than it is for them to research and present a contemporary, and more realistic, portrayal. As Deborah Root (1993) has so succinctly noted, "Native violence is so long-standing and pervasive, it is able to structure many of the images we see on screen, in part because it operates as a way of concealing or drowning our discussions of colonial violence" (46).

When the identity of a people is symbolically demolished through cinematic distortions, it is easy to overlook their humanity and to ignore their status as a set of distinct nations. In the words of Ward Churchill (1992): "The people, as such, disappear, usually to the benefit – both material and psychic – of those performing the symbolic demolition. There are accurate and appropriate terms which describe this: dehumanization, obliteration or appropriation of identity, political subordination and material colonization are all elements of a common process of imperialism. This is the real meaning of Hollywood's stereotyping of American Indians" (239).

Traditionally, the Inuit, too, have been subjected to their share of humiliating media stereotyping and often out-and-out exploitation as a result of being positioned by Southerners as "exoticized objects" from the unknown Arctic. In 1901, for instance, a group of Inuit were transported to the United States and displayed before visitors at the Buffalo Exhibition. Captured on film by Thomas Edison, they were paraded among plaster icebergs in temperatures of up to 90° Fahrenheit.

Subjecting Inuit and other First Peoples to this kind of exhibitionary practice was not anything new at the time. Kenn Harper's excellent 1986 book, *Give Me My Father's Body: The Life of Minik, The New York Eskimo* (due to be released as a feature film), documents the tragic case of a Polar Eskimo who was taken to New York from his home in northwestern Greenland in 1897 by US explorer Robert Peary and exhibited in the American Museum of Natural

History where he eventually died. Then there is the well-documented case of Ishi – the last "wild Indian" of the tiny Yahi tribe of California – who was taken by anthropologists to reside at the University of California's Museum of Anthropology, where he lived under the constant gaze of curiosity-seekers. In each of these cases, the racist exploitation of ethnic differences is both apparent and appalling. No doubt, it was guided by a sense of curiosity about "the exotic" and by the archaic notion that First Peoples' cultures, as well as their physical bodies, were artifactual – something that could be put on display, that could be inhumanly "frozen in time."[4]

That said, the Inuit tended to be more romanticized than their Indian and Métis counterparts both on film and elsewhere in the media, and this for several reasons. For one, Inuit had historically had much less contact with non-natives, and when contact did occur, the incredibly difficult climactic conditions meant that non-natives were generally in a position of being physically dependent upon the Inuit, not to mention somewhat in awe of the Inuit ability to survive in such a harsh environment.

The Inuit population was also small compared to that of the Indians and Métis. This meant that the Inuit tended not to "get in the way" of settlers seeking to appropriate and develop Northern land on behalf of the Canadian government. It also meant that the Inuit could be positioned as a culture on the verge of extinction. As such, the Inuit cultures fit neatly into the salvage paradigm. Finally, the unattractiveness of Inuit land to most Southerners – resource developers and sovereignty-minded federal government administrators being the two exceptions – meant that the Inuit had not had to resort to violence to defend their land against invading parties.

As a result of all of these factors, Inuit and non-natives managed to resolve their potential and actual cross-cultural conflicts in a relatively peaceful and diplomatic manner, albeit with the latter subtly maintaining their assumed position of "natural superiority" over the former. At a symbolic level, the relatively few films that were made about Inuit cultural life tended to reflect this easy, if unequal, relationship. Assessing the period up to 1975, Pierre Berton (1975) could only identify about half a dozen and all of these were filmed in the Arctic, were semi-documentary in fashion, and used native Eskimos as actors (108).

The most famous of these films is *Nanook of the North*. Sponsored by Revillon Frères (fur-trading competitors of the Hudson's Bay Company) and filmed in the region of what is now called Inoucdjouac in Northern Quebec, the original seventy-five-minute silent film depicted life in the Arctic as typified by one family's daily routine. Beginning with the words, "No other race could survive ... yet here live the most cheerful people in all the world – the fearless, lovable, happy-go-lucky Eskimo," the film crystallized the stereotype of the Inuit people for generations. Premiering at the Capitol Theater in New York City on 11 June 1922 and distributed by Pathé Pictures Exchange, a description of the few scenes that were actually simulated by the filmmakers gives a sense of the lengths to which they were willing to go to live up to what they believed to be the public's conception of "real" life in the North. As an excerpt from the catalogue accompanying a 1980 retrospective of director Flaherty's life and work explains: "It would appear ... that none of the leading characters were identified by their actual names; that Allakariallak's (Nanook's) clothing was not indigenous to the region; that the contrived sequences were highly amusing to the Inuit; that the seal hunt was contrived. It is also possible that the walrus hunting sequence had been shot in 1914 or 1916 as part of Flaherty's earlier films, either in the Ottawa or Belcher Islands" (Vancouver Art Gallery 1980, 62).

Despite some simulation, however, *Nanook* presented a fairly accurate depiction of life in the Arctic and brought to many Southern audiences their first glimpse of that remote and enigmatic world. Even before the final edit had been completed, Flaherty's screenings of the uncut rushes were being received with interest and enthusiasm in the South. As early as 31 March 1915 a headline in *The Globe* read, "Movies of Eskimo Life Win Much Appreciation: Remarkable Series of Pictures Shown by Mr R.J. Flaherty," with the accompanying article opening with the following paragraph:

Probably the most remarkable "movies" ever shown in Toronto and surely the first of their kind ever shown in Canada were those put on at Convocation Hall last night. It was the pictures of Eskimo life in Baffin Land secured and exhibited by Mr Robert J. Flaherty, head of the Sir William Mackenzie Arctic Expeditions. Every scene brought applause from the large audience of scientists, archaeologists and laymen to whom the pictures were a source of wonder and instruction. (quoted in Vancouver Art Gallery 1980, 62)

On the same day, *The Evening Telegram* wrote: "Splendid moving pictures showing Esquimo family life, ceremonial dances and traveling with dog sleighs over snowy wastes on the world's second largest island were those given at Convocation Hall last night by R.J. Flaherty, F.F.G.S. Besides the moving pictures there were some excellent portraits of artistic excellence depicting types of this remote people" (quoted in Vancouver Art Gallery 1980, 62).

What stands out in these critical reviews are the ethnographic descriptions. Far from addressing *Nanook* as a film, the reviewers were clearly treating what they saw as ethnographic footage designed to educate and inform and intended for Southern consumption. Unlike films being made about the Indians during this same time period, *Nanook* was not put together primarily for entertainment purposes. Rather, it conformed to the documentation requirements as prescribed by the salvage paradigm. In highlighting the hardships *and* humour of life as a "real" Eskimo, it made the "real" peoples of the North come alive. But, in its framing of these "exotic" people of the North as somehow "other," it also succeeded in perpetuating unequal relations of power in Canadian society.

The National Film Board of Canada carried on this tradition of making ethnographic films about the peoples of the North, and under their direction a number of classic documentary films have been produced. In particular, the *People of the Seal – Eskimo Summer and Eskimo Winter* series, produced by Michael McKennirey and George Pearson (1971), and the *Netsilik Eskimo* (1963–65) series, directed by Gilles Blais under the ethnographic direction of Dr Asen Balikci of the University of Montreal, are outstanding for their attempts to depict Eskimo life with a minimum of cultural reconstruction and a maximum of respect.

Consisting of a total of twenty-three films and constructed from footage shot of the Netsilik Eskimos, both series fall into the salvage paradigm category. Note, for example, the N F B's description of *People of the Seal – Parts I and II*:

Two films, co-productions of the B B C and the N F B of Canada, compiled from some of the most vivid actuality footage ever filmed of the life of the Netsilik Eskimos in the Pelly Bay region of the Canadian Arctic. Together, they provide insight and understanding of *a primitive culture now almost vanished*, as they show the incredible resourcefulness with which the Netsilik (People of the Seal) have adapted to one of the world's harshest environments. (N F B 1979, 17; my emphasis)

In line with the salvage paradigm, this N F B text stresses how the series depicts life as it was lived "before the coming of the white man" (15). The fact that this necessitated a reconstruction is emphasized, as is the point that the Netsilik "readily agreed to live in the old way once more and showed considerable aptitude in recalling and representing the earlier way of life" (17).

Unlike the NFB documentaries, with their emphasis on ethnographic details, Hollywood films made around this same time tended to show the cultural life of the Inuit from a more entertaining perspective. However, as a film like Nicholas Ray's *The Savage Innocents* (1959) demonstrates, they generally ended up doing more to promote the uncivilized "eaters of raw meat" stereotype than anything else. An exception was Phillip Kaufman's *The White Dawn* (1974), which more readily succeeded in providing a fair – almost ethnographic – representation of Inuit life as lived in the particular period depicted.

Since the mid-1970s, depictions have become progressively "truer" to the actual lived experiences of the Inuit. This is largely due to Inuit insistence that they have a voice in the production and distribution of films made about them. Long-time Northern activist Peter Raymont's films *Sikusilarmiut* (1974) and *Magic in the Sky* (1981), for instance, attest to this new relationship between Inuit and the Southern media of film animation and broadcasting television technology. By introducing viewers to early experimental film and video productions made by Inuit, both films succeed in awakening audiences to the possibility that the Inuit can produce and distribute these products for Inuit audiences. In a sense, Raymont's films mark the transition into the period when the Inuit began appropriating Southern technologies and using them to promote their own aesthetic and organizational goals and communication needs.[5]

Interestingly enough, Peter Raymont's later film – *Between Two Worlds* (1990) – shows another aspect of this transition, and that is the impact of the transfer of Southern social and cultural patterns, as well as technologies, into the North. Based on the tragic story of Joseph Idlout – the man who was featured as "the great Inuit hunter" in Doug Wilkinson's *Land of the Long Day* (1952) – *Between Two Worlds* documents Idlout's decline as his lifestyle becomes less and less valued by the non-natives taking over the social, economic, and political projects of the North. As the value of the furs and skins that have marked his contribution to the Arctic economy drops, Idlout's strength seeps out of him: he becomes a victim of alcoholism and loses his cultural pride. There is terrible irony in the fact that Idlout committed suicide in the same year that he was immortalized on the back of the two-dollar bill. What is striking about *Between Two Worlds* is that it is filled with old footage extracted from earlier, more stereotypical, portrayals of the Inuit, yet is accompanied by a politically astute running commentary that charts the decline of the traditional Inuit way of life. Unlike those films that romanticized and exoticized life in the North, it neither glorifies nor denigrates the

Inuit. Though not made by an Inuit person, its depictions quite accurately capture the lived and complex experiences of the Inuit in relation to the non-native intruders into their territories. This leads to the question of what First Peoples of Canada have made of the diverse, and often conflicting, discourses and practices that have circulated about them, and how they have chosen to challenge and counter both the misrepresentations *and* the absences.

PROTESTING THE PAST; PRETESTING THE FUTURE

Hollywood stereotypes ... have not gone unremarked by the victimized communities. Native Americans, very early on, vocally protested misrepresentations of their culture and history. A 1911 *Moving Picture World* reports the sending of a Native American delegation to President Taft to protest erroneous representations and even ask for a Congressional investigation.

Robert Stam (1993, 16)

The Inuit are probably the most photographed people on earth. The first time I saw a white man, he had a camera and it seems whenever government officials or tourists came North, they always had cameras. They projected what we considered to be the wrong images and stereotypes ... Southern film-makers tend to romanticize a lot of things and they overdramatize. What is probably considered to be very ordinary by our people is taken as being extraordinary by Southern standards. It creates a wrong image.

John Amoagalik (quoted in Raymont, *Magic in the Sky*, 1981)

Be it American Indians protesting the way they were being depicted back in 1911, or more recent complaints like that of Inuit politician John Amoagalik, First Peoples have continuously put pressure on non-indigenous media producers and authors to correct the unfair and inaccurate portrayals that have been made of them. Moreover, First Peoples have made numerous attempts to (re)present themselves to their own peoples and to the rest of the world in a manner that they feel reflects their culture and ways. Peter Pitseolak (born in Cape Dorset in 1902), for instance, was a pioneer photographer/historian whose photographs were among the earliest images of self-portrayal to emerge from the North. When he first picked up a camera in 1942 and began to frame his unique perspective through its viewfinder, Pitseolak was in fact laying the foundation for much of what would come to pass in the years that followed.[6] Stories behind this evolution of indigenous media use in Canada, particularly in regard to television access and development, make up the substantive content of the remainder of this book.

Peter Pitseolak, Inuit photographer, with his camera in Cape Dorset (NWT). © Canadian Museum of Civilization, photo Aggeok Pitseolak, 1946, No. 2000-180.

In the last three decades, especially, First Peoples have become highly politicized about their communication rights. Their articulate criticisms of others' misconstrued and often racist representations of them have appeared in print, have been presented before regulatory and funding agencies, and have been vocalized in community forums. Unfortunately, mainstream North American media still shows innumerable traces of this racism in its recycled films and in its current discourses, practices, and employment opportunities. Canada's administrative record, too, might be superior to that of the USA, but it is still far from being adequate. For First Peoples, then, the task has been twofold: to counter past representations and practices, and to politically engage with what is happening today.

As regards the latter, one of the greatest challenges has been to identify the silences that surround contemporary First Peoples' issues – silences that have led to First Peoples' erasure from public and political life and hence from them being considered as equal members of Canadian society. In other words, if challenging the obvious distortions in media representations is one thing, the task of identifying and documenting those far more subtle absences is quite another. Stuart Hall (1992) highlights some of the problems associated with this task in his discussion of how he and his colleagues went about examining racism in the British media:

We had to develop a methodology that taught us to attend, not only to what people said about race but, in England the great society of the understatement, to what people could not say about race. It was the silences that told us something; it was what wasn't there. It was what was invisible, what couldn't be put into frame, what was apparently unsayable that we needed to attend to. If you want to ask, "what can content analysis teach you?" well, one of the questions you have to ask is, "what about the people who appear to have no content at all – who are just pure form, just pure, invisible form?" You can count lexical items if they're there; but you need a different approach if you really want, as it were, to read a society and its culture symptomatically. (14–15)

When applied to the Canadian context, the dilemma that Hall lays out here became a question of convincing policy-makers that "absence" – i.e., not having any aboriginal content to *count* and being a population without discursive or visual power – was a significant issue that would eventually have to be tackled in order to avoid negative social consequences. But who would take up the challenge of talking about this absence to policy-makers and to the general public? Who would identify these consequences and demand that aboriginal peoples should have both access to and a presence on the airwaves?

Although Ward Churchill (1992), in the following passage, talks from a US perspective, his comments apply equally to the First Peoples' media case as it has evolved in Canada: "While it's true that the immortal words of General Phil Sheridan – 'The only good Indian is a dead Indian' – have continued to enjoy a certain appeal with the American body politic, and equally true that dead Indians are hardly in a position to call the liars to account for their deeds, there are a few of us left out here who just might be up to the task" (241).

Enormous as this task initially seemed, First Peoples in Canada have taken it up and have developed the political savvy required to use existing intervention processes to "bring the liars to account" in a highly sophisticated manner. More than that, though, they have taken concrete steps to counter their false and often racist (mis)representations, as well as address the equally damaging silences and absences, through taking control of their own media content, processes, structures, and administration.

What is interesting, however, is that instead of taking on the most obvious guilty party – the Hollywood film industry – it was first to radio and then to television broadcasting that First Peoples turned to (re)locate themselves within media discourses and practices. One of the reasons behind the choice of television as the visual medium in which to intervene was that it, unlike older media forms, was less historically yoked to a legacy of racism. This is not to say that racism did not exist in Canadian television broadcasting; it did, and still does, play old films that reproduce distasteful stereotypes yet again. The main attraction of Canadian national television broadcasting, however, lay in its accessibility: when live television arrived in the North's most remote communities in 1973–74, this relatively new medium had not yet become entrenched in a tradition of inaccessibility to the degree that film production had. Building upon this notion of accessibility, a large component of the cultural agenda of Northern broadcasters has been to apply the participatory principles and practices characteristic of Northern radio development – a medium that had, early on, demonstrated its capacity to be reflective of aboriginal cultures and languages – to television.

As hard as the struggle has been, the First Peoples' media case has become an international exemplar of self-development. Though a significant amount of work remains to be accomplished in order to stabilize and expand First Peoples' television broadcasting and audience reach in this country, the process – as the rest of this book illustrates – is well on its way. Let us now turn to a short history of Northern radio to gain a sense of the already existing mediated environment into which television was inserted in Northern Canada in the early 1970s.

3 Building Media Infrastructure in the Canadian North: Early Deliberations and Policy Actions

If it is true that southerners are not mentally northern-oriented, and that their orientation is erroneous, or at least is different from that of northerners themselves, or that they are constantly torn between aspects of a double illusion, is it not therefore dangerous to permit southern Canadians to make major decisions concerning the country's North and to impose a form of government on northern areas? Moreover, do not the perceptions that the main northern groups hold of their own cultural differences beg that they rise up against the excesses of "homogeneous Canadianization?"

Louis-Edmond Hamelin (*Canadian Nordicity: It's Your North Too*, 12)

By the 1950s, Southern-produced films and print media had been circulating stereotypical images of the North outside the purview of Northern First Peoples for decades. In this context, it was public radio – transplanted into the North towards the end of the decade – that presented itself as a relatively open linguistic medium, and First Peoples turned to it for culturally relevant information about their lives. The way radio was introduced made it immediately possible for aboriginal peoples to participate in its development as local broadcasters. Radio was inexpensive, both technologically and culturally.

CBC NORTHERN SERVICE: THE INTRODUCTION OF RADIO IN THE CANADIAN ARCTIC

Until the formation of CBC Northern Service in 1958, the Canadian Armed Forces and the Department of Transport, with some program assistance from the CBC, provided the only radio broadcast service in the North. The federal government's concern for Canadian presence and sovereignty in the Far North precipitated the takeover of military and community radio stations by CBC Northern Service. Having been politically committed to cooperate with the United States' continental defense strategy in the Far North since

J.D. Soper and David Wark at the radio, Cape Dorset, Baffin Island, NWT, 6 September 1928. National Archives of Canada/PA-101350.

the mid-1940s, Canada found itself in the difficult position of having to exert its sovereignty *over* the region while simultaneously supporting an American military presence *in* the territory. Interestingly enough, this dilemma – though exacerbated at that particular moment as a result of the Cold War – would not go away. Writing over two decades later, Richard Diubaldo (1981) was stressing how:

Canada can no longer reasonably expect to maintain her Arctic territories in a state of vacuum, and hope at the same time to preserve her sovereignty over them *in absentia*. If her somewhat tenuous claims to these territories are to be guaranteed in the face of the direct and urgent interest which the United States has expressed ... then it follows that she must be prepared to carry out such development by herself or *with a calculated degree of assistance*. In brief, Canada must now either herself provide essential facilities and services in her Arctic territories or provide them cooperatively, or abandon almost all substantial basis to her claims upon them. (99, original emphasis)

Herschel Island – Building Services – Communication. "Wireless Station, Herschel Island, Arctic Coast (NWT)," 1930. National Archives of Canada/PA-100701.

Returning, though, to that period in the late 1950s, the presence in the North of the Royal Canadian Mounted Police and of some military staff – there to fly the flag, control pollution, and monitor foreign traffic – had helped to visibly demonstrate Canadian sovereignty. What the Canadian government had still not offered its Northern residents, however, was a mass-media service that would ensure a Southern cultural influence in the region.

Short-wave radio broadcast reception was still notoriously poor in the late 1950s. The federal government became alarmed by the fact that, besides being isolated from the main flow of national life, citizens of the North often received clearer and more up-to-date broadcasts from the Soviet Union and, to a lesser extent, the USA, than from Canadian stations. The Commissioner of the Yukon expressed his concern about the Cold War in 1957, when he suggested that it would not be at all surprising "if the operators of the Soviet radio service looked upon our North land as an interesting battleground of Soviet and American ideologies through the medium of radio, while Canadian viewpoints are totally absent" (Government of Canada 1957, 297). At around this time, it became critical to the federal government that they structure a relevant Canadian radio service for the North that would reflect Southern interests. Due to the insurmountable geographical and atmospheric barriers, it was technically impossible to develop a conventional land line system

"Jim Stafford, Left, and Unidentified RCMP Constable Listening to Northern Messenger Service, Chesterfield Inlet, NWT." N.d. National Archives of Canada/ C- 64900.

within the Eastern Arctic. As a result, early federal broadcasting initiatives focused on the west, with the east having to await the intervention of satellite technology in 1972 before it could significantly improve its broadcast reception service.

In 1958, CBC Northern Service took over transmitters in Yellowknife, Whitehorse, and Dawson City. Although some programming was designed specifically for the North, stations still had to rely on the short-wave service from Sackville, New Brunswick, for their news broadcasts and for various topical programs. As the land line was extended in the west, this region became less dependent on the short-wave news services. The east, on the other hand, remained tied to the short-wave network.

In 1960, the first Eskimo-language (Inuktitut) broadcasts occurred on CBC. In 1961, the idea of a "sub-regional" production centre (which would feed smaller stations with regional programming) was established.

A modern radio broadcasting building in Nain, Labrador, 1985. Used with permission of OKalaKatiget Native Communications Society.

An illegal community radio station started broadcasting from Pond Inlet, Baffin Island, in 1964. Because it was an inexpensive radio station that broadcast culturally relevant programming, those in charge of the local Inuit initiative never bothered to get a license from the Board of Broadcast Governors.[1] Years later, two pilots flying over Dorval Airport in Montreal inadvertently discovered the station. Apparently the pilots heard the Inuktitut programming and could not identify the language. Thinking it was Russian, but not aware of any Soviet plane in the vicinity, they asked air traffic control to locate the source of the interference. It turns out that the radio waves had travelled all the way from Pond Inlet due to atmospheric abnormalities. When it was reported to the CRTC, the station underwent the "normal" processing procedures and the Commission granted them a license.

The idea of native-language community radio quickly spread across the North. Whereas, by May 1972, the short-wave service was broadcasting 16.4 percent of their programs in Inuktitut (Mayes 1972, 93), community radio stations could do all of their programming in local dialects.

Because setting up local and regional CBC radio services in the North was both easy and relatively inexpensive, radio broadcasting never presented as challenging a set of problems as did television. This might explain why the

Mark Nochasak (radio producer) and Sarah Townley (president of OKalaKatIget Native Communications Society) in radio studio (1998). Used with permission of OKalaKatiget Native Communications Society.

CBC has, since radio's inception in the North, consistently responded favourably to requests for culturally relevant, native-language radio programming. In part because costs are low and in part because the technology is so accessible, radio content has tended to be tailored to the information needs of native peoples. Emphasis is on local and national news, regional weather, road and flying conditions, flood and fire warnings, and personal messages – like health reports on relatives who are hospitalized down South, for instance. Not only have Native staff members been trained in radio production techniques and quickly reached managerial positions within CBC Northern Service; Radio has proved to be a more "appropriate" information technology than television, because it conforms to the communications priorities of Northern residents. More than that, it set the attitudinal context for the coming of television. What this meant was that when television finally arrived in the North, people who were accustomed to listening to radio messages that conformed to their information needs fully expected a television service that would do the same.

MOTIVES FOR EARLY NORTHERN TELEVISION SERVICE

Initial television broadcasting facilities in the North were developed in settlements that were of military, economic, or administrative significance to the South. Basically, the four Northern operations that were economically viable were resource extraction, hydroelectric development, administrative and logistical support centres, and military bases. In population centres that responded to the expansion of these operations, non-native workers and corporate representatives (supported by Department of Indian and Northern Affairs staff) demanded entertainment facilities comparable to those in the South. Work camps and communities regularly had film screenings, but these did not fulfill the population's need for information about current world affairs. At the time, administrators believed that having access to television would boost the morale of the transient workforce. They also thought it would help to stabilize the population by making them feel more connected to their homes outside of the North.

The strongest pressure on the CBC to provide television for Northern communities came from the mining companies and the Minister of Northern Affairs. The mining companies hoped television would help to retain their workforce in the North, which sometimes had a turnover rate of as high as 200 percent a year. In 1966, then Chair of the Economic Council, John Deutsch, echoed this hope when he explained how "the provision of television was needed to attract workers from southern Canada into isolated northern outposts" (Cowan 1969, 11).

During the late 1950s and early 60s, partial television service had been set up in areas outside the Northwest Territories where land access was possible. In 1962, the CBC provided kinescope recordings to Flin Flon and The Pas (Manitoba), which had a combined population of twenty-two thousand. In 1965, the Iron Ore Company of Canada, with the assistance of Hollinger Ungava Transport Ltd, set up its own television transmitters in Schefferville (Quebec) and Labrador City (Newfoundland) and later extended a microwave system to Sept-Iles (Quebec). At this point, questions arose regarding programming control and accountability. From the federal government's point of view, if *most* of the programs were to be drawn from the CBC (as planned by the industrial corporations), but not *all* of them, then there was a danger that viewers would hold the CBC responsible for weaknesses in the service that resulted from these latter. Furthermore, if the intent of the federal government was "to bring the North and the undeveloped regions of Canada into the mainstream of Canadian life by providing them with television," then it was obviously in the government's interest to give the publicly owned CBC control and management of television services in remote and isolated regions (Cowan 1971, 1). As far as the industrial corporations were concerned, their management preferred to pay for "an expert" broadcasting service that would relieve them of the responsibility of supervision (Government of Canada 1965, 194). To expedite this, the corporations initiated negotiations with the CBC to provide programming to the new transmitters, and the Board of Broadcast Governors issued a license to Hollinger Ungava Transport Ltd. This license stipulated "that the licensee shall operate the station as part of a network operated by the CBC and to [sic] the condition that the station shall broadcast only those programs provided to it by the corporation" (Feaver 1976, 12).

This provision, then, both allayed the fears of the federal government as outlined above and assured the regional unions that program selection in single-industry towns could not be monopolized by private corporation representatives who had little or no experience in this realm. Faced with mounting pressure for an improved service by Northern corporate and administrative interests, and keen to reinforce Canadian jurisdiction in the North, the government threw its support behind the CBC's proposal for an interim television service.

Between 1965 and 1966, the CBC studied the feasibility of a television Frontier Coverage Package (FCP) for Northern remote communities. The CBC designed the FCP to be a temporary, pre-satellite television system. It would make use of reliable, inexpensive and readily available videotape technology. FCP stations would consist primarily of a transmitter and an antenna system. A single Northern-based technician could broadcast the four-hour helical-scan videotapes that were to be pre-recorded in the South and "bicycled on a one, two, three or four-week delay basis to various locations in the North for playback over local television transmitters" (CBC 1978a, 3).

In 1967, the first FCP transmitters were set in place in Yellowknife, Lynn Lake, and Havre-Saint-Pierre on a pilot project basis. Initially, they were well received by these three communities, and the enthusiastic response encouraged CBC officials to envisage a network of FCP communities scattered across the North. At stake, however, were how the CBC would determine eligibility for the service and which communities would take priority in the extension of FCP coverage. Obviously, the provision of CBC service in the North could not be justified on a population basis alone, given that most communities had less than the minimum population of two thousand – the latter being the CBC's cut-off point for service eligibility in the South.

Specific guidelines for FCP transmitter eligibility were announced in late 1967. These were based on "the needs of the community, the population, existing broadcast services, isolation, the remoteness, the importance of the community as an industrial centre, and the relative cost of providing live service as opposed to the FCP service" (Stach 1970, 163).

Although the CBC attempted to apply these criteria objectively, it has to be said that, more often than not, it was economic considerations that influenced the initial allocation of broadcasting facilities in the North (Feaver 1976, 15). This is evident in the following comment issued by the CRTC: "If we find that the provision of broadcasting service is essential for the development of that [*sic*] economic project, then we are prepared to change a priority to provide the service" (CRTC 1968, 20, cited in Feaver 1976, 15).

The CBC's final community selections were made in consultation with the three government departments directly involved in Northern development – Transportation, Northern Affairs, and Mines and Resources (Feaver 1976, 15). In total, twenty-one communities received the Frontier Coverage Package during the period that it functioned. (See appendix A for a list of these communities.)

Programming for the FCP consisted of a cross-section of Southern programs geared towards children's, teens', and adults' *presumed* interests. News, sports, and special events were eliminated from the schedule because of the delay in playback. The programming made no accommodation for the inclusion of native-language programming; nor were relevant Northern subjects given particular importance in the schedule. This was regrettable, according to CBC Northern Services' first administrative director, Andrew Cowan (1970), who lamented First Peoples' silence over the matter at the time: "One could wish that the Original Peoples of the North were as articulate in expressing their demands and as effective in having them realized as their white fellow citizens. The fact that they are neither demanding nor critical of the broadcasting service does not mean that they neither desire it nor deserve it" (7).

Efforts by Mr Cowan to obtain money for the production of native-oriented programming proved futile. The CBC did not allocate any financial resources for such endeavours. While open *in principle* to the idea of community access to the transmitter as a means of program and cultural diversification, lack of funding meant that only philosophical and technical support were allowed for under the terms of CBC Northern Service's management policy.

Significant, here, was the fact that the CBC, with the backing of the federal departments of Indian and Northern Affairs, Transportation, and Mines and Resources, only responded to demands for television from those communities that conformed to the federal government's Northern development priorities. Gaining access to FCP service, in other words, was intrinsically linked to the government's economic, administrative, and transportation interests in the North. Suddenly, territory that had always been low on the government's service priority list had become symbolically important. Despite outside appearances that it was the CBC that was ultimately responsible for selecting the FCP communities, the truth is that the CBC was but one of *many* consultative bodies taking part in the decision-making process. If, at the time, the inability of CBC Northern Service to command a reasonable budget from the federal Cabinet was a clear indication of just how weak its position in the overall scheme of things was, its subsequent paralysis in native programming policy was a case of the chickens coming home to roost.

Equally significant is that early demand for television in the North did not come from the permanent aboriginal populations. In part, this is because their basic information needs required other kinds of communication facilities like the telephone, trail radio, and native-language community radio (NQIA 1974; ITC 1976). For the most part, however, the silence of aboriginal communities can be attributed to the fact that the CBC and the federal government did not even consult local native populations about the decision to expand television service into the North. Indeed, the federal authorities bypassed native people entirely because the latter did not yet constitute a strong and formidable lobby group.

In summary, initial consultations for FCP transmitters consistently neglected the communication needs of the native population and focused instead on the non-native transient communities; criteria for selection of eligible communities closely reflected federal economic development policies and ignored local priorities; the CBC Northern Service failed to convince federal authorities of the potential negative impact that television could have on native cultures if their need for at least some native-language programming was not met; and, finally, technical extension of service quickly took precedence over programming considerations. Underlying all of this was the fact that the prime motive for introducing mainstream broadcasting into the Canadian peripheries was to render the North more "manageable" by making the resource towns' non-native population feel like they were an integral part of Canadian society. The possible impact that this decision might have on First Peoples living in the regions surrounding these towns was not even considered. In fact, it was not until the Northern First Peoples residents organized a cohesive political lobby in response to discussions taking place around the implantation of the first Northern satellite that procedures for introducing new communications technologies into the North began to be questioned and scrutinized by policy-makers themselves.

CANADA'S DOMESTIC SATELLITE SYSTEM AND ITS IMPORTANCE FOR THE NORTH

The domestic satellite system had been a major preoccupation of Inuit and other First Peoples' communities since discussions leading up to its launch in 1972 began back in 1968. To better understand the nature of satellite policies in Canada, it is important to clarify the distinction between the *potential* and *actual* technical capabilities and uses of the satellite. Most critical, here, is that *all* satellites can potentially facilitate two-way interactive communications for both telephone and broadcasting purposes. However, early decisions made about Canada's domestic satellite only took this latter feature into account for telephony, thereby limiting broadcasting services to "receive-only" functions. The impact of this policy limitation was profound and significantly contributed to the transformation of Inuit and Amerindian cultures and perceptions. Indeed, it was a policy decision rationalized on the basis that, in the 1968 Broadcasting Act, S.3(c), only the right *to receive* broadcasting services was enshrined. In these early years, notions of local and regional access were not considered either in the legislation, or in practice. However, some discussion took place around the question of access when it came to establishing the Canadian domestic satellite system.

Satellite technology has had a significant impact on recent Canadian communication history, in that it has made possible the integration of the North into the larger communication networks of the south, east, and west. Until the advent of communication satellites in August 1960 (Echo I of the USA was used for relay of telephony, facsimile, and data), Canada had little choice but to base a communication system on long-haul microwave relays (UNESCO 1972, 8). The drawbacks of microwave relays are numerous: construction of the system is expensive and difficult in the northwest, and, in the rugged terrain and permafrost of the Eastern Arctic, it is impossible; the number of signals that can be carried are limited; unstable weather causes atmospheric interference; and maintenance costs are prohibitive. It was, therefore, out of the question to consider the establishment of South/North/South or North/North communication systems until the technology of satellites was sufficiently advanced to be implemented in the northeastern regions of Canada.

By the time the issue of a domestic communication satellite became a matter of utmost importance in Canada, the government had already been involved with two national satellites – Alouette I (1962) and Alouette II (1965) – and, with the USA, had co-sponsored a series of experimental satellites known as Isis, designed to collect and send back data about the ionosphere. By 1966, a number of experimental studies had been conducted by government and industrial groups (such as Bell Canada and Northern Electric) on the parameters of satellite technology (Hindley et al. 1977, 154). It was apparent by this time that Canada was in a leadership position in the international aerospace industry. If Canada wanted to maintain that position as well as improve the Canadian communication system, it would be necessary to draw up a domestic satellite policy (Feaver 1976, 21).

To this end, a classified federal study entitled *Satellite Communication in Canada* was conducted, followed in 1967 by the establishment of a government task force to transform this work into policy recommendations (Hindley et al. 1977, 154–5). In 1968, a White Paper on a national satellite communication program was released to the public. Four points critical to the anticipated program as described in the White Paper were: (1) the system's establishment would involve the federal government as a major participant; (2) the system would, however, be a commercial venture, and the government would have only fractional ownership; (3) participation would be shared with approved telecommunications common carriers; (4) Telesat Canada, the resulting company, would be jointly owned by the federal government, the telecommunications common carriers, and the general public through the purchase of its equity shares (Hindley et al. 1977, 155).

Emphasizing the ways in which a satellite could contribute to the growth, unity, and wealth of Canada, the task force stressed the need for quick decision-making. Allocation of place slots in the orbit circuit was a matter of prime concern given that there is only one orbit for geo-stationary satellites to circle over the equator, with a finite number of satellite parking stations to be shared by several nations.

Under pressure to move ahead quickly, and eager to maintain its leadership position in the space technology industry, the Canadian government established Telesat Canada by an Act of Parliament on 1 September 1969. Telesat Canada's assigned objective was "to establish and maintain a system of domestic communications by satellite in Canada" (Telesat 1980b, front cover). This federal decision to establish a domestic satellite program was taken in consultation with technical support staff.

The Anik A satellite system (at a cost of $90 million) made Canada the world's first state to consistently utilize a synchronous satellite for domestic communication purposes. The Soviet Union had broadcast television coverage of the fiftieth anniversary celebrations of the Bolshevik revolution in 1967 but only adopted geosynchronous satellites later on.

The contract to build the Anik A series of three satellites, which were to operate in the 6/4 GHz frequency range, was awarded to Hughes Aircraft Ltd of California, with the participation of two Canadian firms – Spar Aerospace Products, Ltd, and Northern Electric Company, Ltd (Hughes Aircraft Ltd 1972, 4). According to the Hughes Aircraft Ltd literature, each of the three satellites were designed to provide twelve high-capacity microwave channels for color television, or, alternatively, any channel could be used for up to as many as 960 one-way telephone calls. Of the thirty-seven ground stations to be built, approximately twenty-four of them were to provide live television programming to isolated Northern communities.[2] These ground stations were to be equipped with receive-only capability, although in some Telesat literature vague reference is made to "future plans" to add "transmit-and-receive message equipment, and possible television transmit service" (Hughes Aircraft Ltd 1972, 2).

Ground stations capable of receiving TV only and built to the standard required by Telesat would cost $150,000 as compared to the one- to two-million-dollar cost for ground stations capable of carrying radio, television, and telephone traffic. The complexity of the additional equipment required for two-way voice communications accounted for this cost differential. However, as Charles Feaver (1976) explains:

The television receive-only (TRO) ground stations proved to be suitable only for resource extraction communities and other towns which already had telephone service by terrestrial systems. If small, isolated communities were provided with the television receive-only ground stations, they would find themselves in the unusual position of being able to watch live colour television but having to depend on totally unreliable high-frequency two-way radio systems for contact with the outside world.

As someone in Rankin Inlet said, "You can die watching Bugs Bunny, not being able to contact a doctor."

... As a result, some of the larger resource-based communities in the North, which already had telephone service via land-based systems could be served with inexpensive television receive-only ground stations, but many of the smaller settlements needed the more costly telecommunications-capable ground stations. (39–40)

The convergence of these factors served to make the provision of television and telecommunication service to Northern communities less "economically practicable" than had been originally anticipated (Feaver 1976, 40). However, to communication experts at the time, these were unknown and the distribution satellite appeared to respond to the distinct problems and needs of the vast Canadian territory in an economically feasible fashion:

The rapid development of satellite communications is of immense importance to Canada. The capacity of the communications satellite for carrying high-quality telephone, television and data-transfer signals between widely separated points is peculiarly relevant to the geography and demography of Canada, both in supplementing terrestrial connections between urban centres and, even more importantly, by bringing telecommunications services to scattered and otherwise inaccessible communities, particularly in the north. (Government of Canada 1971, 62–3)

On 14 April 1969, in a House of Commons debate over the introduction of the Canadian satellite Anik (which means "brother" in Inuktitut), Eric Kierans, then Minister of Communications, presented his "Northern vision for the 1970s." The satellite, he noted, was to meet four basic communications needs:

1   To provide economic television coverage for the North and underdeveloped regions of Canada;
2   To provide telephone and message communications service to the North and other underdeveloped regions to bring these areas into the mainstream of Canadian life by high quality telecommunications services;
3   To extend television service in both English and French to all Canadians; and
4   To establish a second and supplementary link to our existing east/west microwave network. (Kenney 1971, I: 20)

In the course of the debate, demands for a two-way communication system abounded, with little consideration being given to either the expense of such a proposition, or the policy implications. Jean Chrétien, then Minister of Indian Affairs and Northern Development, pointed out that once the domestic satellite was in place, any Canadians previously isolated in remote communities could become involved in multiple aspects of Canadian life (Chrétien in Kenney 1971, I: 20–1). Improved communications "to, from, and within the North," according to Kierans, would enable citizens to participate in the democratic institutions of Canadian society (Kierans in Kenney 1971, I: 20).

Although the rhetoric was convincing, federal satellite policy plans were still clearly linked to Northern economic development interests (Bergeron in Kenney 1971, I: 20), and in the North, questions began to be asked in response to the federal government's decision to launch a domestic satellite. Indeed, that the decision had been taken by the federal government alone and that at no point during the early discussions had First Peoples been consulted to determine whether or not their communication needs and priorities would be met by the government's satellite plans became serious bones of contention.

Views of satellite dish –
McLeod Lake, BC – one of
fifty-six sites for reception
of Terrace, BC, television
service. Used with
permission of Art King,
Department of Canadian
Heritage, Government
of Canada.

In this light, what *were* those new Anik services that were seen to be *desperately needed* by Northern residents? And to precisely *which* constituency in the North – the native or the non-native – was the government addressing these new services?

Three initial customers had been singled out to rent Anik's channels. The telecommunication carriers rented four channels, two of which were designated for medium and low-density service to the North, with the other two being reserved for a high-density telephone data service between Vancouver and Toronto. The Canadian Overseas Telecommunication Corporation (COTC) rented one channel for transmission of signals between Toronto and the transatlantic cable terminus in Halifax. And the CBC rented three channels: one for the distribution of French network service across the country and to the North, and two for English network distribution across Canada and to the North (Loftus 1973, 681). No native-language or culturally relevant

McLeod Lake – satellite dish configuration in the village. Used with permission of Art King, Department of Canadian Heritage, Government of Canada.

SOME BASIC INFORMATION ABOUT SATELLITES

Communication satellite systems operate simply. They are much like microwave relay systems, except that a major component is positioned in outer space – in equatorial orbit – with the system comprising "both the satellite itself with the necessary control and tracking facilities (space segment) and the associated earth stations (ground or earth segment)" (Telesat 1980a, 12). Earth stations are composed of two basic elements: an antenna focused on the satellite and a package of electronic equipment protected in a trailer. The two functions of this equipment are to receive and transmit signals (9).

Signals are sent to the satellite from antennae on Earth. The satellite amplifies these signals and sends them back into the Earth's atmosphere where they are picked up by receiving dishes. Satellite systems provide capacity for the simultaneous use of many channels for such services as telephony, telegraphy, and television signals and are subject to fewer constraints than existing terrestrial systems. For instance, satellites carry a far greater number of signals and distance is no obstacle; they are less expensive to service; atmospheric interference does not generally impede their functioning; and they require less hardware and maintenance.

Satellites that make one full revolution every twenty-four hours are called synchronous because their orbit period is synchronized with the Earth's rotational

continued ▶

programming was planned. The CBC would broadcast Southern programming to the North, with no allowance being made for schedule adjustments. Clearly, the CBC was addressing its services to the non-native constituency.

As far as the Arctic was concerned, twenty-five communities were to be involved in the Anik program. Of these, the twenty-one communities that were already receiving the delayed FCP television service would have new access to live television broadcasts from the South. The remaining four communities would receive live television as well as a more sophisticated telephone service to replace their radio telephones. "Thin-route" (smallest and least costly earth station) service to an additional number of small, isolated communities would offer one to six long-distance telephone or data channels as well as a channel to receive Southern Network radio (Kenney 1971, I: 23). New basic services consisted of live television, FM radio with regional production centres to supplement short-wave service, and telephone facilities period (12). A geostationary satellite is one that remains at a given longitudinal point (fixed position and altitude) of 35,680 kilometers (or 22,300 miles) above the equator – at which point coverage or visibility of one-third of the Earth's surface is possible (Telesat 1980a, 12). Having numerous advantages over other types of satellites, geostationary satellites seem to be favoured by most nations, including Canada (UNESCO 1972, 9).

There is an inverse relationship between the power of a satellite and the sensitivity of the receiving equipment: the more powerful the satellite, (i.e., as the number and quality of transponders increase), the simpler, smaller, and cheaper the receiving dish required on Earth (UNESCO 1972, 9). The three basic system options, which roughly correspond with developments in satellite technology, are: (1) communication satellite systems for point-to-point communications; (2) distribution satellites; and (3) the direct broadcast satellite system (UNESCO 1972, 9–10).

Generally speaking, point-to-point communication satellites operate as "extensions of the terrestrial networks for the provision of long-distance wideband telecommunication services." They differ from terrestrial systems in their capacity to serve multiple routes through a single facility and their capability of reallocating channel capacity among these routes. Covering approximately one-third of the Earth's surface, these synchronous satellites can provide point-to-point communication, regardless of distance, within the area covered. Because of the

continued ▶

in a limited number of communities selected on a population basis. Why did the federal government decide upon these particular services as opposed to others? To which pressures was it responding? And how would it handle the introduction of services into predominantly native communities? These were questions that were foremost in the minds of Northern First Peoples.

Early native participatory history with CBC Northern Service radio programming had led First Peoples to expect that FM radio would eventually become an accessible medium that could be used to their benefit. Confidence was therefore high that, in their access to FM radio, they would have the chance to become producers of native-language programming. The issue of Southern-based television, however, was cause for concern among First Peoples and constituted, for them, the more objectionable aspect of the satellite plan and its implementation.

strict international regulations imposed on these satellites to avoid interference with terrestrial and other space services, signals arriving on Earth tend to be weak and, therefore, require very precise and electronically sophisticated earth station equipment. To this end, "Satellite antennas must have high gain, capture a minimum of radio electric noise and be precisely pointed in the direction of the satellite." As a result of these constraints, expenses for the point-to-point satellite are somewhat prohibitive (UNESCO 1972, 10).

Distribution satellites differ from point-to-point satellites in that they reduce the coverage territory to less than one-third of the Earth's surface, thereby making it possible to provide a stronger signal regionally:

> Distribution systems ... function primarily ... for providing connections to and/or between a number of earth stations in a given area either for two-way communications (telephony, teleprinter, etc.) and/or for distribution of television programmes over a large area. In the latter case, the role of the earth station is to receive the transmission from the satellite and transform it for rebroadcast via a normal-type television transmitter. The distribution satellite does therefore replace the normally used microwave links for the transportation of television programmes to the transmitters, but in a more flexible and potentially cheaper way than terrestrial methods. (UNESCO 1972, 10)

Direct broadcast satellites imply yet a different pattern of use:

> Television (or sound radio) programmes transmitted from an earth station to a powerful satellite would be broadcast from the satellite for reception by individual receivers, without the need for intermediate earth stations (UNESCO 1972, 10).

In other words, direct broadcast satellites (DBS) bypass the conventional need for rebroadcast facilities and can broadcast directly to homes with fairly small, privately owned receiving dishes. Recently, the DBS satellite system has been upgraded and, due to digitization and compression, can home-deliver ten times more signals than it used to, using the same amount of bandwidth. ∎

4 | Public Mediations and Northern Television

When we turn to the sweeping long-term changes which telecommunications may produce at the national and global levels, we are in a realm of high politics. Yet it is in facing fundamental and long-term questions that the political mechanism ... seems weakest ... This brings us to the crucial role of journalists, authors and academics, in raising and analyzing questions concerning the social impact of telecommunications. Unless these questions are common currency and widely understood ... there is little hope of our responding wisely to these challenging opportunities and dangers.

A.A.L. Reid (*Telecommunications in the 80's and After*, 12)

When plans for a Canadian domestic communication satellite became public in 1969, First Peoples and academics (mainly social scientists) expressed a great deal of concern about the potential impact of the satellite on native cultures. Many studies were conducted (Kenney 1971; Telecommission 8(c) 1971; Mayes 1972) to evaluate the goals of the program and to attempt to influence the direction of federal planning. The basic preoccupation was not whether the satellite was necessary but rather the uses to which the satellite would be put and its potential social impact on the native population. What kinds of shifts in perception and culture would result from the new media inputs, in particular English-language television broadcasting? Was the government planning to use television as a systematic means of modernizing and promoting national development? Given that this was what was happening in Third World countries during the same time period, would local access for community input be prohibited or encouraged? And was the government prepared to compromise its initial intentions in order to include the stated communication needs of the First Peoples in their long-range planning?

In the fall of 1970, the departments of Communications and of Indian Affairs and Northern Development, with the support of several academic groups (among them, the Boreal Institute of the University of Alberta and the

Arctic Institute of North America), jointly organized the Northern Communications Conference in Yellowknife. The purpose of the Yellowknife Conference was to focus public attention on the relevance of communications to Northern residents' needs. It was an extremely important conference because it was the first formal indication of a willingness on the part of the government to listen to the Northern viewpoint. Two hundred delegates (non-native and native) from various regions of Canada, representing technological and social science interests, attended this meeting in which information was sought to guide Northern communication policy formation. The outcome of the conference was a unanimously endorsed set of recommendations on Northern communication priorities (Government of Canada 1971, 51). These recommendations, which conformed only in part to those previously established by the federal government, provided the framework for subsequent research efforts in the area of Northern communications (see appendix B for a list of all the recommendations).

Topping the list of priorities was improved intraregional communications (telephone and teletype links) to support health and emergency services. Efficient telephone contact between remote villages and centres with hospitals was considered imperative. Also mentioned were low-cost radio units for nomadic hunters or trappers (to be used in the case of emergencies). Reliable interregional and local-exchange telephone connections were also considered a priority.

The importance of radio as a means of mass communications in the North was discussed at this meeting. CBC short-wave radio was criticized as being unreliable and subject to long outages due to atmospheric interference. It was convincingly argued that a Northern orientation to radio programming could be established by encouraging local community participation and by broadcasting in the various native languages. Relaxing the Department of Communications' technical standards and the CRTC's regulatory policies were suggested as ways to encourage the establishment of Northern community stations. Priority was given to a link-up of community radio with regional and national network services, wherever possible. The relocation of CBC Northern Service to a Northern community, along with an increase in its program control choices and responsibilities, was advocated.

Sixth on the list of nineteen recommendations from the Yellowknife Conference was a strong statement about the extension of live television and FCP service, with a focus on "programming suited to the northern needs" (Government of Canada 1971, 54). It was suggested that an additional channel on Anik be reserved to guarantee that a transmission medium existed to carry Northern network programming and to develop the organization of programming originating in the North. Assessment of Southern programming in a Northern context revealed concerns about the possible negative effects on intergenerational communications within the native cultures.

One year later, in September 1971, the Arctic Institute of North America published the first part of a two-volume report entitled *People Communications in Canada's North*. The report, coordinated and authored by a team headed up by G.I. Kenney, was part of *The Man in the North Project*, a series of studies on community development in the North. *People Communications in Canada's North* had a very critical edge, and it strengthened the argument to reformulate Anik satellite policy to conform to the expressed needs of the people it was intended to serve. Part I of *People Communications in Canada's North* described the importance for Northerners to receive and produce meaningful, culturally relevant radio and television with a local and regional emphasis (Kenney 1971, I: 1–27). Looking at the introduction of mass media in the North from within a "development" context, Kenney's team referred to Wilbur Schramm's classic work, *Mass Media and National Development* (1964). They supported Schramm's recommendation that lateral channels of communications "between villagers and villages for discussions of mutual problems and solutions" be established (Kenney 1971, I: 17). Mass media, Kenney quotes Schramm as saying, "must ... provide channels by which these people may discuss with their fellow villagers and with other villages what policies and practices they shall adopt; and it must provide channels by which the needs and wishes of the villagers may be carried up the hierarchy to form a part of the higher level decisions" (16). With the exception of the telephone, it was clear that such a lateral channel was missing in the Anik system – possibly because it might have planted the seeds for an autonomous native development program.

Systematic consultation and discussion with Northern residents, the report emphasized, should be part of a coordinated federal policy planning protocol designed to facilitate the development of an improved and appropriate Northern communication system. To proceed democratically would necessitate the establishment of an ongoing educational, technical, and cultural information exchange between government, native, and non-native groups in the North.[1] This exchange would help to incorporate the communication priorities of all sectors into the goals and objectives of the satellite policy. The federal government, according to the findings of *The Man in the North Project*, would have to initiate a concerted liaison effort with Northern residents.

In the second part of the report, entitled *Solutions* (published several months later), Kenney's team encouraged the government to acknowledge the communication work done by popular regional groups. They suggested that this recognition could take the form of funding Northern communication projects and societies. It was the DOC's role, Kenney stated, to "assume the responsibility of coordinating an equitable communication improvement program involving the seven provinces and two territories in the North." He maintained that "because of the economics of the Northern situation, it is believed that governments have certain special responsibilities to assist financially such ventures." Furthermore, he argued that it was the CRTC's role "to provide the guidelines and rulings necessary to ensure adequate and equitable development of the radio and television media in the North, in keeping with the needs of the people" (Kenney 1971, II: 5).

In this second part of the report, Kenney reiterated his position:

The priorities of spending vast amounts of money to bring live TV to certain northern locations must be balanced against expenditures that would attain socially valid goals in terms of communications as desired by the people – for example, satellite channels in conjunction with community radio stations, regional and local programming for radio and TV, community videotape projects, improved telephone communications, educational television, etc. ... [I]t is extremely important that the use of the system in the underdeveloped North be significant in social terms." (3)

To substantiate the feasibility of his approach, Kenney – an engineer by profession – proposed a schema and elaborated the details of such a mixed broadcasting system. Noting that it would utilize a special channel on the satellite, he went on to explain how this system would involve a different arrangement of earth stations from the one proposed by the federal government. Basically, Kenney's system proposed to establish regional and local radio and television broadcasting stations within the North. These stations would use the satellite for linkage. He estimated that the cost of this modified arrangement would run at approximately $1 million for the television production centre and approximately $200,000 for each of the four radio program centres. This was substantially less than the proposed $90 million Anik budget (Kenney 1971, II: 9).

Though the Kenney system of mixed broadcasting appealed strongly to native and Northern activist groups, it did not result in any concrete actions being taken by federal planning bodies. Their approach to the Anik A series

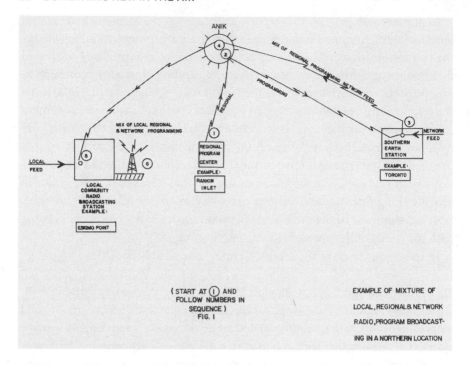

"Kenney's System of Mixed Broadcasting" diagram. Kenney, G. I. 1971.
Communications Study: Man in the North Project. Part II, 36. Montreal: The Arctic
Institute of North America. Courtesy of Gerry Kenney.

was set. Aside from its telephone functions, Anik was perceived to be a distribution satellite. As such, it would deliver information to the North in one
direction only. Plans to use it to facilitate social change or to diffuse innovations were not considered. For federal planning bodies, it was enough that
the system would be broadcasting a potpourri of Southern-oriented programming.

This is not to say that the reports of the *Telecommission Study* (including
that of the Yellowknife Conference) and *The Man in the North Project* had no
impact at all on the federal planning bodies. On the contrary, these reports
awakened planners to issues that they would have to seriously consider in
future communication endeavours in the North. CBC Northern Service and
the CRTC were certainly aware of the many references to culturally relevant
native-language programming and the desire for local and regional participation in future broadcast undertakings in the North. In fact, back in April

1971, as if to prove its willingness to respond to Northern needs, the CRTC had issued a public statement that asked for suggestions about how radio and television services could be extended to the North. In their communiqué, the CRTC also recommended the establishment of an emergency service for communities of five hundred people or more (Juneau 1971, 6). This policy recommendation further realized the CBC's long-range plan to provide CBC service, "in the appropriate language, to all areas of 500 or more, using an independent appropriation from Parliament" (CBC 1968–69, 73). The plan was formalized as the Accelerated Coverage Plan in 1974.

These minor responses attest to some attempt to modify the unilateral decision-making process of Northern communication planners. They also show that in the early days, the CRTC was somewhat flexible in its approach.

NORTHERN AUDIENCE RESPONSE TO TELEVISION SERVICES

While Anik has been able to improve phone and radio communication in the North, it has also made it possible to unleash the juggernaut of network television on isolated Northern communities in a time frame that has everything to do with the availability of technology and little to do with local preparedness. Unfortunately, the money that was plentiful for the provision of hardware and distribution systems has been non-existent for the provision of relevant Northern television programming.
Doug Ward, director CBC Northern Service, June 1979

People don't watch signals; they watch programs.
Pierre Juneau, chair of the CRTC, 17 June 1971

Anik A-1 was launched on 9 November 1972. On 5 February 1973, the FCP system was discontinued in the Canadian west, and live colour television programming was delivered via satellite for the first time. This increased the hours of broadcasting from four to approximately sixteen hours per day. In April 1973, Anik A-2 (designed to provide in-space protection for, or a back-up to, Anik A-1 clients) was installed and direct television service began in the Eastern Arctic. Anik A-3, with its increased capacity, was set in place in outer space in 1975 – approximately the same time that Hermes, the joint Canadian-American Experimental Communications Technology Satellite, was launched.

Initially, Northern audiences were in fact seeing inter-station newsfeed relays, sent from Toronto to network stations across the nation. Because transmitter feed had to be switched from one time zone to another in order to allow for other uses of the satellite, programs were repeated twice a day. Early technical problems with this system of television delivery necessitated basic changes in the network control centre. As a result of these modifications, time slots became available for local and regional programming. According to the CBC:

Material [needed] to program and fill all local and regional time periods ... amount[ed] to approximately one hour per day of programs, plus all station break periods. The Northern Service, in the absence of any capacity for the production of television material, has been using regional exchange programs, National Film Board films, off-air pickups from the CBC stations in the south, and programs supplied by the French services division. (CBC at CRTC, 18 February 1974, 9)

The bottom line was that CBC Northern Service could only afford to produce two five-minute programs per week of specific Northern programming. Apart from *Tarqravut* (broadcast in Inuktitut for audiences in the Northeastern Arctic) and *Our North* (in English, for northwestern audiences), programs beamed to the North were the same as those being shown to Southern urban audiences.

A paucity of financial resources, limited production facilities, and a small Northern population precluded the development of a network of Northern television production centres. Such a network might have helped to offset the invasion of Southern-oriented programming.

When television was introduced into the North in the 1970s, shifts in economic, demographic, transportation, religious, political, and educational patterns – as well as an increase in native/non-native interaction – had already combined to produce radical psychosocial and cultural changes (Wilson 1981). This makes it hard to determinine the exact impact that television had on Native and Inuit communities.[2] The fact that little institutional audience research was undertaken across the North until the Northern Native Broadcast Access Program began to do mandatory Native Communications Society audience evaluations in the mid-1980s to assess the value of their funding program from an administrative perspective makes it even harder.

However, informal discussions that I conducted with locals through the 1970s and into the early 80s, along with some academic studies conducted by Northern-based researchers, do provide insights into how audiences were responding to the arrival of television. It quickly became evident to me, for instance, that soap operas were the favourite genre, providing as they did both "juicy" entertainment and a means to learn about the lives of non-native people. In Frobisher Bay and other parts of the North, *The Edge of Night* so riveted audiences that institutions could not conduct community activities or run services when the show was being broadcast. A silent rule was soon established: if you wanted anyone to attend an official meeting, it had to be planned around the television soap-opera schedule. The same applied to broadcasting of sporting events. Ten minutes after such programs would finish, meeting rooms, classrooms, grocery stores, banks, and other public places would be full again, buzzing with activity, and life would be restored to "normal." Though detective and police shows, musicals, and news programs were also viewed regularly by both adults and children, these didn't seem to have the same impact on viewers as soaps and sports programs.

Programs designed for affluent Southerners and carrying advertising that fuelled the rising expectations of consumer-oriented individuals could not help but create conflicts within an indigenous cultural context. Soon after the introduction of television, feelings of frustration, as well as a deep sense of alienation, grew out of the inevitable tension created as a result of *wanting* a Southern lifestyle, yet being unable to *actualize* it in the North. The North thus became a media lab: a site where social scientists could investigate the impact of Southern and other foreign cultural programming on a "media-illiterate" population.

Their research findings fit nicely into a post-Second World War model of cross-cultural programming analysis. An initial set of findings, as evidenced in the work of Herbert Schiller (1969; 1978), Ariel Dorfman (1975), and Armand Mattelart (1975), concluded that the media were powerful agents of social change. The media were seen to benefit the producer-countries, who designed their messages to integrate Third and Fourth World receivers into their social, cultural, and political value and market systems. From this dependency/media imperialism perspective, the mass media were seen as indispensable tools that enabled producer-countries to stop using coercive political techniques in receiver-countries and to rely, instead, on persuasion through media exposure. One of the major weaknesses of this paradigm was that though it considered *some* of the effects that the media might be having on those to whom programming was targeted (in this case, Southern, non-aboriginal audiences), it did not take into account the effect(s) the media might be having on those who were *incidental* viewers, like the peoples of the North. This oversight was addressed in a subsequent paradigm, as epitomized in the *Limited Effects* approach of Katz and Lazarsfeld (Katz 1980; 1987). In focusing on what receivers brought to the media (i.e., on their active reception patterns, as well as on the audience's specific utilization of the messages received), this model allowed for the possibility that audiences might well *resist* predictable media impacts and might even use the media as an organizing stimulus or catalyst for developing strategies of cultural persistence. In other words, in suggesting that each program segment generated a multitude of possible readings that were dependent on the viewer's own values, Katz and Lazarsfeld challenged the notion that a single message would necessarily be interpreted in a common way throughout the world of receivers. Certainly, the wide range of meanings derived from much-studied popular programs such as *Dallas* or *Sesame Street* – which have been transplanted into a number of cultures without much cross-cultural adaptation – support Katz and Lazarsfeld's findings.

Here, I would go even further and suggest that not only are there multi-tiered meanings in any given mediatext – which can be appropriated and transformed by viewers – but these meanings can serve to either weaken or strengthen one's cultural identity. In other words, we can do what we want with television: either use it to figure out ways to become more assimilated into mainstream culture or react against it, nurturing in so doing, the emergence of a distinct cultural identity that stands in proud counter-distinction to "the norm." In their recognition of television as yet another apparatus of Southern domination, First Peoples' reactions were not as predictable as Schiller, Dorf-man, and Mattelart might have expected. Katz's Limited Effects theory, on the other hand, not only allowed for more fluidity in terms of reactions to the medium; in addition, his later writings about the media, cultural continuity and change (1979) turned out to be very much in line with what First Peoples eventually "did" with their early television viewing experiences.

While these kinds of issues were being debated in US communications schools in the 1970s, most Northern-based researchers were using empirical sociological approaches to gain an understanding of cross-cultural reception. For instance, before the activation of the satellite, Gary Coldevin of Concordia University in Montreal was collecting data for what he anticipated would be the beginning of a series of longitudinal studies on the impact of television on Inuit adolescents (Coldevin 1977a, 145–53). Later, Gary Grantzberg conducted a study on the cultural role of television among Northern Algonkians in which he compares television to magic (Grantzberg 1982). These studies documented the increasing "out-group identity, stress, and even a

"Simqaanak Watching Television in the Arctic." 1981. Used with permission of Jerry Giberson.

sense of 'helplessness'" felt by Northern native peoples as a result of "disruptive cultural images" (Roth and Valaskakis 1989, 224). Focusing primarily on the impact of television in the Eastern Arctic, two segments of the Inuit population were generally targeted in these academic studies: one, children and young adults who were fluent in both Inuktitut and English and, two, the adults whose second-language vocabulary was limited to a few key words.

What emerged from this work is that of the many factors affecting a change in the Inuit lifestyle, television was among the most important. Gary Coldevin noted that television seemed to have a more profound psychological and social impact on children than on adults, because of children's greater vulnerability to novelty (Coldevin 1977a, 153). My own findings, based on interviews conducted with teachers in Frobisher Bay in 1975, suggested that television viewing was resulting in: (1) an increase in the popularity of both watching and playing competitive games, such as hockey and other televised sports; (2) tardiness of students, as well as general fatigue in the classroom, due to their staying up to watch late-night movies (this in turn resulted in poor concentration and in a loss of interest in schoolwork); (3) a reluctance to attend community activities when the scheduled time competed with that of a popular television program.

Inuit parents expressed concern over the potential loss of native-language skills through the constant exposure of their children to entertainment in a second language. In addition to worrying about the effects that television violence would have on their children's behaviour, they feared that television would cause a rapid integration of their children into a Southern lifestyle – thereby creating cultural dissonance and a generation gap. The predominant preoccupations of Inuit parents at the time were that television was destroying the Inuit culture, that it was making their children forget their language and their past, and that it was seducing them into embracing "the white man's ways." At the same time, parents acknowledged that television could be of educational benefit to their children and that it would build up their culture rather than destroy it if television were used in such a way.

Television viewing, it was noted, also brought increased visual knowledge of the outside world to the Inuit. This often occurred, however, "without the necessary accompanying comprehension of its verbal and cultural components" (ITC 1976, 30). As one parent expressed it: "When we can understand the English language we know when a child shouldn't be watching television and we can arrange for him to do other things or go out with him. But when you don't understand English and your child does, you cannot do anything about it" (22).

As the above quote suggests, non-English speaking adults were frustrated by their inability to comprehend the audio component of the broadcast. However, by concentrating on the juxtaposition of images (as discussed at the beginning of this book) they were able to accumulate some information about the world beyond their familiar territory. Not that interpreting this information was always a straightforward business:

One would think that the effect of shows such as "Police Story" would be, for Inuit who have never been to the South, [the perception] that policemen can just shoot people like they do on television. This is not very seriously taken by the producers or people used to all kinds of television and even by the police force itself, but for someone who has never been South, that could easily be the concept of police down there. It would be a fearful concept to have." (ITC 1976, 26)

Not all the research findings pointed to television having a negative impact on the North. Clearly, young Inuit benefited linguistically from their daily exposure to the English language. Grammatical improvements were notable, according to the teaching staff at Frobisher Bay's two schools (Roth, personal interviews, 1975). Routine viewing patterns enticed children to return home earlier in the evenings, making television a new means of social control. As such, it offered the possibility of facilitating closer family ties (ITC 1976, 16).

As far as adults were concerned, Sheldon O'Connell (1977) found that, among those whose English-language speaking skills were competent, there was an observable "desire for change and travel, a certain restlessness, an increased awareness of international issues and a comparative readiness to offer opinions" (142). Coldevin's findings concurred with this and further suggested that television had captivated the attention of the Inuit population. In spite of this, television was, for the most part, considered "irrelevant to their deep rooted social customs and environment," leading Coldevin (1977a) to conclude that television had not introduced an element of cognitive dissonance into Inuit adults' understanding of their own lifestyle and value orientations (153). In short, "the benefits of electronic media were associated with community-level communications, rather than attitude change, motivation, and skills" (Roth and Valaskakis 1989, 224).

Television messages are received into a context of interpersonal relationships and prevailing communication patterns. A comprehensive analysis of the impact of a medium must explore the existing networks of power in addition to the medium itself. Gail Valaskakis, whose prolific writings on the North have had a profound influence on the formation of public opinion and of policy, has been interested in historical studies of Inuit interpersonal communications that emphasize shifts in interaction patterns resulting from contact with early agents and agencies of change such as whalers, missionaries, the RCMP, and The Bay stores (see, in particular, Valaskakis 1979).

Valaskakis's contributions to the study of the impact of media on Inuit culture reveal some interesting phenomena. In an informative, unpublished paper entitled "Media and Acculturation Patterns: Implications for Northern Native Communities" (1976), she examines the broader role of Southern media within the Northern context and its impact on the young Inuit male population specifically. Her research indicates five critical phenomena occurring within Inuit communities in the 1970s:

1 The functioning of two simultaneous, non-complementary information systems;
2 The variance in individual and settlement acculturation levels;
3 The significantly increased amount and speed of information reflecting dominant Euro-Canadian culture ... and functioning within a model of cultural replacement;

4   Widening generational and sexual divergence in native value orientations, and
     the goals and norms which they reflect; and
5   The shifting of the native perception of traditional concepts, values, and
     lifestyles. (Valaskakis 1976, 6)

With regard to how young Inuit males process differences between foreign
cultural images of men as seen on television and Inuit cultural images (in
particular that of the "real Inuk"[3] male) as encountered in daily life, Valaskakis posits that an *operational synthesis* occurs at a deep cognitive level within
this segment of the population. If, on the one hand, this means that the image
of the traditional Inuk is synthesized with that of a super-masculine hero
image accrued from Southern television programming, it also means that:

Functionally, the synthesis integrates two cultural adaptations which are as divergent as the concepts. And the modern, super-masculine image is chosen not only
because of its mediated prevalence, but because it, like the "real Inuk" concept, operates to counteract the sense of lost powers, decreased value, and frustration young
males feel in relation to rapidly changing female goals. The synthesis is a strategy to
stabilize self-esteem, compete with Euro-Canadian males and alleviate the tensions
in male-female relations, and to integrate himself into the community. (Valaskakis
1976, 10–11)

Though I would argue that, rather than a *total* synthesis taking place, the
two strands of cultural inputs tend to coexist without the one ever being
entirely reconciled to the other, Valaskakis's notion of an operational synthesis might help to explain how Inuit have adapted to two different sets of
cultural stimuli. Valaskakis's hypothesis was, at the time, an important and
unique notion in the literature because it unequivocally confirmed the need
for local Inuit television input and relevant cultural programming that could
ensure continuity of the Inuit cultural image. In the context of André Caron's
(1977) research on the powerful impact of television on Inuit children's cultural images, Valaskakis's findings take on even greater significance.[4]
     Arguing against the federal government's use of television programming
as an "alien culture socialization agent" (Coldevin 1977b, 34), researchers like
Valaskakis urged the federal government to devise a broadcasting policy that
would support an indigenous "cultural reinforcement" position (Valaskakis
1976, 4). Furthermore, Native community input in the broadcast decision-
making process and in the production of relevant cultural and linguistic tele-

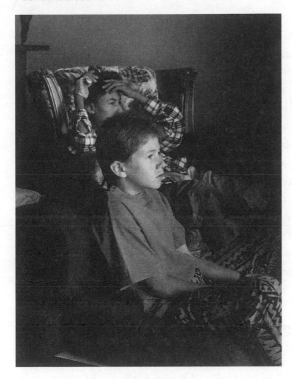

"Wawatie Children Watching Television in Lac Rapide, Quebec, 1997." Used with permission of Laurie Wawatie.

vision programming was recommended as a way of mediating the potentially overwhelming impact of Southern programming (Valaskakis 1976; Coldevin 1977a, b; Caron 1977; O'Connell 1975; NQIA 1974; ITC 1976). The establishment of production, training, and resource centres in the North, along with the formal encouragement of a lateral communication flow, were seen as necessary steps in this process (Valaskakis 1976; Coldevin 1977a, b).

THE ROLE OF THE NATIONAL FILM BOARD IN THE EASTERN ARCTIC

In 1972, Wolf Koenig – then executive producer in the NFB's Animation Department – went to Cape Dorset to shoot a film about the work of Peter Pitseolak entitled *Pictures Out of My Life*. While waiting for the plane in Frobisher Bay, his exposure to Frontier Coverage Package programming confirmed to him that television did not adequately reflect native concerns. Curious as to how television might have modified the cognitive structures and re-ordered the perceptions of the Inuit people, Koenig interviewed residents of Frobisher Bay and Cape Dorsét (Thorvaldson 1976, 2). His informal research led him to the following suppositions: (a) television had indeed transformed the Inuit cultural base – for instance, anecdotal information provided by teachers suggested that English-language use and comprehension among children had improved but that these newly acquired skills were gradually eroding interest in learning Inuktitut grammar and writing syllabics; (b) interest in Inuit culture was on the decline; (c) an increase in consumerism was conspicuous; (d) family ties were loosening due to generational gaps; (e) social interaction patterns were shifting (personal interview with Wolf Koenig, 9 June 1975).[5] Although Koenig was aware that television was not the only factor influencing these transformations, he suspected that it was the one that could be controlled most effectively (Thorvaldson 1976, 2).[6] Anticipating a more intelligent use of television that would also serve the interests of the Inuit, he visualized a project in which they would have access to their own community transmitter:

When in Frobisher Bay, we saw television that was totally irrelevant. We thought it was insane to see white faces. The Inuit saw none of themselves on TV; what they saw had no relation to their world.

Communications is a way people get to know who they are. If there's no identification in dramatic terms, then an individual becomes depersonalized. This results in what they see on TV becoming normal. Normality is outside. "What I see in the mirror becomes abnormal." Your own image tells you lies.

So, we thought about Dorset as a community. It has a tremendous artistic tradition and the people have lots of time. Why not set up a 16mm camera to find its way onto the tube. The psychology is "We could share that same magic box," which means ... "We can be persons." (Koenig, 10 June 1975)

While in Cape Dorset, Koenig committed to establishing a film-training project in which Inuit could learn to produce culturally relevant material appropriate for broadcasting on Northern television. After meeting with members of the younger generation and showing them several animation films, he discussed the possibility of setting up a workshop on animation filmmaking techniques. The group responded enthusiastically, and this encouraged Koenig. During his return stopover in Frobisher Bay, discussions were held with members of the Adult Education Department of the NWT. Their belief that such a workshop might help to counter the negative effects of television led them to provide one-third of the funding for the project.

The NFB pledged another one-third, and the last third came the Department of Indian and Northern Affairs in Ottawa, following negotiations upon Koenig's return South (Thorvaldson 1976, 4). Arrangements for the Sikusilarmiut workshop were finalized by October 1972, at which point John Taylor, an animator-producer with the NFB Vancouver studio, moved North to install equipment in the Cape Dorset film-training work space.

Over the next three years, about six prominent animators emerged out of a population of approximately seven hundred as a result of the workshop; a collection of short films was assembled into a reel entitled *Animation from Cape Dorset*. Though relatively little beyond this one reel of completed work was produced by the Sikusilarmiut workshop participants, the quality of the animation was excellent, even receiving international recognition.[7] The important outcome of this venture, however, was that Inuit youth were learning how to create their own visual media products.

Much of the content of these short films revolved around Inuit cultural patterns and heritage. Hunting, fishing, legend-telling, music-making, and traditional magic were all well documented through the use of innovative animation approaches. Topics of a political, legal, and social nature, however, were ignored, partly because filmmakers were encouraged to stick to topics of an apolitical nature and partly because it was assumed that animation was not the best genre for exploring such areas.[8]

As a result of a workshop evaluation in 1973, the following became apparent: the output of Sikusilarmiut was too small to warrant a regular time slot on CBC Northern Service television; the cost of 16mm film stock and equipment upkeep was prohibitive; transportation costs were exorbitant; film processing involved a series of complex South/North transportation manoeuvres; waiting periods between film exposure and delivery of processed film were lengthy and non-productive; and the difficulty of finding workshop producer/trainers affected production continuity (personal discussions with W. Koenig, 10–11 June 1975). This analysis of the Dorset undertaking suggested the need for another type of training project: better located (for technical reasons), emphasizing "live action" information-oriented programming, utilizing a cheaper and more portable medium (such as Super 8). Two key points prevailed as plans were put into place for this second workshop: the Animation Department wanted to keep their native film-training projects within the North itself, hoping to be able to provide both financial support for trainees and Northern job opportunities for those who had completed their training.[9] The latter considerations were designed to render credible the "job" of filmmaker – an occupation that was at that time foreign to Inuit culture – and to promote the idea that it could lead to employment for Inuit.

Because of its position as the transportation and administrative hub of the Baffin region, Frobisher Bay was considered the most accessible location for a "live action" workshop. The decision to use Super 8 instead of 16mm film meant lower equipment and film costs, lighter and more portable equipment, and total automation with high-quality results; Super 8 was also a responsive and practical medium, capable of withstanding extreme temperatures. In addition, general access to Super 8 equipment in Northern settlements, via the Hudson's Bay Company stores, had already made it into a familiar, hence "approachable" medium.

After confirming its decision to create a second workshop in Frobisher Bay, and after consultation with the Community Council to assure its support, the National Film Board Animation Department renegotiated funding from the same three sources that had sponsored Sikusilarmiut. Unfortunately, unlike what had been done in Cape Dorset, no money was allocated for trainee salaries. This caused much resentment, and resulted in an erratic commitment to the training process as time went on. Nonetheless, the workshop went ahead in the winter of 1974 after the NFB finalized accommodation and staff arrangements.[10]

The Workshop staff consisted of one non-resident producer/liaison officer who oversaw the smooth functioning of the project and one, or possibly two, producer/trainer(s) who resided in Frobisher Bay for a minimum period of six weeks at a time. It was difficult to recruit long-term producers, but, when possible, six-month contracts were negotiated. As for the trainees themselves, no systematic recruitment procedures took place other than a few announcements made over the local radio asking for volunteers. Because anyone who responded was accepted as trainees, no matter what their age or skills, children as young as ten signed up. It was later recognized that curiosity, perhaps, was not criteria enough for taking part. At the beginning, however, this was the sole prerequisite for participation (personal conversation with Wolf Koenig, 6 January 1981).

By the winter of 1975, one interesting and well-edited film entitled *Natsik Hunting* (about a family seal hunt) had been produced. Made by Mosha Michael, *Natsik Hunting* was blown up to 16 mm for National Film Board distribution purposes (Thorvaldson 1976, 4). Other than this, though, few concrete products were finalized during the lifespan of this workshop. However, those Inuit who participated, at least experienced what it meant to "see with camera-in-hand" and to "frame reality." Moreover, the workshops became a context within which local artistic talent could be discovered and supported.

Inherent in both workshops were deep structural problems. As mentioned previously, the limited time commitments of training consultants accounted for a somewhat fragmented teaching approach. As soon as the trainees would get accustomed to the patterns, habits, and teaching style of a consultant, their contract would terminate and a new trainer with a different approach and perspective would assume workshop coordination. Such disruptions to the smooth daily functioning of workshop procedures in turn impacted the level of commitment that trainees were willing to make. The practicalities of community and family life – keeping up activities like hunting and fishing, for instance – meant that trainees often spent a substantial amount of time away from the settlement, hence away from the workshop. Also, some decided spontaneously to leave the community, either moving elsewhere or travelling for an indeterminate length of time, and, in so doing, abandoned film productions in mid-course. The fact that these workshops tended to recruit village "drifters" had an important impact on what happened within the workshops: originally drawn by the novel aspects of filmmaking, the interest of these particular participants tended to lag once it became apparent that an ongoing commitment, as well as a lot of hard work, was expected.

Impact of the NFB Media Workshops

As the first direct effort on the part of a government media production institution to stimulate native film production within the North, it is important to understand the role these media workshops played in furthering the Inuit goal of establishing a more native-oriented medium. It is also interesting to note the reactions of other NFB departments to the Animation Department's training efforts – efforts that didn't so much reflect a desire on the part of the NFB to help the Inuit develop film production skills but rather were the result of one man and his team's singular efforts to fulfill a private vision.

The workshops served mainly to establish a relationship between the National Film Board Animation Department and Inuit people with an expressed interest in the film arts. Those few Inuit filmmakers in training who maintained an ongoing commitment to the projects temporarily became the communication professionals of the Eastern Arctic region. Because the workshops had not evolved from within a grassroots context, they operated without strong linkages to relevant community organizations and therefore were perceived by the local population as an outside agency's project that had been randomly located within their communities (author's interviews 1975).[11]

Initially, these workshops were the only model of a film communications training project within the region. As such, it has been suggested that they deterred, albeit unwittingly, the Inuit from developing indigenous approaches to their own training (telephone conversation with Green, 6 January 1981). Though the National Film Board did not exactly *prevent* the Inuit from changing the direction of their training, the fact that the workshops were designed and run by "experts" from the South might have been enough to postpone, however temporarily, the search for a locally controlled method of developing material for a native-oriented broadcasting system. That said, one might well speculate as to whether the workshop's location in the Inuit Tapirisat (Eskimo Brotherhood) building may have stimulated a future interest in the design of their own communication projects.

Although they were only of passing interest to most departments in the NFB, the workshops elicited an active response from the Media Research Department and *Challenge for Change*. The Media Research department, preoccupied as it was with philosophical questions regarding media use, turned to the workshops to bolster its argument regarding the negative impact of television on indigenous culture. The department was also interested in accumulating data on alternative forms of communications appropriate for native people (Cruickshank and Martin 1974–75: personal interviews).

The *Challenge for Change* program showed interest for other reasons. A bit of historical background is necessary here, not only to understand the differences that arose within the NFB concerning the workshops but also to provide a context for understanding later indigenous efforts at local film training, the development of which reflected, to some degree, the *Challenge for Change* prototype.

Created in 1966 in response to a government policy directive, the *Challenge for Change* program was coordinated by an interdepartmental committee comprised of seven federal government departments and the National Film Board. Concerned about the relationship between the media, community organization, and community development, the program's stated objectives were to improve communications, create greater understanding, promote new ideas, and provoke social change (Hénaut 1972, 3). To this end, portable media – usually videotape recorders but sometimes Super 8 film – were seen as tools that could be used by a social animator to diffuse conflict, resolve problems, and assure promised action. As such, the uses to which the media were put were process-oriented, with final products being seen as nothing more than documentary evidence of the process undergone by a given community. Projects supported by this program depended largely on community initiative, leadership, and support at the local level. The NFB acted merely as a media/technical service in this context and ideally perceived its involvement as a consultative body available at a community's request only.[12] As for the medium and the producers, they were regarded as technically supportive elements in the movement towards the resolution of sociopolitical conflicts; they were seen as catalysts for social change. Filmmakers, in other words, became technicians and looked to the community for direction when it came to making the final product. Naturally, this radical departure from the notion of the film producer/director as a professional specialist to a resource person/technician offended many institutionalized filmmakers who were accustomed to having full artistic and editorial control over their productions.

The *Challenge for Change* program, looked at simply as a working model, might best be described as an instrument designed by political and social professionals to achieve certain defined tasks. Its major goal was to experiment with innovative designs for community integration and dialogue through the use of communications media. Following through with the working model analogue we can visualize the program both as system and as process. The system had static elements – a management structure, an inventory of equipment, people to carry out the projects. The process was sociopolitical, emerging from active elements existing in the community and triggered by the presence of a new element that, like a catalyst in the chemical process, made a reaction possible instead of causing it or actively combining with the energies peculiar to the community in question.

The emphasis on experiment and innovation suggested that projects would not take on characteristics of permanency, that they were visualized as having an end-point where they could be evaluated, changed, terminated, or recycled. In order to guarantee a sustained emphasis on innovation, no one project could be so large as to drain off resources needed for other experiments (Driscoll 1972, 23).

Foremost among the opponents of the *Challenge for Change* "politicized" philosophy of media (and the use of VTR in general) was the Animation Department, which defined film as an art product and filmmaking as a specialized and professional activity. The Animation Department's interest up North was basically artistic. A secondary concern was to facilitate the process of cultural preservation by providing the opportunity to develop a set of historical and cultural records for the Inuit people.

Not surprisingly, then, those involved in the *Challenge for Change* program criticized the product-oriented "technical" training approach being promoted by the Animation Department in the workshops of the Eastern Arctic, proposing in its place the idea of a process-oriented media consciousness-raising program. They insisted that teaching the technique of filmmaking involved being aware of and integrated into the sociopolitical context in which the training took place. Film technology, they felt, was something that was integrally connected to a culture, a specific way of seeing and recording the world. To separate mechanical technique from cultural perception was to create an arbitrary and false dichotomy.

The Animation Department's response to this critique was that a consciousness would organically emerge as familiarity with the technical possibilities of the equipment developed. There was no need to deliberately intervene in this process with consciousness-raising techniques. In this respect, Koenig's approach was similar to that of John Grierson, who maintained that in teaching members of another culture "how to hold their cameras steady and shoot simply, as their own native powers of exposition direct[ed] them ... a real 8mm revolution anchored in necessity" would emerge (Grierson in Hénaut 1972, 5). If this philosophy had motivated the Animation Department to go North in the first place, it is also what Koenig repeatedly emphasized to workshop instructors, as well as to Peter Raymont, who became executive producer for the two workshops.

At a practical level, the filmmakers/teachers experienced a great deal of difficulty extricating their own way of seeing from the demonstration of technique. They were not quite certain where the demarcation line was, or if it existed at all. Some were quite sure they were entangling the two and, after a while, ignored whatever artificial boundary existed (personal conversations with Blumer and Raymont 1974–75). This situation might have been ameliorated had trainers been given a cross-cultural orientation course before heading North.

For their part, the *Challenge for Change* group identified these contradictions, articulated the fuzziness of what they saw as the Animation Department's ideals, and openly criticized the effort as a whole. They questioned in whose interest and with what local support the workshop endeavour had been undertaken. Their concern was whether or not the random participants in the program would come to recognize the project as their own and attempt to take control of its direction. In other words, would they transform the project into a community media workshop supported on a grassroots level by local community organizations and residents, or would the workshop continue to remain under the control of the NFB administration? Would they stay isolated as an independent NFB entity in the North or would they develop strong linkages within the community?

This internal conflict between *Challenge for Change* and the Animation Department manifested itself within the Board in subtle ways. *Challenge for Change* made a direct effort (through my liaison work in Frobisher Bay in 1975) to set up an independent relationship with Inuit people, but this was unsuccessful, largely because the Inuit perceived the Animation Department as the National Film Board in its entirety. Unintentionally and temporarily, the Animation Department might have acted as a gatekeeper, curtailing the possible widening of Inuit contact to include other NFB Department interests in the Baffin region.

Internal competition over Eastern Arctic spheres of influence continued until mid-1975, at which point the Media Research and *Challenge for Change* departments organized a timely conference on Northern communications and on how best to support further media development in the North. The Cape Dorset workshop closed in 1974, and the Frobisher live-action workshop transformed into a drama production unit called Nunatsiakmiut, which would later be integrated into the Inuit Broadcasting Corporation when it was licensed in 1981.

Though it is difficult to evaluate the precise degree to which academic research and early demonstration projects such as the NFB's influenced Inuit public opinion, it is likely that it played a significant part in motivating Inuit leaders to begin a comprehensive (re)assessment of their communication priorities in the mid-1970s. What is clear is that First Peoples (mostly the Inuit) recognized that data collected about media effects and the results of the NFB pilot projects would not, in itself, bring about the desired changes to the broadcasting system. Well aware that it was only through viewing communications as *interaction*, as opposed to technological *extension*, that they could move the struggle from a technical to a politically based challenge to the ruling relations within the media in Canada, it became important to First Peoples' representatives that they enter into a critical dialogue with federal government policy-makers and bureaucrats. To this end, "bridge discourses" – to borrow Nancy Fraser's (1989) term – which could mediate relations between unilingual aboriginal communities and the federal government, would have to be initiated and developed. "Go-betweens" – natives who could speak their own and at least one of the official languages of Canada and/or non-native "interested parties" (activists, media researchers) who were acceptable to First Peoples' community leadership – would play this bridging role. By situating themselves "between" the two worlds, the task of these go-betweens would be to knit together the disparate discourses of governmental regulatory policies, results of early media experiments, and Inuit and First Nations' cultural concerns.

THE IMPACT OF INUIT LOBBIES ON NORTHERN COMMUNICATIONS

Two Inuit organizations were critical in researching and publicizing Inuit communication needs and access priorities at this time. Mandated by their constituency groups to improve communications facilities and services, both the Inuit Tapirisat of Canada[13] (ITC) and the Northern Quebec Inuit Association (NQIA) worked persistently to bring federal government communications priorities in the North into line with those of the Inuit themselves. Through legal and political channels, interventions at CBC/Bell Canada license application hearings, confrontations and negotiations with CBC Northern Service and CBC management, and organizational publications, these groups battled to bring their research and viewpoints into the public forum.

As early as 1973, the ITC leadership was making proposals about acceptable percentages of Inuktitut-language programming on the CBC. At its annual assembly in Baker Lake, NWT, in August 1973, it went so far as to recommend that all subsequent applications by the CBC for licenses to broadcast in NWT Inuit settlements be refused until the CBC was prepared to broadcast eighty percent of its programming in Inuktitut (ITC 1981, 1: 5). The ITC's original quota of eighty percent was somewhat inflated, given the paucity of resources available to the CBC for Northern television productions. Its quota argument was important in principle, however, because it reflected its members' understandings of the important relationship between cultural reinforcement and broadcasting.

Even more outspoken about the need for Inuit control over Northern communication resources was the Northern Quebec Inuit Association (NQIA), under the direction of Josepi Padlayat. Originally from Salluit, Northern Quebec, Padlayat was appointed Communication Officer for the NQIA in

Josepi Padlayat played a critical political role in controlling entry of CBC Television into Northern Quebec in the early 1970s. Used with permission of Tom Axtell.

1973, just after the Inuit of Northern Quebec had developed some sense of where their communication priorities lay. In order of importance, these had been established as:

1   Communications between communities;
2   Communications between the land and the communities;
3   Communications within a community;
4   Communications from the South to the communities. (NQIA 1974, 3)

Amid discussions of how to improve the quality of communications services for its people, the NQIA learned of the CBC's application to the CRTC to license and operate satellite-fed television repeaters in Fort Chimo (Salluit) and Poste-de-la-Baleine (Whapmagoostui) at a cost of approximately a half-million dollars (Feaver 1976, 44–5).

An intervention was prepared. On 13 March 1973, Padlayat appeared before the CRTC, where he argued against granting the two licenses and questioned

Map of Nunavik, formerly known as Nouveau Québec. Used with permission of Makivik Corporation, Montreal.

the representative basis upon which the CBC had made the applications. No prior consultation with the Inuit people of the region had taken place; nor had the CBC planned for local programming input. The NQIA could not comprehend the CBC's intention to provide live colour television before it had developed an adequate Northern Quebec radio service as CBC had done in the Western and Eastern Arctic. Furthermore, the use of English *and* French as the languages of programming was objectionable. The Inuit's preferred second-language choice was English. Padlayat ended his intervention by requesting that consultative meetings between the CRTC, CBC senior management, and Inuit representatives be held before any licenses were granted (NQIA 1974, 4).

Responding to Padlayat's intervention, Marcel Ouimet, then CBC's vice-president of Special Services, admitted that the existence of the satellite had indeed molded the television-oriented direction of Northern broadcasting developments, even if the CBC acknowledged that television should not necessarily be given priority over other communications services. Ouimet's admission was a historic moment: it was the first time a senior representative of CBC had publicly made this link. In Ouimet's words: "I think in all sincerity that priority was given to television presently because of the launching of this satellite. If the satellite had not been launched, I believe we would still be waiting for television, at least live television ... [I]f it hadn't been for Anik, I think that at this time [television] wouldn't have been a priority" (Feaver 1976, 45).

A meeting between the NQIA and CBC senior management consequently took place with the support of the CRTC, though it was later described as "offensive" in tone and substance by NQIA representatives (NQIA 1974, 5). Following this initial meeting, the CBC and the NQIA disagreed over whether future meetings should be scheduled to take place before or after the language of proposed CBC programming had been determined. To the Inuit, the CBC's refusal to meet until *after* the Corporation had decided on the language of programming showed a lack of good will on their part, and made them question whether it was worthwhile carrying on negotiations with the CBC.

On 16 March 1973 the CRTC demonstrated its concern over Inuit communication priorities by announcing that, "The Commission accepts the contention that further discussion ... is required in the interests of the population of the areas affected and therefore defers a decision on these applications until these matters have been clarified" (NQIA 1974, 5).

ᑲᖑᕐᒥᐅᑦ   (TAQRAMIUT)
THE NORTHERNERS;
LES SEPTENTRIONAUX

Above and right: front and inside covers of *The Northerners*. Northern Quebec Inuit Association. Montreal: NQIA, 1974. Used with permission of Makivik Corporation.

Still uncertain over whether they should continue negotiating with the CBC, the NQIA decided to propose their own communication system. This new system would take into consideration the inventory of priorities that the NQIA had previously outlined. Headed by Padlayat, a task force on communications was formed and set out to draft a document that would clearly lay out to broadcasting authorities the background information necessary to formulating communication decisions in accordance with Inuit opinion. *The Northerners*, published in 1974 by NQIA, was the first formal Inuit assessment of Northern communications. As such, it represented an important step in the consciousness-raising process of both the Inuit and the federal government broadcasting authorities. It was also the first profile of Inuit community opinions about the inadequacy of Northern communications services to be published and widely circulated.

Without exception, all communication facilities in 1973 were criticized for not serving Quebec Northerners adequately. The Inuit vehemently disap-

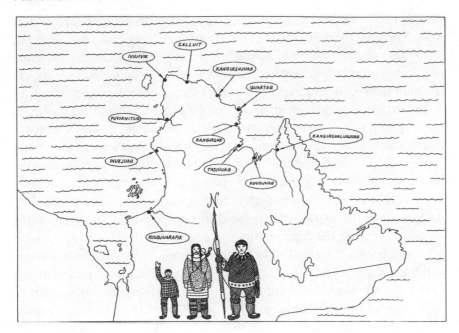

proved of the erratic telephone service and the poor quality of short-wave reception. The insufficient quantity of Inuktitut content on short-wave was also a concern. They concurred with Padlayat's argument to the CRTC that the establishment of a set of locally controlled radio stations (one per community) would be far more beneficial for Northerners than was television reception. They further proposed that this network of radio stations be tied in with a central Inuktitut Radio Production Centre, which might act as an information clearing house. Emergency or safety communication requirements (trail radio, a better telephone system) also took precedence over television on their list of priorities.

The Inuit proposal would have brought radio to four thousand Inuit, three hundred Cree, and six hundred Caucasians in Northern Quebec. It was less expensive than the CBC's plans for TV and FM radio broadcasting reception, and it strongly conformed to Inuit-perceived communication needs. "We are here and we are ready, even anxious, to take our place in our own way in the mainstream of Canadian society," they stated, "but we cannot do so until we understand the broad political and social trends in the society at large" (NQIA

1974, 133). Information in Inuktitut, most easily communicated by radio, was needed in order for the Inuit of Northern Quebec to make informed decisions about their future. Josepi Padlayat, as the NQIA communication representative, was neither intimidated nor frustrated by the bureaucratic responses to the Inuit interventions with regard to the federal extension of service plans.

The NQIA's experience had clear ramifications throughout the North, in terms of both its model spillover effects and its impact on the CBC's approach to extension-of-service procedures. It is important to be aware of the NQIA's communication study and the CRTC intervention. These events marked the beginning of a series of Inuit interventions into what the federal government had hoped would be a smooth technological extension of service policy. As a result of the NQIA's efforts, the CBC was pressured into establishing a policy of asking the communities to be served if they wanted television service *before* the CBC applied for a CRTC license. The choice, however, was still limited to "service" or "no service." A modified, local programming option was not considered feasible. Finally, and most importantly, the NQIA's opposition and its subsequent publicity inspired other native organizations – in particular the ITC – to begin re-examining their own communication priorities in relation to the observable positions of the CBC and the CRTC. At this time, other Inuit people across the North also began to recognize the possibility of actively participating in the transformation of their communications services.

In February 1974, CBC network license renewal hearings took place in Ottawa. Native leaders from the NWT took advantage of the opportunity to express their displeasure with the CBC satellite service television programming being received in some of their communities. They complained that the five minutes per week of Inuktitut-language programming was lost amidst 116 hours of foreign-language programs. They also criticized the antiquated documentary films that were selected by CBC Northern Service to fill in local time slots. They forcefully argued for a programming service that would meet Inuit relevance criteria – one that would highlight, in Inuktitut, Northern news and public affairs (Feaver 1976, 47-8).

Given these repeated requests for more Inuktitut programming, it would seem logical that subsequent financial investment in CBC Northern Service television would have been directed towards the improvement of program content. Instead, the CBC, the Cabinet, and the CRTC focused on an extension-of-service plan and on putting the capability of the satellite into effect. No modifications to the CBC programming schedule were projected.

THE ACCELERATED COVERAGE PLAN

[The Accelerated Coverage Plan] wasn't seen as an anti-northern move. In fact, I'm sure it was seen as a positive northern move. There were northern communities, especially resource communities, white resource communities, in mid-Canada, that were going to benefit from this project.

But if you are saying, we are going to provide television to every community of 500 or more, how do you write into that ... [that] we'll provide it for every white community of 500 or more. It would have been impossible ... [T]he juggernaut of technology ... makes things possible that ... [even] when they appear to be implemented democratically in fact wreak havoc on aboriginal communities.

Doug Ward, director of CBC Northern Service, 1976

In April 1974, the Cabinet approved $25 million dollars for the extension of the CBC service in English or French to all Canadian communities with a minimum population of five hundred. The Accelerated Coverage Plan (ACP) was an addition to the normal coverage plan. Its basic objective was "to compress in a five-year time frame coverage development that would have taken ten to twelve years under normal circumstances" (CBC 1974b, 1–2). It was a technical program that involved extending satellite hardware into the remote corners of Canada. It promised FM radio and live television broad-casting to those communities that had not previously qualified for service.[14] Projected capital costs of the ACP were $50 million. Half of this amount came from Cabinet appropriations and the other half came from the CBC budget (Feaver 1976, 54). The ACP annual operating budget was originally estimated to be $12 million (Feaver 1976, 53).

To determine the order in which communities would become eligible for the CBC service, several factors were considered. These included: population, geographic and cultural isolation, capital and operating expenditures, and provincial equalization (CBC 1974b, 1, 3, 7). Eventually, a priority formula was developed. This formula made geographic and cultural isolation the main criteria for eligibility. Given that cultural isolation was measured by considering the availability of other media, Northern regions that received only short-wave radio were selected to receive service first under the ACP. The order in which Northern communities were to be hooked into the satellite network was kept confidential until the application for each individual license was submitted to the CRTC. At such time, the CBC would contact the given community and present it with a choice between a Southern television package (with no plans for local programming input) or nothing at all. James

"Shadows of Technology. Wemindji, James Bay." Used with permission of Lorna Roth.

Arvaluk, the ITC president at the time, objected to this procedure on the grounds that consultations with native community leaders should precede the CBC's selection of communities. His objections were acknowledged, then ignored.

By 1 July 1976, the CRTC had approved 101 ACP projects in fifteen communities (most of them in the North). Only one Northern community refused television: Igloolik, located in the Baffin region. A March 1975 referendum to determine the community's attitude to receiving television via the ACP resulted in fifty-three votes against television, forty-nine for it, and seventeen undecided. Local input to the radio repeater in Igloolik was requested in television's place (Feaver 1976, 57).

Several factors contributed to the Igloolik Settlement Council's support of the vote results. These included: (1) their fear that English would become the dominant language of the community; in particular, that it would negatively affect their children's perception of Inuktitut; (2) their concern that community activities, meetings of various organizations, and cultural pursuits, including craftwork, would decrease in popularity if the time scheduled for these activities competed with favourite television programs; (3) their disapproval of young people staying up so late to watch television that it might interfere with their school or work (ITC 1976, 36).

The Council also expressed concern about the detrimental effects of television on interpersonal relationships, the unhealthy implications of watching television for long hours, and the possible negative influence of violent programming (36–7).[15]

In spite of the example of Igloolik and despite a general concern about the potential negative impact of television, all other communities in the Northwest Territories either requested television before the CBC approached them or immediately agreed to the CBC's package deal without formal opposition.

Critical consciousness found other outlets, however. In July/August 1976, the ITC published a Special Communications Report in its bi-monthly, bilingual magazine, *Inuit Today*. Similar in style and content to the NQIA's *The Northerners*, the issue documented a communications study funded by the Donner Canadian Foundation. Written in the words of representative Inuit from across the Northwest Territories, the bilingual text (English and Inuktitut) described responses to the media available in their communities and offered constructive criticism of mail, radio, telephone, television, and newspaper services. Subsequent wide circulation of this magazine helped start an ongoing dialogue among Northerners about the quality and impact of Northern communications service. Central to this dialogue was the need to modify Northern communications policies and undertakings to meet Inuit priorities. This publication provided the basis for an informed Inuit public, and it laid the foundation for broad Inuit support of the ITC's proposed involvement in the federal communications planning process.

THE NORTHERN BROADCASTING PLAN

The CBC, in consultation with the CRTC and DOC representatives, had been given the mandate in 1973 to develop both a three-year and a long-range Northern Broadcasting Plan. This was in response to native and academic pressure for local programming. The working group produced two proposals. The first recommended funding for Northern regional and subregional radio programming, as well as extending radio service to communities of two hundred or more. It also recommended a policy of community access, upon request, for both radio and television. Budget estimates were approximately $20 million for capital investment and an additional $20 million for operating costs. Funding was to be federally allocated for this Northern Broadcasting Plan. The Cabinet's study of the CBC's original submission in 1973 led to its request for revisions of the plan on the basis of its high cost.

The CBC's second Northern Broadcasting Plan differed in two ways. First, it placed a higher priority on radio access, thus eliminating the overall possibility of community television upon request. Second, to reconcile Northerners who had lobbied for relevant programming with Cabinet members who had demanded a lower budget, the CBC planned to establish a Northern regional production studio in Ottawa that would take the place of its previously proposed idea of community access to the satellite transmitter.

Despite the reduced cost of this alternative plan, it too was rejected by the Cabinet in 1976. Once again, the main objection was its high cost. However, First Peoples opposition to the central Ottawa studio also played a crucial role in the rejection. This was their reaction to the proposal: "The studio they are planning to put up in Ottawa ... we don't want that put up. We would rather have the money put to the Inuit in the North to produce their own programs instead of going to a studio in Ottawa which isn't even up North" (CRTC 1976, 104).

Another reason behind the Cabinet's negative response to the Northern Broadcasting Plan was that it dealt only with broadcast improvements in the Northwest Territories and the Yukon: it did not accommodate those Northern parts of the provinces that were still deprived of even the token amount of Northern programming produced by the CBC. The Cabinet returned the plan to the CBC and requested a new one which would incorporate these regions. Work towards the development of yet another comprehensive CBC Northern Broadcasting Plan terminated here.

The CBC was left in the precarious position of being responsible for all matters concerning Northern broadcasting. It had not been granted a budget to support either pan-Arctic or locally produced native programs for television on a systematic basis – nor were funds from government departments allocated for "sponsored" programming, which could then be distributed by the CBC (Feaver 1976, 63). If broadcast content that was relevant to aboriginal populations was to be developed, it would have to be initiated by those outside the immediate institutions of power. In order to build evidence for changed priorities in broadcasting access, content, and distribution, it would be up to the First Peoples to demonstrate their capacity in the broadcast sector. The communications tool that evolved to mediate relations between First Peoples and the various levels of governments involved in Northern development was the Demonstration Communications Project.

THE DEMONSTRATION "COMMUNICATIONS" PROJECT AS A TOOL FOR MEDIATING SOCIAL RELATIONS

As the debate around the potential social impact of satellite communications entered the public domain, efforts to broaden and improve understanding of media applications in the North took shape. These efforts took the form of a series of projects, experiments, and field tests using pre-satellite (conventional) technology: HF two-way radio, FM radio broadcasting, portable VTRs, and 16mm and Super 8mm film.

Generally speaking, these experiments were designed to test the technical and social parameters of community-oriented media usage and control patterns. Media projects created a dynamic cultural and linguistic record and fostered participation in community development processes. They included demonstration projects that were conducted to provide a knowledge base about the possible innovative uses of new broadcasting technologies in the North. Northern projects tended to fall into three broad categories: field experiments to test the viability of new equipment and to explore alternative forms of communications for the North; projects designed to mitigate the potential negative effects and influence of Southern programming on native cultures; projects associated with the use of community media for organization and development purposes.

Field Experiments to Test the Viability of New Equipment and to Explore Alternative Forms of Communications for the North

THE NORTHERN PILOT PROJECT (1971–74). Sponsored by the Department of Communications, this project consisted of a series of experiments designed to clarify the communication needs of indigenous people living in the isolated regions of Northwestern Ontario (Indian territory) and the Keewatin district of the NWT (Inuit homeland). Its overall objective was to recommend policy options for the planning, establishment, operation, and evaluation of communication facilities.

NAALAKVIK I (1978) IN NORTHERN QUEBEC. This was an interactive audio experiment using the Hermes satellite to link eight radio stations in Nouveau-Québec. It was operated by Taqramiut Nipingat Inc., the Native Communications Society originally started by Josepi Padlayat of the Northern Quebec Inuit Association, with the assistance of Paul Lumsden, a communications consultant with whom he worked closely.

Some members of the Inukshuk project team at work in Frobisher Bay, 1981: Lyndsay Green, operations manager; Keith MacNeil, studio supervisor; John Amagoalik, director of communications. Used with permission of Tom Axtell.

PROJECT INUKSHUK (1978–81). This represented a massive undertaking by the ITC. It was approved in November 1978 as part of DOC's Anik B experimental program and allocated more than a million dollars for its budget. The purpose was to train Inuit film and video producers, to establish Inuit production centres in the North, and to conduct interactive audio/video experiments utilizing the 12/14 GHz capability of the satellite to link six Arctic settlements.

Projects Designed to Mitigate the Potential Negative Effects and Influence of Southern Programming on Native Cultures

TWO NATIONAL FILM BOARD PRODUCTION WORKSHOPS. The National Film Board Production Workshops in Cape Dorset (film animation, 1972–74) and Frobisher Bay (live-action Super 8 mm, 1974–75) were the outcome of Southern initiatives but nonetheless prepared the way for Inuit-organized undertakings.

Other members of the Inukshuk project team at Baker Lake, 1981: Harry Sutherland, trainer; David Simailak, Inukshuk project director; Gail Valaskakis, project evaluator. Used with permission of Tom Axtell.

THE NUNATSIAKMIUT [PEOPLE OF THE BEAUTIFUL LAND] *COMMUNITY TELE-VISION PROJECT* IN FROBISHER BAY. This TV drama project lasted from 1975 until the licensing of the Inuit Broadcasting Corporation in 1981. It was the outgrowth of the two NFB undertakings.

Projects Associated with the Use of Community Media for Organization and Development Purposes

Examples of projects associated with the use of community media for organization and development purposes included the *La Ronge Community Television Project (1971–74)* in Northern Saskatchewan, the *Pond Inlet Community Television Project* (PIC-TV), begun in 1977, and *The Northern Pilot Project* (described above).

Since much widely available documentation exists to substantiate the work achieved within the context of these projects, it is unnecessary to go into

Cameraman Noah Nakashook at work, with Inuit children watching. Baker Lake,
Inukshuk Project Photo, n.d. Used with permission of Tom Axtell.

detail here about each of them (see Hudson 1974, 1977a,b; Robbins 1974,
1977a,b; Valaskakis, Wilson, and Robbins 1981; Roth 1983; and individual
organization reports, available upon request). Suffice to say that the projects
were successful in training staff, in producing culturally relevant aboriginal-
language programming, and in establishing the technical infrastructure to
link several communities laterally so that local residents could participate
in intercommunity discussions. Through federally sponsored projects such
as these, First Peoples were able to begin the historical (re)construction of
their traditional folklore and heritage through programming that reclaimed
active use of their own languages and lived cultures. Community development projects and experiments also provided broadcasters and sponsors with
important data on viable and alternative uses of new technologies.

The pursuit of a more representative way of providing media services to
the North led, somewhat serendipitously, to communications projects becoming the acceptable method of mediating between the divergent policy goals
of the federal government (including the CBC) and those of the aboriginal
population.

Media projects between 1971 and 1981 provided Northerners and government sponsors with the empirical data needed to show that First Peoples were ready to take on the various responsibilities of network operations. The information accumulated throughout this process further demonstrated the readiness of native peoples to participate in the policy-making process. The self-organized project thus represented an agreeable mechanism for the initiation and facilitation of Northern broadcasting policy negotiations. In the end, the media demonstration project data provided the basis for challenging the official federal lack of a broadcasting policy that incorporated the cultural information and entertainment needs of native communities. The project results convinced government bureaucrats to change policy objectives by making them aware of unanticipated possibilities. Communication projects consequently served to broaden, deepen, and improve knowledge of media applications in the North.

5 | Policy-ing the North[1]

Walker, there is no road
Roads are made by walking

Antonio Machado[2]

To work with a government implies neither subjection nor global acceptance. One can simultaneously work and be restive. I even think that the two go together.

Michel Foucault (cited in Burchell et al. 1991, 48)

First Peoples' community groups[3] turned to the self-organized communication project as a response to the federal government's lack of provision for a culturally and linguistically inclusive broadcasting service. Successful projects met the basic communication needs of First Peoples' communities, demonstrated their administrative and management skills in television production, and expanded technical and community-based knowledge about media use. Accumulated evidence of project successes became the basis for a policy dialogue between First Peoples and the federal government, including the DOC, the CRTC, and the Secretary of State's Native Citizen's Directorate.

The idea and practice of First Peoples' self-representation in broadcasting promised to weave the notion of diversity into the overall fabric of policy and to pave the way for aboriginal cultural coexistence with the Euro-Canadian broadcasting system in the North. While some federal bureaucrats felt that this was a positive and progressive goal for broadcasting and cultural policies, others considered these objectives to be threatening and continued to resist any changes to the overall system. This is no surprise. Unity of beliefs or value systems between the federal government's staff, management, and Ministers is never a given. In the end, the successful evidence accumulated

from First Peoples' media projects served the additional purpose of contributing to a policy consensus within a resistant civil service.

First Peoples wanted an aboriginal broadcasting policy because it would
constitute a landmark in Northern communications development – tantamount to a formal recognition of the distinct status of First Peoples. From the
perspective of their status as pre-Canadians, enshrining specific aboriginal
access rights in a revised or new Broadcasting Act could only strengthen the
cultural and racial tolerance objectives in Canada initiated with the Bilin-
gualism and Biculturalism Commission (mandated in 1963 by the Pearson
government). Such a move would also acknowledge their *special* status as
national, separate, and distinct cultures different from other ethno-cultural
and recent immigrant communities and would help to clarify the long-
standing confusion over who was to be considered under the rubric of multiculturalism policies. However, there were many civil servants, politicians,
and CRTC bureaucrats at the time who firmly believed that if aboriginal
broadcasters were to be given a special place in legislation and granted separate licenses on a regional basis, there would ensue a flurry of requests from
the "ethnic" communities who might argue that they, too, deserved *special*
status. To avoid the potential loss of control over the scarce airwaves that
might have occurred, these particular civil servants did not waiver in their
opinions for a long while.[4]

A special status for First Peoples had to be marked symbolically, and this
could only happen if policies targeted to First Peoples' needs were written into laws with the power of enforcement. It became imperative to First
Peoples that they have broadcasting policies that were grounded in legislative
instruments. Once these policies were written into a new Broadcasting Act,
assurances of special status in law could be argued. Without these guarantees
in writing, First Peoples would not have a strong enough legal basis to argue
for their distinct inclusion in the national broadcasting system.

For two decades, researchers, consultants, and lobbyists (First Peoples and
non-aboriginals) worked to pressure government policy-makers to enshrine
aboriginal broadcasting policy into law. Advocacy became a common feature
of public writing about Northern broadcasting – studies that originated from
within academic institutions being no exception. In fact, writing about broadcasting to and within the North has, in a sense, always meant planning and
proposing *policies* in favour of Northern First Peoples' broadcasting access
rights. Many of the Northernist academics who were writing in the early
1970s wrote from an activist perspective (Valaskakis, Coldevin, O'Connell,

Wilson, Stiles, and myself, among others), and an implicit sense that First Peoples' access rights *always* "mattered" became embedded in the resulting corpus of scholarship. For years, those producing this corpus moved back and forth between critical and administrative research and field work. Strong affiliations were built among ourselves, and with the few empathetic people within the federal government who were supportive of First Peoples' broadcasting rights. Together, we worked to "policy" the North: to survey and, in a sense, to *police* the airwave regulations and regulators. "Policy-ing" the North involved identifying loopholes and locating gaps in governmental policy discourses into which arguments for Northern broadcasting access rights could be inserted. Once deliberation about these possibilities commenced, it was only a matter of time before civil servants became convinced that transmission rights should be inscribed in new policy and legal frameworks.

What follows is the historical evidence that documents the phases in the Northern television policy-ing process culminating in the enshrinement of aboriginal broadcasting in the Broadcasting Act of 4 June 1991. Broadly speaking, we can divide the lead-up to this important moment into five key stages: (1) the early evidence of CRTC support for Northern native broadcasting; (2) the Therrien Committee Hearings and the report on the extension of service to Northern and remote communities; (3) the recognition of aboriginal broadcasting in policy and licensing decisions; (4) the lobbying strategies and phases directly related to aboriginal broadcasting as it became recognized in legislation; and (5) the Broadcasting Act of 1991.

STAGE ONE – EARLY EVIDENCE OF CRTC SUPPORT FOR NORTHERN NATIVE BROADCASTING

[H]ow do you channel, how do you select the opinions that are going to be expressed from all those that are going to be kept out? You know there's a door there, a door to the studio, there are millions of people who are kept out of the studio, they have no access to that microphone, they have no access to those cameras, and some people have a lot of access.
Pierre Juneau, ex-chairman, CRTC, 1972

In contrast to the Cabinet's decisions against separate parliamentary allocations for the CBC's production and distribution of native cultural programming, CBC Northern Service had always supported the attempts of native lobby groups to influence federal regulatory agencies in principle. In practice, corporate budget constraints and a technological policy focused on service extension meant that CBC Northern Service was only able to demonstrate its advocacy by writing letters and briefs to the CRTC, by conducting discussions with key federal policy makers, and by providing technical support, when possible, to indigenous communication projects.

The Inuit Tapirisat's early recognition that the CBC could not afford to invest money in Inuktitut programming led it to take its own initiatives with the CRTC. At the same time, it sought support and credibility by collecting data from its media project successes.

The record of the CRTC's advocacy for Inuit broadcasting is long and detailed, with the documentation showing commissioners' consistent support for both the Inuit critique of Northern television programming objectives and Inuit regional programming initiatives. For example, the CBC 1978 TV license renewal decision reflected the CRTC's concern with an adequate Northern broadcasting service. There, the CRTC called for an improvement in programming for native communities and made it clear that any further influx of Southern television, though technically feasible, should not be contemplated until an appropriate and adequate primary First Peoples service had been put into place (CBC 1980, 9).

Clearly, the commissioners were aware of the necessity for a more balanced approach to the differing communication needs of the North. This was evident from the many briefs presented to them by Northern residents and interest groups arguing for a transformation of broadcasting structures. Several questions remained. Who was to be responsible for its design? What changes should take place? Who would finance and administer the new system? And how and when would it come into being?

The 1968 Broadcasting Act placed the financial responsibility for Northern television programming directly with CBC Northern Service. Federal cutbacks in the early 1970s had paralyzed the Corporation's budget, however, making it unable to materially support Inuit programming initiatives other than small projects (such as setting up a regional production centre in Yellowknife). Given these constraints, novel alternative strategies were needed to break the deadlock.

STAGE TWO – THE THERRIEN COMMITTEE ON EXTENSION OF SERVICE TO NORTHERN AND REMOTE COMMUNITIES: THE HEARINGS AND REPORT

In early 1980, the CRTC resolved to establish a public forum at which the television programming options of Northern lobbies and interest groups could be outlined, examined, and debated in an effort to design changes in

Northern media infrastructures. On 8 January 1980, a nine-member committee was struck to report on how television services to Northern and remote communities in Canada "might best and most expeditiously be increased ... (and also to) deal with issues related to satellite distribution of programs and pay television" (CRTC 1980, x). Headed by Réal Therrien, then vice-chairman of the CRTC, this committee represented a critical turning point in policy-making for two reasons. First, the Commission agreed to hold hearings in the North – something it had never done before. Second, John Amagoalik, an Inuk from the Baffin Region, was invited to become a panel member. The decision to include Amagoalik set an important precedent – demonstrating both openness and good will on the part of the Commission.

Amagoalik's commitment to Inuit-controlled broadcasting initiatives was unquestionable. His strategic leadership in the ITC communications program (along with David Samailak, director of the Inukshuk Project) had resulted in the passage of a number of critical resolutions concerning the acceptance of new television channels within Inuit communities. According to ITC, the requirements that should condition expansion of television in their territory would be (1) that Inuit communities control the new channels through local broadcasting societies and (2) that any revenue generated by these channels be allocated to the community broadcasting society for the production of Inuit programs (Valaskakis et al. 1981, 401). Amagoalik's participation with the Therrien Committee implied that the CRTC recognized these needs for a more inclusive and radical approach.

The Therrien Committee received nearly four hundred briefs from interested parties across Canada. It held public meetings in Baker Lake (NWT), Whitehorse (Yukon), Geraldton (Ontario), Goose Bay–Happy Valley (Labrador); and the National Capital Region (Ottawa/Hull). The meeting at Baker Lake – the first of the series – was a coup for the Inuit. It provided the committee members with an opportunity to experience first-hand the broadcasting service available to Northern residents and to listen to their briefs in a more meaningful geographical setting.

At Baker Lake on 28 February 1980, the ITC presented a new proposal. This proposal included the following seven-point plan, which was geared towards the establishment of an Inuit Broadcasting system:

1   The establishment of a special programming fund;
2   The distribution of Inuit broadcasting productions;
3   The construction of an up-link transmitter in an Inuit community;
4   Community access to the television transmitter;

5 The use of video tape for education and community development purposes;
6 The extension of services to all communities;
7 Community control of additional channels on the satellite. (CRTC 1980, 29–30)

The proposal advocated a reduction in the number of hours of CBC Northern Service operation to between ten and twelve per day. This would liberate four to six hours of programming time, during which Inuit productions could be aired. The basic idea, which became reality in the 1990s, was to establish one satellite channel dedicated to the North, with CBC Northern Service sharing satellite time with Inuit broadcasters. Initial annual funding was projected to be $2 million, increasing to $5 million within a five-year period. The funding could be generated by revenue from Southern pay-television channels (Valaskakis et al. 1981, 403).

In its proposal, the ITC argued that because the CBC had been unable to provide a Northern television service that met Inuit communication needs, programming would have to be produced by Inuit organizations themselves and funded by sources other than the CBC. The proposed Inuit Broadcasting Corporation was essentially a continuation and expansion of the television broadcasting service provided under the Anik B Inukshuk project. It was presumed that, with the transfer of control to the proposed Inuit licensee, the satellite and broadcasting infrastructure already set in place in the five participating communities could remain on-site.

The CRTC responded with interest to this submission and Therrien himself noted the importance of a pan-Arctic Inuktitut-language broadcasting network: "I understand that in the past many of the ITC briefs have given concerns about [the] delivery of programming [and] the distribution of programming, but I think this is the first time you are putting forward ... the idea of a third network and ... the sharing of channels" (CRTC 1980b, 37).

At a second joint presentation before the Therrien Committee in Ottawa (1 April 1980), the ITC and the Taqramiut Nipingat Incorporated of Northern Quebec reiterated the Baker Lake proposition. However, formal application for an Inuit Broadcasting Corporation network television license did not go forward until 1 December 1980. This gave the CRTC some time to contemplate the feasibility of the plan.

The CBC's Position at the Extension of Service Hearings

The CBC's presentation at the hearings in March 1980 (held in Ottawa/Hull) once again acknowledged the financial difficulties attached to extending basic

services to the last 2 or 3 percent of the population (CBC 1980, 9). Specifically, it noted, "There is a need for northern regional television programming
that will provide important communications jobs for northerners, and that
will build bridges across the North, interpreting native perspectives to other
northerners, and vice versa" (CBC 1980, 10). Recognizing that it was not feasible for them to provide a more comprehensive program service alone, the
Corporation management suggested the possibility of a partnership between
itself, Parliament, the federal government, the Northern Territorial Governments, the peoples of the North, and the CRTC (CBC 1980, 11).

Plans for broadcast resource development included the production of new
programs, the procurement of programs from Northern producers, and the
versioning of Southern network programs that best reflected the South to
Northern native-language speaking groups. The CBC expressed the desire to
televise Northern programs to Southern audiences via the national network
and suggested that the government fund native regional production and
distribution groups. The CBC saw this as a way of enabling native-controlled
organizations to create their own programs and thus ensure the maintenance
and reinforcement of their cultures and languages. The Northern Service
"[w]ould be prepared to telecast the programs produced by such groups on
an 'access' basis, to the extent that time is available on our satellite channels"
(CBC 1980, 12).

An important point of the CBC's presentation was that the collaborative
effort needed to extend service to the North had already begun to take shape.
In 1979, the NWT and Yukon governments had embarked on their own public
service communications programs, which were designed to deliver television
and radio services to communities not covered under the ACP. The federal
departments of Indian and Northern Affairs, Communications, and Supply
and Services were supporting pilot projects that focused on Inuit television
production. The Secretary of State, through its Native Communications
Program,[5] was also sponsoring some Inuit television productions, along with
other native media projects, and, as already noted, the National Film Board
of Canada had demonstrated interest and support in Northern communications development by participating in the design and operation of its two film
workshops. Technical assistance to Nunatsiakmiut (a community television
project in Frobisher Bay), to PIC-TV (a community television project in Pond
Inlet), and to the Inukshuk project also indicated the NFB's supportive attitude. To further Inuit plans for an improved Northern broadcasting system,
David MacDonald, then Minister of Communications (1979), established an

interdepartmental committee with representatives from the Department of Indian Affairs and Northern Development (DIAND), the Department of Communications (DOC), the Secretary of State (SOS), the CBC, and the NFB. The committee investigated costs and options for Northern First Peoples television production centres. Members believed that the submission of system blueprints to native groups and to the Cabinet was a necessary step before final infrastructure and policy decisions could be made (CBC 1980, 15).

The CBC believed that the efforts of these institutions, when combined with the data accumulated through technical and social experimentation (including native-controlled communications initiatives), could bring about a major transformation of Northern television programming. The CBC refused to be considered the only agency responsible for transforming the Northern communications system. Insisting that having sole responsibility was financially unfeasible and politically untenable, it argued that any efforts had to be strategically coordinated. The CBC also expressed strong opposition to the ITC and the Joint Action Committee's proposal that revenues from pay-TV be redirected into subsidies for Northern television programming. Native communications should be a top priority for federal government funding, the CBC argued, and should not have to depend on the success of pay-TV undertakings in the South for funding. Opting for the latter solution would, the CBC insisted, represent an abdication of the federal government's obligation to the aboriginal peoples of Canada (CBC 1980, 16).

The NFB's Position on Northern Native Broadcasting at the Therrien Committee Hearings

As noted in chapter 4, the NFB's institutional and project support for Northern media activities was extensive in the 1970s and these were outlined in detail in its formal presentation to the Therrien Committee. While reviewing its historic relationship with the North in the areas of film production and distribution, the NFB representatives statistically profiled hundreds of their agency's films that were native in subject matter or in which native crews had participated (NFB 1990, 4). The representatives made reference to the NFB's 1979 *Outpost Film Library Catalogue* (a listing of available films assumed to be of interest to audiences in remote communities) and to the uniqueness of its Northern film distribution system – a system that, in addition, had to contend with incredible transport challenges. They also outlined the NFB's involvement with education and training programs for aboriginal media projects (NFB 1990, 5). At this time, the NFB was also participating as a member of the ad hoc Interdepartmental Committee on Northern/native Television Programming. The NFB mentioned this as evidence of its ongoing commitment to lobby for changes to the Northern communication system.

Underlying NFB activities in the North were a set of three principles that, for the first time, traced out the framework for a new Northern Support Project. Simply stated, these asserted that: (1) the preservation and development of native cultures is a national trust that must not be compromised; (2) local access to television should be controlled by the local community; (3) Native programming should be encouraged to develop as an alternative to Southern programming as much as it is feasible (NFB 1990, 6–7).

In addition, the NFB stated its belief that "native programming projects, including training and development programs, should be under native control" (NFB 1990, 7). If this confirmed the NFB's support for the ITC resolution passed on 7 September 1979, which recommended Inuit control over the influx of new television channels into Inuit territory, the Northern Support Project was also the NFB's way of consolidating its existing Northern operations. Though the person designated as project coordinator would be located at the NFB's headquarters in Montreal, the primary objective of the Northern Support Project was to promote the making and distribution of native cultural and aboriginal-language productions:

The project will attempt to take a coherent approach, within the capabilities of the Board, to Inuit audio-visual production needs as defined by the Inuit. It will attempt to be flexible so it is best able to meet those needs without adding the pressure of another infrastructure in the North. The Project will attempt to increase the efficiency and impact of the resources the Board already devotes to northern operations and it will develop new services within the principles stated above.[6] (NFB 1990, 7–8)

Planned in conjunction with the ITC proposal for an Inuit Broadcasting television network, the Northern Support Project constituted an important step in the National Film Board's Northern policy.

The positions of the Inuit, the CRTC, CBC Northern Service, and the National Film Board of Canada made clear that the public and the political will to re-order the broadcasting service were in place. Nor were these the only voices that responded to the Therrien Committee's mandate to poll existing public opinion. Numerous other groups (native and non-native) concurred with the need to develop a stronger voice for First Peoples in the broadcasting system. That the Committee extended the public meeting in Hull by twelve days to accommodate all the presenters testifies to the lively debate that was generated by the Therrien Committee hearings. The almost unanimous demands for training programs, for native-language and native-oriented program production, and for community control of programs impressed upon committee members the native organizations' determination to receive and often pay for broadcasting services that would both meet their needs and give expression to their cultural identities. However, it remained to be seen how the committee would react concretely to this convergence of public opinion.

The Hearing Outcome: The Therrien Committee Report

In July 1980, after considering the material presented, the Therrien Committee issued a report entitled *The 1980s: A Decade of Diversity-Broadcasting, Satellites, and Pay-TV*. This was the first formal document to outline a framework for a Northern communication policy. Several recommendations of this report are important to note in detail:

Recommendation 1. The CRTC should immediately call for license applications for the delivery, in remote and underserved areas, of a range of Canadian satellite television services that would be attractive to Canadian audiences.

Recommendation 2. As a purely interim measure of an experimental nature, the federal government should arrange and pay for one composite public service channel of alternative entertainment programming to be delivered by satellite to remote and underserved areas as authorized by the CRTC.

Recommendation 3. Immediate action should be taken to ensure that the national radio services be made available in all parts of Canada as soon as possible. The Committee has further concluded that there are some broad principles that should govern planning for the extension of broadcasting services to remote and underserved areas of Canada and the following recommendations embody those principles.

Recommendation 4. Canada must fulfil its obligation to provide opportunity for its native peoples to preserve the use of their languages and foster the maintenance and development of their own particular cultures through broadcasting and other communications.

Recommendation 5. The extension of broadcasting services to northern and remote areas must not rely upon subsidies from pay-television.

Recommendation 6. It must be recognized that residents in remote areas may have to contribute to the cost of receiving all but the national broadcasting services, and such contributions must be kept down to the lowest feasible amounts.

Recommendation 7. Approval for the introduction of any new satellite service must take into account the essential need to provide, maintain, or expand facilities for community and regional services.

Recommendation 8. Planning for the broadcasting system of the future must be flexible enough to accommodate technological, legislative, and structural change.

Recommendation 19. The CRTC should encourage license applications from native communities or organizations to operate broadcasting undertakings in predominantly native communities, in order to promote native-language programming and production by native people.

Recommendation 20. Any predominantly native community should have the right to decide on the channels to be delivered locally; to eliminate complete channels; and, on any particular channel, to eliminate a program or substitute one of its own choice. (CRTC 1980, 3–27)

Regarding the issue of access, the committee argued that it was not enough to provide access "without the assistance of trained staff and technicians, and funds to produce the programs" (CRTC 1980, 27). To pay for Northern production costs, the Therrien Committee suggested that "the approved budgets of the CBC and the NFB should be supplemented by Parliamentary appropriations to be used exclusively for the development and support of broadcasting services by and for the native peoples of Canada" (CRTC 1980, 22).

The committee also considered the possibility of assistance from the private sector of the broadcasting industry, such as the donation of surplus equipment and training staff. It proposed that federal funding for Native Communication Societies should be granted by a single federal coordinating body rather than the multitude of federal and provincial sources that existed at the time. Native Communication Societies that had demonstrated their experience and the determination to organize their own broadcasting undertakings should have priority in the allocation of funding. As well, it was recommended that they should be given the right to negotiate funding arrangements according to their distinct needs and circumstances (22).

In concluding its review of Inuit broadcasting initiatives, the Therrien Committee made one final recommendation. Laying the foundation for the future development of Inuit broadcasting, this was that "consideration should be given to providing financial and other support, on the largest feasible scale, to the creation of an Inuit broadcasting system to operate a network of services available in all Inuit communities" (24).

The context had been set. Not only had the ITC's and TNI's lobbying efforts paid off; the success of the Inuit communication projects had also convinced federal communication policy-making authorities of the capability of Inuit production and administrative staff and of the feasibility of indigenous broadcasting undertakings. Public and institutional support for an Inuit television network was widespread. All that was missing was a television network broadcast license – the license to go ahead.

STAGE THREE: THE RECOGNITION OF ABORIGINAL BROADCASTING IN POLICY AND LICENSING DECISIONS

In October 1980, the CRTC acknowledged the Therrien recommendations and separated the issue of pay-TV from that of service extension. It then proceeded to call for license applications for radio and television programming to serve the North. The ITC responded by filing an application for a network television license to operate an Inuit television service. Its application also constituted an intervention against other applicants.

On 14 January 1981, the ITC appeared in Ottawa to intervene against the CBC's application to establish a second television channel, CBC II/Télé-2. In its submission to the CRTC (ITC 1980), the ITC had asserted that the CBC had not fulfilled its mandate to meet the objectives of the Broadcasting Act and the needs of the Northern native population. It went on to state "that the North should have one relevant television service before other television channels are brought into Inuit communities" (8). The ITC argued for the leasing of a separate channel on the satellite to be rented by the CBC that would be dedicated solely to Northern service and shared with an Inuit television broadcasting corporation. This would resolve the potential difficulty of splitting channel access time three ways (between the CBC's east/west national network feed, CBC Northern Service, and the Inuit Broadcasting Corporation). The ITC informed the CRTC that should the CBC remain intractable on this issue, it would be "forced to consider the introduction of more southern English language television channels into our communities." It therefore asked the commission "to make carriage of Inuit programming a condition of any license to serve remote and underserved communities where the satellite transmission coverage area of such licenses includes Inuit communities" (9). As a condition of the license, the ITC also requested some financial support ("a significant contribution") for Inuit program production (12).

In its reply to the CRTC, the CBC indicated its willingness to negotiate with the ITC and TNI for the dedication of a Northern satellite channel on Anik D. The CBC even went so far as to agree to intervene at the ITC's license hearing in its favour. CBC administrators also agreed to approach the federal government to obtain funding for a shared channel on Anik D (to be dedicated to Northern programming). Finally, as an interim measure, and to demonstrate its good intentions, the CBC agreed to make satellite time available for Inuit broadcasting on Channel B, commencing on 1 September 1981 (Valaskakis et al. 1981, 406-7).

On 22 July 1981, the CRTC issued a license for an Inuit television broadcasting network, to be incorporated under the name Inuit Broadcasting Corporation. In rejecting the ITC's proposal to fund Northern television through the revenues of pay-TV, the CRTC challenged the ITC to develop other means of financing. In response, and as a possible way of ensuring long-term funding, the ITC drew up a proposition that designated communications as a topic for negotiation under land claims.

The Treasury Board's approval of ITC's funding submission was made public on 1 July 1981. The ITC and TNI were to receive $3.9 million to sustain an Inuit television service. The service would be initiated through the Naalakvik II and Inukshuk projects' infrastructure for an interim period of two years pending the finalization of a land claim settlement. A meeting was subsequently held at Baker Lake to establish a national Inuit broadcasting network through the incorporation of the Inuit Broadcasting Corporation (IBC) as an independent entity.[7] Its board of directors would include representatives from all the Inuit regions across Canada, including Labrador.

The IBC decided to set up its headquarters in Ottawa in order to be close to government agencies responsible for issuing information and to have easy access to the negotiations process. A Northern uplink was installed in Frobisher Bay in 1981. It became operational on 11 January 1982, when the Inuit Broadcasting Corporation officially launched its programming service.

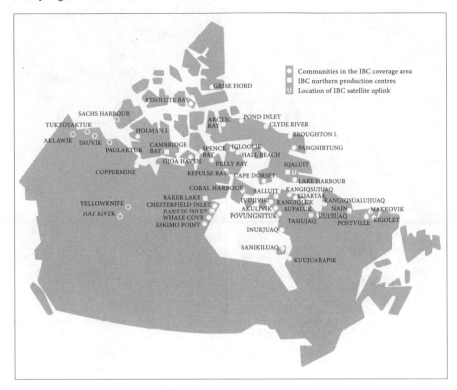

Map of Inuit Broadcasting Network – Service Areas. Source: IBC Pamphlet, n.d. Used with permission of Inuit Broadcasting Corporation.

The IBC began broadcasting four hours per week: one hour on Saturday mornings and a daily half-hour slot at midnight. Pending satisfactory scheduling of appropriate hours, which still had to be finalized with the CBC, it hoped to be producing ten hours per week by April 1983.

Several problems emerged at this point, the first of which concerned scheduling. In fact, until Television Northern Canada began operating in 1992, the Inuit Broadcasting Corporation continually faced constraints with regard to working out appropriate schedules with CBC Northern Service administrators, who, in turn, had to contend with east/west network schedule restrictions. If, however, Inuit audiences often complained about IBC's placement *after* CBC's east/west network had finished its daily programming, it had to be admitted that even inconsistent access to Northern programming – complete with the future promise of a shared channel dedicated to broadcasting

Peter Tapatai as Super Shamou on the front covers of English and Inuktitut versions of the Super Shamou comic book. N.d. Used with permission of Inuit Broadcasting Corporation.

material of cultural and linguistic relevance to the North – was a remarkable step forward from the days of the early CBC Northern television service.

Beginning in 1981, the IBC had been operating five regional production and broadcasting centres throughout Northern Quebec, Labrador, and the Northwest Territories airing approximately seven hours of programs per week on CBC Northern Service. Its target audiences were unilingual older Inuit, adults aged between twenty-two and forty-five (whose language skills were most threatened by acculturation), and children from seven to ten years old. Several IBC programs created at that time were highly imaginative and of excellent quality. One of these – *Super Shamou* – was about a hybrid character who conjoined elements of the traditional Inuit Magic Man and the North American pop-culture hero Superman, in order to solve problems, teach moral lessons, and act as a behavioural role model for Inuit children. Though only a limited number of programs were made in the original television series, *Super Shamou* is now considered a collector's item and Peter Tapatai – who played the title role – is still recognized and associated with

Peter Tapatai, program producer, talking with community coordinators Jayco Anaviapik and John Aulatjut. Used with permission of Tom Axtell.

the part in and out of the North. Furthermore, spinoffs like drug and alcohol education posters and comic books featuring cartoon images of Super Shamou validated Inuit alcohol and drug rehabilitation programs, largely due to the appeal that this original character had to children of all cultures living in the North.

Another popular children's program created in those early days, *Takuginai*, continues today on APTN. Entertaining, educational and aesthetically appealing, this multimedia show aimed at young children, incorporating puppetry and live action, is testimony to the talent for puppet design and storytelling found in Inuit communities. Originally, the Inuit responsible for *Takuginai* received training from producers of *The Muppet Show* on how to "give spirit to one's hands" when manipulating inanimate puppets. Now, two decades old, the series addresses Inuit children from a cultural perspective that takes into account both traditional and modern aspects of life in the North.

The IBC was not the only aboriginal organization to make gains in its status as broadcaster during this period. In 1981, the Council for Yukon Indians and

Takuginai team takes time to pose with their puppets. Source: Art King, Department of Canadian Heritage. Compliments of Inuit Broadcasting Incorporation.

the Dené of the NWT applied to the CRTC for a radio network that would simultaneously deliver programming in several native languages. Approval was granted and a license was issued in April 1981. The Yukon Indians organized Northern Native Broadcasting, Yukon at this time, and the Dené submitted a request to DIAND for funding to research and develop a network plan. In Quebec, le Conseil des Attikamek-Montagnais was established with monies from Le Ministère des Communications du Québec. It delivered five hours per week of regional radio programming in two native languages to eleven communities. WaWaTay Native Communications Society operated a regional radio production centre out of Sioux Lookout, Ontario, and served a network of twenty-one local radio stations. Other regional native organizations and Societies also strengthened their arguments for a coherent national

MY EARLY HISTORY WITH *TAKUGINAI*

It was winter 1986. As part of a much larger team, including a trainer and trainees in video, audio, scriptwriting, puppet and set design, as well as curriculum, psychological, pedagogical, and communications consultants, I had been hired as an audience researcher for the Inuit Broadcasting Corporation. The network management was planning to establish a children's television program geared towards viewers aged four to seven and wanted a new IBC Program Team to do a pilot series of three programs and evaluate them with school and community audiences in three Northern regions. The idea was to produce a relevant program reflecting a range of Inuit language dialects and cultural practices, so that the Frobisher dialect, which tended to dominate Arctic television, would not be seen as the only – and best – version of Inuktitut.

Most of the team travelled together for two sets of consultations in Igloolik, Salluit, and of course Frobisher Bay/Iqaluit. The first revolved around planning; the second took place at the testing stage. On our initial trip, we met with a wide range of people – school teachers, parents, elders, young children, and teens. We conducted focus groups and interviewed many on an individual basis, asking them what kinds of content they thought would be relevant and at what level they thought the program should address the viewers linguistically, given that in Inuktitut, there is an adult and a children's dialect. The consensus was that the show should reflect multiple dialects and that the language level should be adult-oriented. I found this interesting, given that the show was being designed for four- to seven-year-old viewers. Would the four-year-olds capture the essence of the messages or would it be above their heads?

Our interviews also revealed that adult IBC viewers did not want their children to be exposed to the tempo and rhythms of a show like *Sesame Street*, which, they felt, might attract their children to too fast a pace of life. They were worried that the speedy presentation of information, along with the slickly packaged formula for teaching literacy and numeracy, would induct the Inuit children into a quick style of communications and a set of expectations tied too closely to the advertising industry – in other words, to the values of a Southern, consumer-based society.

It happened that, when working with IBC on this contract, I went to New York on some other business. While there, I met with *Sesame Street*'s Children's Television Workshop (CTW) animators to talk to them about cross-cultural adaptations of their program. I discovered that these consisted of adding a local character or two and incorporating a few key words in the native language of the community. Period. For their part, the CTW crew were much more interested in IBC's plan to replace programs that reflected the core assumptions of mainstream television with programs that were representative of indigenous cultural values, unfolded at

continued ▶

a slower pace, and were respectful of the Inuit attitude towards time. The interest of the *Sesame Street* producers in IBC's approach strengthened the team's confidence to go ahead and produce the program according to their own cultural norms and standards.

With the language policy and Inuit perspective more firmed up, and after many team planning sessions, three fifteen-minute programs were produced for the evaluation process. They consisted of several core stories, presented in different formats so that they could be compared, discussed, and assessed by viewers in terms of impact and preference. A wide range of techniques and approaches were used, including animation, art backdrops, traditional storytelling (i.e., without props), live acting, kids painting and drawing, dancing and singing, video inserts of community activities such as bike riding, snowball throwing, team sports, and demonstrations of how to do cultural activities the Inuit way. A team of three audience researchers (myself and two production team members) and often several teachers and classroom assistants then carefully watched children watching the programs. Our observation guide consisted of a grid of behavioural responses, onto which we would mark reactions as viewers responded to a particular change of scene, to a character, to a sound effect, etc. The children were then interviewed in Inuktitut for further information about their program responses. We showed these pilot programs to hundreds of young viewers of all ages in the three communities, and also held public screenings for those interested in what IBC was doing.

Interestingly, one of the segments consisted of an elderly Inuit man telling a very long story in a monotone voice, while seated in a simulated igloo to an audience of about twenty children aged three to twelve (at this stage, the target age for the show was still not 100 percent certain). The story lasted about five full minutes, during which time the children, much to my surprise, sat mesmerized. The fact that the elder was speaking in an adult dialect made the children's attentiveness even more intriguing to me. When I inquired about it later, I was told that even though the three- and four-year-olds wouldn't understand much of the story the first few times they heard it, they would have many more opportunities in life to listen to this story. Consequently, each time they would be exposed to this very same story, they would derive more and more meaning from it until they reached an age where they would fully understand its significance. Though the approach used in this sequence was not chosen for inclusion in the final program, I felt that I had learned much about the audience I was researching as a result of this experience.

Out of the feedback gathered, the team constructed the television program *Takuginai*, the goals of which are to tell legends, to keep Inuit culture alive, and to educate children about critical issues such as dealing with gun and road safety (for more information, consult: www.nunatsiaq.com/archives/nunavut000230/nvt 20218_16.html).

continued ▶

The *Takuginai* team has developed several interesting characters who have become familiar to audiences all across the North and increasingly in the South, now that it is shown on APTN. These include Grandma Malaya, Grandpa Issacie, and Magic Michael, who performs magic tricks and various stunts that keep even the older viewers laughing. Working with Leetia Ineak, a puppet designer and artist, the team – headed at the time of the program's inception by Blandina Makkik of Igloolik – also came up with a puppet character called Johnny the Lemming, whose main purpose was to smooth out the dialect issue. Johnny travels every summer to the various Arctic communities on the sealift supply ship. Although originally from Iqaluit, he engages in sexual relations with lady lemmings in various ports of call. This, as might be expected, leads to the proliferation of lemming babies who Johnny visits every year while touring the North on the sealift ship. Given that the ship stops in almost all of the Inuit communities at one time or another during the open-water season and that each community has its own dialect, Johnny is the character who shows viewers how important it is to know, respect, and communicate in more than one Inuktitut dialect. *Takuginai* has been on the air on a regular basis since 30 November 1987 and receives segments from all four IBC centres located in Igloolik, Taloyoak, Rankin Inlet, and Baker Lake. ■

aboriginal broadcasting policy. All they needed to actualize their plans for native broadcasting were financial appropriations.

Meanwhile, private industry was looking to the North for new markets. During this period, Canadian law prohibited private ownership of satellite receiving dishes and the unauthorized retransmission of programming received from US satellites. Yet, many native communities received US television channels on satellite dishes purchased outside of the purview of the regulators. Video playback units were common in native homes, and tapes were easily rented through Northern video clubs and stores. As the Therrien Committee travelled across the North, it became obvious to its members that there had been a proliferation of illegal/pirate satellite dishes as a community strategy for expansion of received services. Those working in the licensing and regulatory arenas began to recognize that an increase of relevant Northern programming would be necessary to bypass the embarrassment of having to deal with a series of court cases around the transgression of CRTC, DOC, and Ministry of Transportation satellite-dish regulations.

MY EXPERIENCE WITH A PIRATE SATELLITE DISH

In 1981–82, I worked in Wabannutao (Eastmain) in James Bay as a supervisor-trainer for the local elementary-school principal who had just been promoted from a classroom teacher. The community at the time had a population of 250 and my student was the only female school principal in what was then a new Cree School Board. The Cree had taken control of their own education system in 1979–80 and had made some substantial changes to localize the administrative and senior staff. I had an eighty-day contract with the new School Board during this period and was in my second year of work in the village.

One day, the principal asked me to stop going to the school building. She informed me that she felt confident in her skills and no longer needed my services on a daily basis. We both realized that her training had given her the confidence and strategies she needed to be on her own and so I agreed to be available if and when she needed my support. Because I could not break my contract and leave town, this meant that I suddenly had a lot of time on my hands – twenty days of time, to be precise. There wasn't a lot to do, so I resorted to watching television.

Wabannutao is one of those towns that didn't qualify for the Accelerated Coverage Plan service, having a population of under five hundred. Residents would have had to wait for a long time before they could actually get a legal satellite service, so several ambitious townspeople got involved in purchasing a dish from the USA. It wasn't a very expensive or sophisticated dish, but it served its purpose. It was mounted on a square concrete block of about 12 x 12 feet. In order to change channels, the actual dish had to be lifted, tilted, and moved manually according to various channel coordinates that some ingenious mathematician in the village had figured out. Scrawled in black paint across the four top edges of the block were the names of the community's favourite television channels: WGN Chicago for sports programming, Home Box Office and The Movie Channel for films, CBC for Southern Canadian programming, CTV, ABC, CBS, and NBC. Most of the channel markings were for US-based channels, some of which I had no idea even existed since I didn't have satellite access in Montreal.

Watching television in Wabannutao was like watching TV nowhere else. Sitting inside my overheated trailer, I had no option but to watch whatever the band chief and his cohorts wanted to watch, given they were the ones who had control over the only knob in town – the actual displacing of the satellite dish itself. No matter how modern our sets were, we had no choice but to leave the TV on channel 3, the receiving channel for whatever was coming in over the airwaves at a given time.

From my perspective, this is how channel-switching operated: I would be sitting in the trailer all toasty-warm and enjoying a film – *Tootsie*, for example – when

continued ▶

all of a sudden, I would hear the sounds of snowmobile motors approaching and I would know that, within minutes, I would lose my channel because the band chief and his friends were heading towards the satellite dish. It would always be at the best part of the film, the reveal-all moment, when the channel would suddenly switch – inevitably to a sports program. Not my favourite kind of viewing, by any means. So there I would sit, totally frustrated, knowing that I wouldn't find out what happened until I rented the film in a video store a month later, after I returned to Montreal.

One Monday night, a friend's film was being screened on CBC's *Man Alive*. I called the band chief and begged him not to program in sports for that time slot. No luck. I called the village priest to ask him to speak with the band chief. No luck either. I was a stranger in the town – without status or privilege. I missed the film.

The only person who seemed to have power over the chief was his grandmother, who would put her foot down and insist that he allow her to continue watching "her" program. It was obvious when this happened; after the initial switch to sports programming, a second posse of snowmobiles would approach the dish, and the television would switch back to the original channel.

However, I'd say my most extraordinary viewing experience in Wabannutao was connected to the village's one transponder, which shared programming hours equitably between evangelical preaching and hardcore pornography. This meant that from 6 a.m. to 6 p.m., one could watch Billy Graham preach to his heart's content. At 6 p.m., the programming would automatically switch (without the manual intervention of the satellite-dish snowmobile posse) to the most violent S&M hardcore pornography one could possibly imagine. Basically, if you had the TV on, this is what you watched – and that meant everybody in the community, including the children.

I once asked a friend in the village what her grandmother had said when she first saw the pornography. Her response was that her grandma was surprised that "white people take off their clothes to make love." ■

The Cancom Decision

In response to the legitimate demands by Northern communities for an improved range of broadcasting services, Canadian Satellite Communications Inc. (Cancom) was granted a network license on 14 April 1981. CRTC's Cancom decision (CRTC 1981b) set local access for native programmers as a condition of license. In its decision, the commission emphasized "that the extension of southern-originated broadcasting services to the North, and to native communities in particular, carries with it a concomitant responsibility to facilitate the development of Northern and native-originated broadcasting services" (CRTC 1981b, 12).[8] As it went on to explain:

The Commission notes the extent to which CANCOM has recognized this responsibility by the commitments of assistance that it has made and expects it to take all necessary and appropriate steps to implement such commitments and to report to the Commission in this regard within three months after the introduction of its service (CRTC 1981b, 12).

The requirement for mandatory local access to the Cancom service was based on the implementation of Section S. 6(1)(f) of the 1968 Broadcasting Act, which stated that "every licensee shall distribute, on its basic service, to the extent of the channels available on that service, ... a community channel."

The community channel was to be reserved for local access to community groups. In villages and towns up North, where Cancom signals were to be rebroadcast via cable, access to this channel would be an asset. However, it would do nothing to simplify the complexities involved in the regional distribution of signals. To deal with this issue, the CRTC drew upon S. 18 of the 1968 Act, which stipulated that "no licensee shall alter or curtail any signals in the course of their distribution, except as required or authorized by its license or by these regulations." The CRTC framed the Cancom decision obligations in this way:

The Commission ... notes the commitment of CANCOM to permit deletion of any of its signals in predominantly native communities. The Commission has frequently affirmed that local control over the influx of southern-originated programming in native communities is of vital importance. It is, therefore, a condition of license that CANCOM permit an affiliated undertaking located in a predominantly native community to delete the distribution of any southern-originated broadcasting signal and to substitute native-produced programming therefore. CANCOM is also required to reduce its monthly fee on a pro-rata basis to any such affiliated undertaking that decides not to receive one or more of these television signals. (CRTC 1981b, 252)

In the case of Cancom, it would not be the licensee who would alter signals in the course of their distribution. Rather, it would be the native programmers (in consultation with the affiliates) who would determine the times of local access. This was a particularly interesting shift in the CRTC's position: significantly, it preceded the announcement of a Northern Broadcasting Policy by two years.

The licensing of Cancom offered an important alternative legal range of programming to CBC Northern Service. Potentially, it offered a second option for native broadcasters looking to distribute their programming. The CRTC later integrated Cancom into its plans for Northern native broadcasting, but at this point it was not clear whether the members of the Commission were even aware of how important a role Cancom was to play. Nonetheless, the CRTC had set in place one of the key non-native private players in the facilitation of native broadcasting distribution.

Recognition of the Special Status of First Peoples Television Producers

The fact that IBC became a network at this time is significant. However, if a more inclusive system of indigenous broadcasting were to be set up in the North and provided with its own budget – one separate from that of ethnic broadcasters in the South – governments and the public would have to acknowledge the "special status" of First Peoples, thereby also accepting the distinctions between the two constituency groups.[9]

In 1982, a federal study called the Applebaum-Hébert *Report on Federal Cultural Policy* had already acknowledged that Indian, Inuit, and Métis peoples had gained a "special place in cultural policy":

In the formulation of principles for cultural policy in general, and with special regard to cultural diversity in particular, it is important that no one group have privileges, priority or precedence over others. We have come to believe, however, that a special place in cultural policy should be reserved for peoples of Indian and Inuit ancestry. This should be so for several reasons. To begin with, the cultural traditions of the original peoples are uniquely rooted in this country, as compared with those more recently derived from other cultures. In the second place, the federal government has by treaty, law and custom a special responsibility for the well-being of these peoples. Finally, and most important of all, the original cultural traditions have a set of values and aesthetic standards which have not been easily accommodated within the usual structures and practices of federal cultural institutions.

... This committee is convinced that Native artists must be recognized first and foremost as contemporary Canadian artists, whatever their field, and that federal policy should

give special priority to promoting both traditional and contemporary creative work by
artists of Indian and Inuit ancestry. (Applebaum et al. 1982, 11, original emphasis)

This was the first formal pronouncement of any significance to demonstrate federal appointees' support for a separate status that could be used
to argue for a distinct Northern Broadcasting policy. Though it came from
the researchers of a task force report and not from functionaries within the
bureaucracy or from Cabinet, it represented an opinion from those closer to
the sources of power than had previous statements of this kind.

The 1982–83 Consultation and Discussion Paper

We might liken the onslaught of southern television, and the absence of native television, to the neutron bomb. This is the bomb that kills the people but leaves the build-
ings standing. Neutron-bomb television is the kind of television that destroys the soul
of a people but leaves the shell of a people walking around. The pressure, especially
on our children, to join the invading culture and language ... is explosively powerful.
Rosemarie Kuptana, CRTC Hearing, December 1982.

In 1982, the federal government undertook a series of consultations with
sixteen native organizations to determine their broadcasting needs. The
result was the 1983 Federal Government Discussion Paper. Declassified on 2
September of that year, the document summarizes the objectives of aboriginal organizations vis-à-vis government agencies' support of native broadcasting. Included are the following five points:

1 The government should sponsor special Northern native production services;
2 Regulations should be developed which require broadcasters serving significant
   native audiences to provide free access to their networks for the distribution of
   native programming;
3 Regulations should be developed which allow local government organizations to
   control the introduction of new broadcasting services in predominantly native
   communities;
4 Programs offered by Employment and Immigration for training native radio and
   television producers should be expanded and maintained; and
5 Consultation should be continued with Northern native organizations on
   Northern broadcasting. (Government of Canada 1983b, 29)

The Federal Government Discussion Paper set out various options and cost estimates. It argued that a critical decision would be necessary to frame aboriginal communications rights, with special attention being given to whether broadcast production and distribution services should be funded through land claims treaties or through a government-administered program. The paper further stated that the only differences between the two options had to do with the method of program and funding delivery and with where accountability lay. Given that, as of 1982–83, no direct requests for the inclusion of broadcasting had been submitted to the federal government by native nations during constitutional negotiations, it was recognized that a governmental intervention into financially supporting the development of aboriginal media would have to take place to allow it to break into Northern Canadian broadcasting.

Just prior to the government's 8 March public announcement of the discussion paper's outcome, Cancom submitted a new application for the addition of signals to its service (CRTC 1983). At this point, the CRTC reminded Cancom of its original commitment to native-produced programming and pointed out that these had not yet been met. In an effort to persuade Cancom to renew its interest in extending service and access facilities to native communities, the Commission demanded that Cancom submit a detailed plan and timetable for the implementation of these promises. Receipt of the plan and timetable was to be one of the CRTC's conditions of approval for the 3 + 1 service, which Cancom had applied for.[10] Cancom submitted the required information on 29 March 1983. On this date, the commission noted the initiatives of Mr Ross Charles (Cancom's vice-president responsible for relations with native groups) in helping "to facilitate the production of Native programs" (CRTC 1983, 4). The CRTC expected that native-produced radio programming would be available to Cancom for distribution by the fall of 1983 (4). Television programming by native producers was not discussed outside of the CRTC's request that it be kept informed of progress in this area. The CRTC accepted Cancom's application for the 3 + 1 signal package on 27 April 1983 after having received the requested written documentation from Cancom (CRTC 1983, 4).

The Northern Broadcasting Policy of 1983

On 10 March 1983, after years of aboriginal lobbying and (in)formal consultations, the federal government announced a Northern Broadcasting Policy

(NBP). This policy – the most important document in aboriginal communications in terms of its development – contained five basic principles that
assured significant native participation in both media programming and the
regulatory process.

1   Northern residents should be offered access to an increasing range of
    programming choices through the exploitation of technological opportunities.
2   Northern native people should have the opportunity to participate actively
    in the determination by the CRTC of the character, quantity, and priority of
    programming broadcast in predominantly native communities.
3   Northern native people should have fair access to northern broadcasting
    distribution systems to maintain and develop their cultures and languages.
4   Programming relevant to native concerns, including content originated by native
    people, should be produced for distribution on northern broadcasting services
    wherever native people form a significant proportion of the population in the
    service area.
5   Northern native representatives should be consulted regularly by government
    agencies engaged in establishing broadcasting policies which would affect their
    cultures. (Government of Canada 1983a, 2)

The Northern Broadcasting Policy (1983), with its five principles as outlined above, is typical of policy texts in that it used ambiguous terms that
could be subjected to a range of discretionary interpretations over time.
For example, terms such as "fair access," "predominantly native," and "a
significant proportion of the population" immediately generated arguments
between federal regulators and native broadcasters about their conflicting
points of interpretation. Moreover, how precisely could these problematic
terms be applied in a practical context if there was no consensus about what
they meant? Given the varied and complex range of interests involved in this
negotiation, these kinds of clarification discussions were an integral part of
the Northern policy-ing process throughout the decade.

The most contentious term in the NBP was "access." There were three
kinds of "access" outlined in the policy: access to a broader range of channel
choices comparable in number to those received in the South; access to the
CRTC and federal agencies' policy-making process through a series of ongoing consultations related to the establishment of broadcasting policies and
practices; and "fair access" of native producers to a means of distributing
native-language programs via existing satellite facilities.

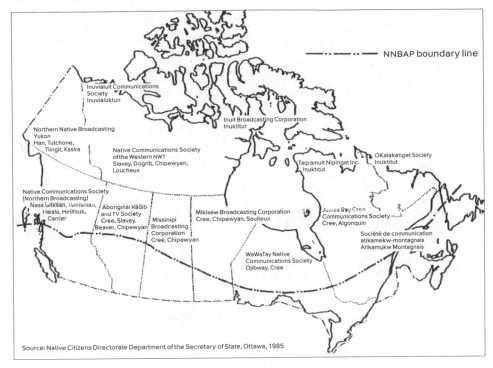

Source: Native Citizens Directorate Department of the Secretary of State, Ottawa, 1985

NNBAP-Funded Societies and Linguistic Regions, 1985. Used with permission of Native Citizens Directorate, Department of Canadian Heritage, Ottawa.

The question remained as to whose version of "fairness" should be applied to all three. And what, for that matter, *was* "fair" access? The latter question, of course, continues to defy easy response.

A major concern at the time was whether or not it would be possible to implement the Northern Broadcasting Policy in the context of the 1968 Broadcasting Statutes and regulations. It could be argued that a basis for principle 1 (of the NBP) in the Broadcasting Act was its assurance of a broad range of programming options for Canadian residents. Principles 2 and 5 (concerning access to the policy-making process) were not elaborated within the Act at all. Nor was a legal ground for this process to be found in the regulations issued by the CRTC. In the spirit of principles 3 and 4 the CRTC could, for instance, use its discretionary powers to justify access to broadcasting services for native programmers. However, in doing so, the CRTC would be bending existing principles enshrined in the 1968 Broadcasting Act.

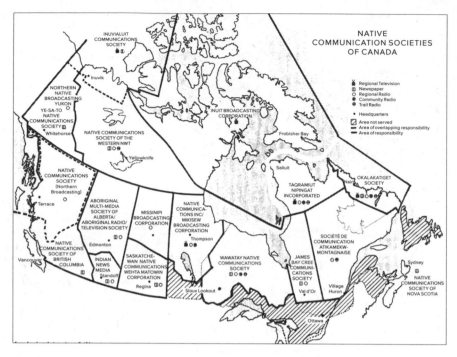

Native Communication Societies of Canada, August 86. Used with permission of Native Citizens Directorate, Department of Canadian Heritage.

These grey areas notwithstanding, a policy vehicle – the Northern Native Broadcast Access Program (NNBAP) – was also announced on 10 March 1983. This was to be the mechanism to operationalize the five principles. Administered by the Department of the Secretary of State, Native Citizens Directorate, the NNBAP management team was expected, over an initial four-year period, to distribute $40.3 million to thirteen regionally based Northern Native Communications Societies for the long-term production and distribution of twenty hours of radio and five hours of television programming per week.[11] Consistent with the decade-long position of the Northern aboriginal lobby, production and distribution plans supported the future entrenchment of aboriginal-language broadcasting rights in the Broadcasting Act. However, the federal government also expected CBC Northern Service and Cancom to deliver the programming as a social cost to their licenses, and this was not to be as easy a matter to settle as anticipated.

That two key aspects of previous discussions were missing from the framework of the NNBAP rendered the policy even more problematic in its initial implementation phases. One was the lack of available funds to provide employment training. The presumption that Canada Manpower and Employment would take on the responsibility of providing funds on an annual basis might have been a realistic expectation during the first four years. However, as time wore on and personnel changed, negotiations for this funding became increasingly difficult. The second was the aforementioned assumption that CBC Northern Service and Cancom would happily deliver Northern programming at times suitable for aboriginal producers. However, the Broadcasting Act of 1968 did not *obligate* either the CBC or Cancom to comply with the CRTC's expectations. Consequently, until changes were enshrined in the Act, native broadcasters would have to rely on moral suasion and "amiable negotiations" to assure the distribution of their productions.

This meant that First Peoples' access to broadcasting distribution facilities was as much a moral question as a technical and political one for the two networks involved. Carriage on their services, rather than the establishment of new networks, would involve modifications to CBC Northern Service and Cancom infrastructures and schedules. Who would assure that these changes take place? Clearly, this was the duty of the CRTC, whose administrative mandate is to supervise and regulate Canada's broadcasting industries. However, policy implementation occurs within a legal, as well as a regulatory, framework. Policies would have to conform to existing statutes of the current Broadcasting Act and legal regulations as issued by the CRTC. If policies were created for which a basis was not found in current legal documents, amendments to the Broadcasting Act or changes in regulations and licensing procedures might enable the policy to be implemented with greater facility and less likelihood of challenge. Legislative change takes place rather slowly, however.

In 1984, the CRTC was informed of the difficulties that some of the Native Communications Societies were experiencing in getting access time on Northern distribution systems. It formed a Northern Native Broadcasting Committee to identify and discuss broadcasting-related problems experienced by the NNBAP groups. Although the CRTC was aware of distribution challenges, it wasn't until much later that public hearings would be held in various locales (including the North) to try to resolve these. In the meantime, it was decided that the CRTC would react to each distribution problem to the best of its capacity on a case-by-case basis. The Commission recognized the complexity of the issues and began to view a combination of public, private, and community-owned stations as a possible solution. The CRTC went so far as to support requests by the CBC and the Native Communication Societies for a dedicated Northern satellite channel transponder in principle. From a practical perspective, funds as high as $10 million over four years would eventually have be allocated by the federal government to accomplish this goal. Several years passed between the first mention of a dedicated transponder and the actual setting aside of funds for it in 1988.

STAGE FOUR: TOWARDS THE RECOGNITION OF ABORIGINAL BROADCASTING IN LEGISLATION

1986 was a significant year in the development of Northern native broadcasting support at the policy and governmental levels. Two key reports were released and circulated, adding further strength to arguments for the enshrining of native communication rights in a new Broadcasting Act.

The Caplan-Sauvageau Report on Broadcasting Policy

In separating First Peoples from multicultural minorities in the Caplan-Sauvageau report, the researchers behind it demonstrated the political will to respect the "special status" position of First Peoples in the broadcasting sector. The chapter on native broadcasting argued forcefully for the creation of a significant place for native broadcasters within the Canadian broadcasting system. After outlining the basic issues for future decisions, the report made the following recommendations for new Broadcasting legislation:

1   The Broadcasting Act should affirm the right of native peoples to broadcasting services in aboriginal languages considered to be representative where numbers warrant and to the extent that public funds permit.
2   The Broadcasting Act should give the CBC a clear mandate to provide broadcasting services in representative aboriginal languages where numbers warrant and as public funds become available. Furthermore, we recommend the CBC establish an autonomous aboriginal-language service, as there are now distinct French and English services.
3   As production levels warrant and as public funds become available, a separate satellite distribution system should be established to carry native-language

programming produced by independent native communications societies and the CBC. As an interim step, we recommend that native communications societies [sic] and the CBC Northern Service share a satellite transponder dedicated to service northern communities.

4 A research and consultation process should be carried out among aboriginal people in the South in order to identify regional needs and to establish a general policy of native broadcasting for the whole country.

5 In extending the Accelerated Coverage Plan, the CBC should give special consideration to serving isolated aboriginal communities that request service, regardless of size.

6 Native-language broadcasting should be administered at arm's length from the federal government and should be provided with sufficient funds to cover the cost of all essential related activities such as training. (Caplan and Sauvageau 1986, 519–23)

Concern was expressed in the Caplan-Sauvageau study that native language programming would be subject to the vagaries of department priorities, budget allocations, and bureaucratic bottlenecks as long as the NNBAP remained affiliated with the Secretary of State, Native Citizens Directorate. Although it focused on separate services for native broadcasters, the task force also suggested that better aboriginal representation be developed in mainstream broadcasting. It did not offer program advice in this regard but planted the seeds of what was to come.

The Lougheed Evaluation Report

After four years of operation, and one year after the Caplan-Sauvageau Task Force had begun its research, the NNBAP and each of its client Native Communications Societies underwent a thorough evaluation process (conducted by Kendall Lougheed & Associates in 1986). Reaching remote areas whose combined native population totalled more than 200,000, NNBAP-funded Societies were found to be producing 5,530 hours of regional radio programming and 747 hours of aboriginal television. This was quite impressive.

The final evaluation report was laudatory in terms of NNBAP's production accomplishments and the commitment of its audiences. The Societies were found to be significant cultural and educational contributors to the growing awareness of native languages and issues (such as land claims, self-government, and educational and environmental concerns). The report saw the

Societies as essential tools in the development of cultural identities and political empowerment. It did, however, raise several negative points. First, the NNBAP had created tensions between those First Peoples who lived above the Hamelin line and those south of it. This is because the Native Citizens Directorate had used a modified version of the Hamelin line (north of about 50°) to divide the Northern communities that were considered eligible for funding from the Southern ones that were not under the rubric of federal communications programs. People south of the line were, therefore, ineligible for broadcast funding. Communities had argued to the evaluators that the modified Hamelin line criterion for NNBAP was arbitrary: it was unfair that, because of location, some nations (for example, the Algonquins in Northern Quebec) were divided in terms of access to broadcasting resources. The report also identified training and distribution as key problems along with the Secretary of State's underestimation of the funding needed to cover production costs. The Societies needed more money to produce consistently good-quality programming.

The Report pointed out the complexity of the climate in which native broadcasters were operating. The DOC created broadcasting policies; the CRTC regulated and supervised the implementation of those policies; the Secretary of State, Native Citizens Directorate, administered and guided the programs designed as vehicles for the policies; CBC Northern Service, Cancom, and provincial/territorial broadcasters carried the signal based on individual negotiations with each Broadcasting Society; training was sponsored by Canada Manpower and other subsidizing agencies (when possible). A rationalization of services was required in order to systematize the procedures.

The Lougheed Report recommended consolidation and increase of federal funding for all communications activities both north and south of the Hamelin line. It also called for a long-term policy on aboriginal broadcasting that would enable NCSs to plan for their futures with more financial and social certainty.

The Secretary of State, Native Citizens Directorate, sponsored the evaluation study and was pleased with the overall results of the evaluation. Consequently, NNBAP funding was renewed for four more years.

In addition, Lougheed's Report identified several pertinent theoretical issues. One related to the notion and meaning of the term *culture* as it was inscribed within the federal government's policy definition. Another key point revolved around the relationship between culture and native languages.

The way the federal government inscribed the word "culture" in the Northern Broadcasting Policy appeared to be deceptively simple and one-dimensional. Folkloric in tone and salvagist in objective, it was problematic in that it could potentially promote exotic and ethno-exhibitionist programming to the exclusion of productions related to politics, economics, education, and other relevant topics supporting cultural retention. More than documenting the process-related complexities of First Peoples' lived experiences, the government's administrative view of "culture" referred to the salvaging of traditional languages and activities in an entirely fixed sense – as if it were possible to freeze time in some historically idealistic or romantic moment before (post)modernity. Paralleling the cases of other First Peoples (for example, the Waiapi people of Brazil), the federal government was coming dangerously close to pushing First Peoples into colonizing their own historical and idealized image in order to retrieve what might have "disappeared from their rituals because of colonization" (MacKenzie 1994, 21). This is like mimicking already existing mimicry of First Peoples' own cultures. Critically examining this relationship between culture and language was thus an important feature of the Lougheed Report, which redefined "culture" in more processual terms as follows:

A patterned response to environment based on selected values. It is rooted in shared social practices and experiences, which are maintained through communication. As [the] environment changes, culture responds with characteristic dynamism ... This dynamic nature of culture has led to a redefinition of traditional culture among most native peoples. For instance, Eastern Arctic Inuit consider square dancing, the mouth harp and accordion, trapping, the Christian Church, syllabic writing, and other activities as "traditional" when in actual fact they have been incorporated into their culture since Euro-Canadian contact. (Lougheed et al. 1986, 4: 16–17)

The report's authors went on to note that "native peoples may define cultural programming more broadly than do southern Canadians" (4: 17) – a statement that demonstrates at least a basic understanding of the kind of issues that emerge from relying on too narrow and confined a definition of cultural broadcasting, as articulated in the NBP. In fact, native peoples in the Western Arctic, the Yukon, and Northwest British Columbia would soon challenge the government's notion of culture, pointing out that it limited them to broadcasting a finite repertoire of ethno-cultural content in languages that, in some cases, had all but disappeared.

On the point of the language/culture relationship, the Lougheed Report went beyond the NBP principles with its assertion that "language is intimately, but not exclusively associated with culture" (Lougheed et al. 1986, 4: 17). The report drew on the 1981 Census to illuminate how English was rapidly replacing native languages in the Southern parts of the provinces, especially among the young. It was also noted that "the languages with the strongest institutional support are the most likely to be retained, although the size of the linguistic community is, at least, as important" (4: 17–18).

The Lougheed evaluators argued in favour of the availability of native-language broadcasting because it would mitigate "against the separation of native audiences in the North, one which does not understand English, the other which does" (4: 18). But the authors did not disapprove of English or French programming in cases where language skills had already eroded. Shared understanding of information, the report argued, should be the goal of programming. The Evaluation Study concluded:

The importance of shared information access in native communities suggests that the extent to which programming is broadcast or printed in a language mutually understood by respective residents is central to its socio-cultural role. Thus, native cultural products can be produced in any appropriate language. In the case of native media, the numbers and age range of the native audience is an additional indicator of its ability to reinforce social cohesion in native communities. (4: 18)

Towards a Definition of Native Cultural Programming

By the time the Lougheed Report was released, problems were already arising in towns that had more than one radio station. In Whitehorse and Yellowknife, for example, English-language broadcasters had begun to feel the effects of having to compete for audiences with native-owned stations. In 1988, dissatisfaction escalated into a confrontation when the two commercial radio licensees complained to the CRTC that the publicly subsidized native radio stations in Whitehorse and Yellowknife were encroaching on their market by playing English pop music and using English as the lingua franca of programming. The two native stations argued that their programming was in the aboriginal language that *most* First Peoples in Whitehorse and Yellowknife spoke – English. Furthermore, they contended that the popular music they were playing was aboriginal music: after all, who was to say that heavy metal or Bruce Springsteen and Céline Dion were *not* native music? Pointing out that these choices were just as "native" as "non-native," they compared First Nations' appropriation of singers or music genres to mainstream society's incorporation of ethnocultural music into *their* own. In this context, key questions emerged for the NWT and Yukon Native Communication Societies involved in this dispute. Who owns musical notes, sounds, words, and languages? And why should aboriginal media be restricted to narrowly defined terms when they are producing their own inclusive *perspectives* on this music from within a multimediated environment?

Here, we have an interesting example of the ways in which media can both assimilate cultures *into* another and separate them one *from* the other. Initially, and according to the federal government's mandate, aboriginal media was to be produced to further distinguish First Peoples from other constituency groups in Canadian society. The easiest way to do this was to limit what Native Communications Societies could program by tying funding to specific kinds of content materials and languages. To First Nations radio producers in Yellowknife and Whitehorse who wanted to reflect the lived cultures of their own communities, these restrictions were ghettoizing. Furthermore, they did not conform with First Peoples multiple fragmented existences. Not that their desire to play the latest pop hits and program in the English language meant that they wanted to become assimilated into mainstream society. Rather, they refused to be limited by administratively imposed constraints that did not reflect the realities of their daily lives. "Behaving" at this point could mean being committed long-term to an *electronic media reservation*.

This particular confrontation marked a turning point in First Peoples communications by challenging what had been hitherto a little questioned ensemble of definitions, practices, and normative assumptions about the NNBAP. More than anything, the two NCSs involved demonstrated how politically savvy and empowered they had become by not having succumbed to initial attempts by the complainants to make them conform to their demands.

Wishing to respond to this important dispute in a comprehensive manner, the CRTC engaged the services of Greg Smith and Associates to undertake a review of Northern native broadcasting from a more complex perspective and to recommend reasonable means of resolving such differences. What was involved, Smith noted in his report (1988), was a rethinking of several critical issues. One was what, in fact, constituted a native broadcasting service, or put another way: how did one define "a native station," "native music," or "a native language"? Another key issue was whether the CRTC should stream-line the licensing procedures for small Northern stations: in other words, should Northern stations be obliged to fill in a *Promise of Performance* form as other stations did?

To be fair and thorough in soliciting critical opinions, it was recognized that these and other questions should be circulated for public deliberation before the federal authorities made a decision. In a *Call for Comments on Northern Native Broadcasting* (CRTC 1989), the CRTC asked for public input on eight questions:

1 Should the Commission establish a more precise regulatory framework for native broadcasting as it has for community radio and ethnic broadcasting?

2 What is an appropriate definition of a "native broadcasting undertaking"? Of a "native program"? Of "native music"?

3 Should native broadcasters be required to file a promise of performance with their applications? If so, to which broadcasters should this requirement apply (e.g., networks only, individual stations)? What should be included in the promise of performance? For native FM undertakings, should substantial compliance with such a promise of performance be imposed by condition of license, as is the case with conventional FM undertakings?

4 What measures could the Commission and/or broadcasters adopt to encourage the funding and recording of music by native artists for broadcast by native broadcasters and others? For example, could a funding mechanism for native-language recordings or other music by native artists be designed which would complement the funding available through FACTOR[12] and the Canada Council? If so, who would administer it and what access criteria would be employed?

5 What regulatory mechanisms can be used by the Commission to assist in resolving conflicts between native broadcasters and private commercial broadcasters serving the same location? Should the Commission, for example, limit the amount of non-native music on native stations?

6 Under what circumstances, if any, should the CRTC place restrictions on the amount or kind of advertising by native broadcasters? What impact would advertising by native broadcasters have on commercial broadcasters serving the same market?

7 Should the CBC permit native broadcasters using its distribution facilities to sell advertising in their programming?

8 To what extent do distribution problems for northern native broadcasters still exist? How can they be resolved in the interests of native broadcasting and of the Canadian broadcasting system as a whole?

While these questions were being considered and a model policy was being circulated for public comment, the Department of Communications and the Secretary of State were busy making other critical decisions.

1990: Deliberations about Southern Native Communications and the Federal Budget Cuts

One of these decisions was that the Department of Communications would commission Lougheed and Associates, along with Greg Smith and Associates, to prepare the ground for a communications needs assessment for aboriginal peoples living *below* the Hamelin line. There were to be two preliminary reports before the actual assessment was undertaken. The first was to be a demographic study identifying the locations of the First Peoples' populations in Canada. The second was to be an Annotated Bibliography of existing research on native communications in Canada. I was subcontracted to put this bibliography together for the two consulting groups.

Amidst these lively and optimistic debates over how to more equitably open existing infrastructures to both Northern and Southern First Peoples, and how to further refine their relations with commercial broadcasters, the federal government announced devastating budget cuts. The Native Communications Program – begun in the 1970s to support print, audiovisual media, and community radio in the South and the North – was cut 100 percent ($3.45 million). Without warning, finances for fifteen native-language newspapers across Canada were eliminated. The NNBAP was cut by 16 percent ($2.2 million), which severely restricted the operations of the thirteen Native Communications Societies. Furthermore, the Secretary of State's Native Distribution Fund of $0.8 million, which assisted in payment for transponder rental, was also cancelled (PEN 1991, 11).

Subsequently, the two preliminary Lougheed/Smith studies were buried, as were further discussions about the equitable development of native communications in the South.[13] The fact that the Lougheed and Smith contract had not yet been widely acknowledged made it easier for the federal government to drop it without attracting the attention of critics in the field. However, the contract had been well under way when the government announced the cuts in February, and the concerns of native Southerners had become a subject of discussion among First Peoples by this time as well.

Plans to develop Southern broadcasting infrastructures fizzled out when the Lougheed/Smith contract was terminated. The Department of Communications could not easily earmark $250,000 for a study of Southern communications needs when the Department of the Secretary of State was pulling back a substantial amount of its support from its two existing Native Communications programs. The contradiction in federal decision-making processes would have been too blatant, and subject to public scrutiny. As a result, the plans for equalizing the allocation of resources were laid to rest before they were even publicized.

The NCSs' anger over the cuts was evident in the brief submitted by the Northern Native Broadcasting, Yukon to the CRTC later that year:

Forty-four per cent of the cuts to the Secretary of State's total annual budget came at the expense of native communications programs, notwithstanding that native communications represents a much smaller fraction of that department's budget.

We believe this action shows a blatant disregard for the role of aboriginal broadcasters and our record in developing social, cultural and linguistic programming for the indigenous people of Canada. Such a decision displays a paternalistic "program mentality" toward the rights of aboriginal Canadians to exercise our languages, culture and traditions. (NNBY 1990, n.p.)

The cuts had a considerable impact on the further development of native broadcasting and distribution services – an impact that was felt until Television Northern Canada (TVNC) became operational in 1991 (see chapter 7 for details of this period). Ironically, in 1988, the group organizing what was later to become TVNC had received $10 million from the federal government to set up a dedicated pan-Northern transponder. In 1990, however, the Native Communications Societies' program production fund was cut.

In other words, Northern First Peoples were to be given a dedicated Northern delivery system, but not enough money to produce material for dissemination. The analogy of giving First Peoples a voice but cutting off their tongues would not be too far afield here. In response, the aboriginal public, along with non-native supporters, went to the defense of aboriginal broadcasting. Non-governmental organizations across the country, such as the

TABLE 2

ABORIGINAL BROADCASTING FUNDING HISTORY

Northern Native Broadcast Access Program 1983–2003

Year	(Operations & Production) Program Funding Level	Distribution Funding
1983–84	4,289,000	0
1984–85	6,734,275	403,725
1985–86	8,470,468	116,532
1986–87	13,358,000	901,000
1987–88	12,481,000	732,182
1988–89	12,564,004	729,996
1989–90	12,493,000	787,189
1990–91	10,494,000	0*
1991–92	10,528,012	747,766
1992–93	10,565,212	713,000
1993–94	10,038,000	115,000
1994–95	10,038,000	115,000
1995–96	9,536,480	52,520
1996–97	8,130,035	44,765
1997–98	7,906,267	43,533
1998–99	7,906,267	43,533
1999–2000	7,906,267	43,533
2000–2001	7,906,267	43,533
2001–2002	7,906,267	43,533
2002–2003	7,906,267	43,533
TOTALS	$186,157,088	$2,049,249

* $1,077,000 used as transitional funding to groups whose funding was eliminated under the native communications program.

Source: Whiteduck Resources Inc. & Consilium; used with permission of the Department of Canadian Heritage, 25 June 2003.

Supporters and members of the OKalaKatiget Communications Society protesting the cuts in 1990. Used with permission of OKalaKatiget Native Communications Society.

Centre for Research/Action on Race Relations (CRARR) in Montreal, called press conferences to criticize the government for its ad hoc decision-making and refusal to consider the many supportive evaluations of native communications.

Even the Canadian Centre for International PEN (an organization concerned with protecting the human rights of writers and journalists) circulated a brief outlining the international legal basis for the reinstatement of the two programs (PEN 1991). Its authors argued for the aboriginal right to cultural development through protection mechanisms such as the International Covenant on Economic, Social and Cultural Rights-Article 15(1), which specifies that everyone has the right to take part in cultural life. Article 27(1) of the Universal Declaration of Human Rights was also used as a basis to promote the reinstitution of the two programs, as was Article 27 of the International Covenant on Civil and Political Rights. The latter states that, "In those States in which ethnic, religious or linguistic minorities exist, persons belonging to such minorities shall not be denied the right, in community with the other members of their group, to enjoy their own culture ... or to use their own language" (PEN 1991, 21).

According to PEN's brief, several international laws recognized the right of aboriginal groups to the special protection of their languages and cultures, including "the use of mass communications in the languages of these peoples" (PEN 1991, 25). What were the consequences of PEN's brief? Other than informing a limited public about the implications of the cuts, this well-researched and well-argued statement more or less fell on deaf ears within federal circles.

Other criticisms and pressures were brought to bear on the federal government as aboriginal broadcasters tried to build a broad public coalition for their cause. They argued about the importance of their service to the goals of self-government, self-empowerment, and the democratization of the information order within their regions. Once again, public and private protests fell on deaf ears. At a private meeting with representatives from the National Aboriginal Communications Societies (NACS, a national umbrella organization designated to speak on behalf of the native broadcasters), Secretary of State and Minister of Multiculturalism Gerry Weiner suggested that if the aboriginal peoples could mobilize as much public pressure to demonstrate support for their programs as had the Japanese in their reparations case, he would reconsider a reallocation of the funding.[14] A public campaign was undertaken. According to Rosemarie Kuptana, then president of the Inuit Broadcasting Corporation, approximately fourteen thousand support letters were mailed to the Secretary of State. Neither of the programs were fully reinstated. The same number of letters were received with respect to preserving the Women's Program, which had been cut at the same time period. This provided enough impetus for the Minister to extend this program! For First Peoples, the most to which the federal government would agree was to prolong funding to the NCS recipients of the Native Communications Programs for three months: during this time they could attempt to diversify their funding, in the hopes of financially saving themselves. Unfortunately, many of the NCSs existed in isolated communities with very small economic bases and depended on public subsidy for their economic survival.

Consequently, the Native Communications Societies were forced to turn to commercial sources of funding. Meanwhile, the CRTC had been collecting comments on its Proposed Native Broadcasting Policy (CRTC 1990b, 12) and was about to announce its new policy decisions to the public.

On 20 September 1990 the CRTC released the actual Native Broadcasting Policy (CRTC 1990b), with a notable shift in title from the previous one of 1983 (the Northern Broadcasting Policy). Calling its new approach "flexible" and "minimalist," the commission took the 1990 cuts into consideration by relaxing the advertising restrictions on native stations as a way of augmenting their limited financial resources. Borrowing from its Community Radio and Ethnic Broadcasting policies, the commission clarified what it meant by an aboriginal broadcasting undertaking. According to the policy, it is:

... owned and controlled by a non-profit organization whose board members are drawn from the aboriginal population of the region it serves. Its programming can be in any aboriginal language or in either or both of the two official languages, but should be specifically oriented to the aboriginal audience it is licensed to serve. It also has a distinct role in fostering the development of aboriginal cultures and, where possible, the preservation of ancestral languages. An aboriginal program is a program in any language directed specifically towards a distinct aboriginal audience, or a program about any aspect of the life, interests, or culture of Canada's native people. (CRTC 1990b, 2)

In communities with non-native stations, native broadcasters were given permission to run advertisements for an average of four minutes per hour each day, with a maximum of six minutes in any given hour. However, should the native service be the sole broadcasting undertaking in a given community, all advertising restrictions were waived (CRTC 1990b, 1–2).

This policy liberated the notion of culture and language from its heritage containment framework and allowed for the potential development of programming based on other considerations that drew on a wider range of subjects, languages, frameworks, and perspectives. First Peoples were satisfied with the Native Broadcasting Policy in principle. But there was still one enormous policy task left – the enshrinement of aboriginal communications rights in legislation and its implementation within an environment of budgetary constraints.

STAGE FIVE: THE BROAD CONTEXT OF CANADA'S BROADCASTING
ACT OF 4 JUNE 1991 AND ITS IMPLICATIONS FOR FIRST PEOPLES'
BROADCASTERS

Up to and including the 1968 Broadcasting Act and its 1976 modification, legislation specified that "all Canadians are entitled to broadcasting service in English and French as public funds become available" (Government of Canada 1968–69, 16 & 17 Eliz. 2, c.25: S 2[e]). The Act also stated that the

While lobbyists were negotiating new terms of reference for the Broadcasting
Act, the Native Communications Societies persistently went on doing their work.
Above: Setting up a video shoot in Labrador – OkalaKatiget Native Communications
Society. Used with permission of Art King, Department of Canadian Heritage; *below*:
Randy McKenzie and Robert Smith setting up a video shoot in the Yukon, NNBY.
Photographer: Robin Armour. Used with permission of NNBY.

national broadcasting service should "be extended to all parts of Canada, as public funds become available" (S.2 [g] [ii]). This meant that First Peoples (as well as the rest of the Canadian population) had the right to *receive* but not to *transmit* programming.

Once the Accelerated Coverage Plan and supplementary territorial subsidies had provided centrally controlled services throughout most of the country, Canadians (particularly minorities) began to look at other ways to talk and write about broadcasting policies and practices. I refer here to the alternative Canadian tradition of constituency-based services. According to Liora Salter, who first used the term to reformulate the notion of community, "constituency" refers to "people sharing multiple overlapping relationships in a system of power" (1980, 113). Constituency groups share a common relationship to institutions of governance and to those who hold power within a given society. They are located at a common distance from the corridors of power.

Between 1968 and the passing of the current Broadcasting Act on 4 June 1991, Canadian policy-makers and regulators struggled with modifications to the 1968 Act and the 1976 version. The objective was to technologically streamline it and to make it more reflective of constituency group rights already enshrined within other Canadian legislation.[15]

During this period, three constituency groups were outstanding in their demands to make the principles of the Broadcasting Act more culturally, racially, and gender-inclusive. Besides Canada's First Peoples, the other lobby groups consisted of ethnic populations and women. Each of these groups demanded more accurate portrayals, whether positive or negative, as well as equitable employment opportunities for themselves within existing White, male-dominated mainstream broadcasting venues.

Along with changes in the technological, regulatory, and sociocultural environments, the result of their concerted lobbying efforts has been that broadcasting services within Canada have changed considerably for them, as well as for community groups. Each of these constituency groups now have collective broadcasting rights enshrined in the Act and on-air services that have materialized from these rights. Although the integration of minorities into the broadcasting sector has been slow, it has definitely gained momentum by the enshrinement of the constituency group principle within the 1991 Broadcasting Act, which specifically states that:

... through its programming and the employment opportunities arising out of its operation, [the Canadian broadcasting system should] serve the needs and interests,

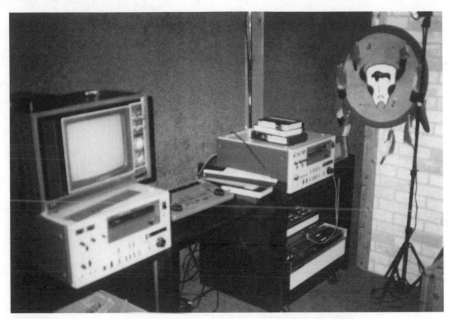

Wawatay equipment setup. Used with permission of Wa-Wa-Tay Native
Communications Society.

and reflect the circumstances and aspirations of Canadian men, women and children, including equal rights, the linguistic duality and multicultural and multiracial
nature of Canadian society and the special place of aboriginal peoples within that
society. (Government of Canada 1991, S. 3 [d][iii].)

The changes in broadcasting legislation marked a turning point in Canada's official recognition of collective over individual rights in broadcasting.
The 1991 *Broadcasting Act* takes Canada's existing commitment to equality
rights inscribed in the Charter of Rights and Freedoms, Section 15 (1982),
the Multiculturalism Act, 1988, the Human Rights Act (1976–77), and the
Employment Equity Act (1986) and applies it to the broadcasting field. These
equality rights include: the right to express multicultural and multiracial
differences; the prohibition of discrimination on the basis of race, national
or ethnic origin, colour, religion, sex, age, or mental or physical disabil-
ity; and the right to equitable job opportunities in the broadcasting sector.
Although it cannot be expected that the Canadian broadcasting system will
change overnight, having strong legislative principles in place for the next

The changing face of Wawatay TV. Wawatay Television production staff: Charlie Chisel, camera man; John Cook, video editor; Joe Beardy, producer; Mike Dubé, assistant video editor. Photographer: Joe Beardy. Used with permission of WWT Native Communications Society.

few decades will give minority constituency groups the opportunities to participate more actively in the production and distribution sectors of the Canadian broadcasting industry. How consistent these opportunities will be remains to be seen, given the extensive budget cuts experienced by non-profit organizations in the 1990s. Nonetheless, in the years since the implementation of the *Broadcasting Act* (1991) the evidence indicates that the Canadian broadcasting system is beginning to open up to a multiplicity of accented voices that had not been guaranteed access to a public medium of expression in the past.

THE SIGNIFICANCE OF POLICY-ING THE NORTH

The stages of the Northern broadcasting policy case represent a complex and powerful historical record showing the movement from an absence of native concerns in the 1968 policy to the full legal enshrinement of Northern First

Peoples' broadcasting transmission rights in the 1991 Act. This recognition by the federal government is significant. It tells us about the relations among the federal state apparatus, Northern First Peoples, other Canadian constituency groups, and the policy-making process itself. Parallel, yet contradictory trajectories within the federal government's decisions (around Northern native broadcasting) are not unusual, as demonstrated in many of the examples provided in this book.

The federal government apparatus is not a homogeneous unified body of opinion. Rather, it is a microcosm of the cleavages (classes, fractions, and divisions) already existent in our social structures, practices, and institutions. The typical messiness surrounding the state's internal contradictions as it operates to create what appears to be a consensus has implications for policy production, implementation, and analysis. In other words, the fissures evident within the administrative apparatus, including the bureaucracy, will undoubtedly manifest themselves in the various aspects of the policy-ing process. The Northern case was no exception.

Here, the federal government demonstrated at least two parallel and contradictory policy tracks: positively responding to the aboriginal demands for broadcasting infrastructures and pulling cultural funding away from aboriginal peoples just when they had begun to tackle issues from a more journalistic and less ethno-exhibitionistic manner.

In the early 1980s, the federal government had demonstrated its good will by financially supporting cultural broadcasting services in regions with significant aboriginal populations, but its support was circumscribed within certain cultural and linguistic frameworks. By the time the 1990s arrived, native broadcasting systems were operating smoothly and were no longer as much of a priority on the federal agenda as they had once been. There were other concerns of greater importance to those in the federal government, such as the Meech Lake constitutional discussions and the political/national questions about First Peoples' expectations and roles within a new confederal system. Aboriginal peoples were also becoming more coherent in their demands for self-government and land claims treaties were in various stages of negotiations around the country. As communications infrastructures became more sophisticated within native communities, First Peoples used them to become more articulate and outspoken when voicing their demands to the federal, provincial, and territorial governments. Leaders like Elijah Harper (who was just about to say "No" to the Meech Lake Accord) were positioning themselves for a confrontation with Conservative government strategists. The Kanehsatake/Oka conflict of 1990 over the appropriation of a Mohawk sacred burial ground for the purposes of expanding a golf club was deepening. A native voice publicly documenting each of these crises would have added a very important perspective to the national debates surrounding these turning points in Canadian history. Because of the financial cuts, broadcast journalists could not afford to cover the issues on-site. Was this silencing process a conscious strategy on the part of federal bureaucrats, or was it just incidental – the consequence of an ad hoc decision?

It is not my intention to propose a conspiracy theory. It is important, however, to place the budget cuts within their overall political and historical context in order to assess the relationship between the cuts and the social milieu. From the beginning of the program in 1983, the NNBAP coordinating team seems to have adopted a casual style and maintained an unusually open enclave within the federal public service, closely supporting the interests of their client groups. The NNBAP staff did not tend to speak in bureaucratic discourse; nor did they follow the typical norms of government interaction patterns. Their informality challenged the government's way of doing things and the normative patterns in which typical policy circles operated. Their dress was more casual than the typical office worker, and their manner of negotiations tended to be in alignment with the nations with whom they were working.

Aboriginal witnesses were encouraged to testify at the CRTC and Parliamentary Committees' hearings by NNBAP staff. Here, they conducted themselves in such a way as to make federal bureaucrats uncomfortable because it contrasted with their own formal, culturally coded ways of being and of doing things. Often, government bureaucrats at the upper level of the hierarchy were thrown off guard by both First Peoples and the NNBAP staff. Basically, these differences were grounded in unique cross-cultural realities, and all parties had to stop periodically and take stock of how they could move their agendas forward. In the case of First Peoples, they succeeded in convincing enough senior federal bureaucrats that their case was exceptional and that they warranted special treatment. At the same time, NNBAP staff had to be compliant with the administrative constraints and priorities of their departments, whose leaders sometimes differed in their political and social opinions. In other words, and in a practical sense, the NNBAP team did not always align themselves with the regnant views and expectations of their Cabinet Minister supervisors, yet they were required to conform to these at times of financial cutback. Certainly, in terms of their public interface, they had to appear as if they were representing the Cabinet Ministers' views. However, it is interesting (but perhaps not all that surprising) to note that the fiscal cutbacks of 1990 were just as much of a surprise to those administering the NNBAP and the Native Communications Program as they were to the aboriginal broadcasters. There were definitely communication gaps taking place on a systemic level within the public service.[16] For example, none of the evaluations of the two programs had ever suggested terminating either one of them. On the contrary, independent evaluators had suggested fortifying them with increased budgets and a wider variety of services as public funds became available on the basis of their successes.

The damage done to relations of trust between civil servants involved in the administration of Native Communications Programs and First Peoples as a result of the cutbacks was immeasurable. It could only be compared to the political mobilization that had occurred around Chrétien's declaration of the *White Paper on Indian Policy* in 1969. The federally instigated fracturing of First Peoples' loyalty to what had become a commonly owned policy project reinforced an even stronger commitment on the part of First Peoples' broadcasters to diversify their funding sources and to expand their audiences in an effort to build both a political support group and an advertising base.

The departments that handled broadcasting policies clearly did not have a coherent policy front; nor was their internal communications process effective in building a strategy for consensus within the civil service. Given the fluidity and overlapping of paradigms within decision-making circles, many First Peoples communities concluded that building a broad consensus around native issues in civil society would be the key to stabilizing and strengthening native broadcasting services. Interestingly enough – and somewhat ironically – it was Minister Gerry Weiner who, in March 1990, informed aboriginal broadcasters of this important strategy: build alliances in the non-native audiences, have *them* visibly and audibly demonstrate their support of native broadcasters, and then he might listen to the message. The challenge that Weiner laid out was to be taken more seriously than even he expected. Indeed, activities that had this goal in mind had already begun in the late 1980s, when Northern Native Broadcasting, Yukon arranged with CBC Newsworld for its half-hour program *Nedaa* to cross over the cultural and regional borderlines on a weekly basis. Moreover, Television Northern Canada – a dedicated Northern satellite transponder – was also in the works, preparing for its launch in 1992 and the possibility of becoming the third national television network in Canada.

6 | *Bridges-over-the-Air*: Aboriginal Television as Cross-Cultural Bridge

In principle, there is no alternative to bridge building. No single oppressed group can possibly win significant structural change on its own, nor can any be trusted to look out for the interests of the others. Moreover, social transformation requires struggle in the sense of engagement with one's opponents.

Nancy Fraser (*Unruly Practices*, 13)

In 1977, a little-known document called *Ikarut Silakkut: Bridges-over-the-Air* began circulating in Northern Canadian centres. The illustration gracing its front cover is of an Inuit man beating a drum on which there is a map of Canada with arrows pointing from the North towards the South. There are two quotations superimposed on the drum. These read: "How, by reversing the South-to-North flow of broadcasting, a cultural passage may be realized by the Canadian Inuit" and "How a return of information from North-to-South – from the Canadian Inuit to the Canadian population as a whole – may become for the Canadian nation a bridge to the *FUTURE COUNTRY*" (Multilingual Television 1985). Written by the first director of research of the Canadian Radio-television and Telecommunications Commission, Rod Chiasson, and illustrated by his daughter Rachelle, *Ikarut Silakkut* described a new cross-cultural radiospace for Inuktitut speakers of the circumpolar countries, including Canada's Arctic, Alaska, Greenland, Siberia, Finland, Norway, and Sweden. Chiasson envisaged a cross-border short-wave radio service that would provide opportunities to create an international, electronically constituted Inuit public. He was presenting the case for the development of a symbolic electronic bridge over the airwaves.

Rod Chiasson's idea was visionary, predating as it did a time when technologies would make the reconfiguring and bypassing of borders and regulations a reality. Much of *Ikarut Silakkut* was inspired by the publication

The Northerners, put out by the Northern Quebec Inuit Association in 1974, and by the idea of decentralized broadcasting, which was closely tied to Gerry Kenney's notion of a mixed satellite broadcasting system as outlined in chapter 4.

Ikarut Silakkut mapped out a multidirectional short-wave radio service linking the North to the South, and the North to the North both within Canada and throughout those circumpolar nations outside of Canada. Chiasson saw radio as a medium compatible with the Inuit oral tradition, and one that would help to preserve the native dialects of the North. Many indigenous Northerners saw this potential at the time as well, but at this point they were still a long way from having a "home-based" service that satisfactorily met local and regional needs for information and entertainment. In other words, it was only *after* such an infrastructure had been put into place and was functioning well that Northerners felt they could turn their attention to the establishment of North-South and circumpolar broadcasting services.

Chiasson's short "cahier" circulated widely among his network of personal connections and even reached the offices of Queen Elizabeth II of Britain, whose personal secretary responded with a short but interested note congratulating him on his international vision (personal interview, 26 February 1994). I first came upon it accidentally, while doing my Masters degree research at CBC Northern Service offices in 1982. Although the plan itself could not be realized at the time, *Ikarut Silakkut* did awaken the cross-cultural curiosity of a limited number of people within and outside of government circles. In 1985, *Ikarut Silakkut* was revitalized and appended to the CRTC intervention that Ontario's Multicultural Television submitted as part of its response to the CRTC's *Call for Comments on Northern Native Broadcasting*. In this new context, its title was "To Make the North Present in the Canadian Consciousness," but the contents of the pamphlet remained unchanged.

In the Multilingual Television intervention, an unnamed, institutional author[1] comments that Rod Chiasson's "future has arrived" (Multilingual Television 1985, 3). The author gives full support to the Chiasson vision, and then describes the Multilingual Channel's ideal vision of the North-South relationship:

Let's go back to the model in "IKARUT SILAKKUT." Let's create a new common meeting ground. Let's not just have the Aborigines talk to themselves. Let's talk north-south-north communications – links between and among our peoples of Canada. Is there not a communications railroad that won't disrupt the programming

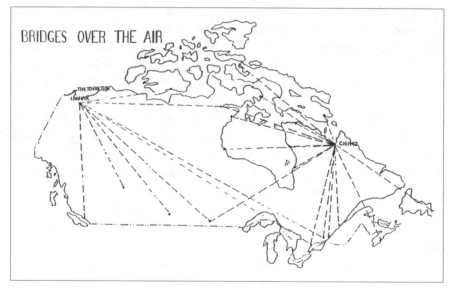

Illustrations from *Ikarut Silakut: Bridges-over-the-Air*, Rod and Rachelle Chiasson, 1976. Used with permission of Rachelle Chiasson. Permission to reproduce the illustration "Shaman Entering the Drum Dance" (c) 1976 by Luc Anguhadluq granted by Public Trustee of Nunavut, Estate of Luc Anguhadluq and by The Winnipeg Art Gallery.

"APPARENTLY WE HAVE ADMINISTERED THESE VAST TERRITORIES OF THE NORTH IN AN ALMOST CONTINUING STATE OF ABSENCE OF MIND."

- THE RT. HON. LOUIS ST-LAURENT, P.M.
SPEECH ON INTRODUCTION OF BILL TO CREATE THE
DEPT. OF NORTHERN AFFAIRS AND NATIONAL RESOURCES
DEC 8, 1953

A PROJECT :

TO MAKE THE NORTH PRESENT

IN THE CANADIAN CONSCIOUSNESS

"SHAMAN ENTERING THE DRUM DANCE"
by ANGUUMALUQ, BAKER LAKE 1977

A SUBMISSION TO
**THE CANADIAN RADIO-TELEVISION
AND TELECOMMUNICATIONS COMMISSION**
*IN RESPONSE TO PUBLIC NOTICE 1985-67 ON
NORTHERN NATIVE BROADCASTING*
BY
**MULTILINGUAL TELEVISION
CFMT-TV CHANNEL 47,
TORONTO**

MAY 24th 1985

"TO MAKE THE NORTH PRESENT
IN THE CANADIAN CONSCIOUSNESS"

plans of what we call "conventional" broadcasters? Can we broadcasters, private and public, cable operators and satellite carriers not jointly create a broadcasting project "to make the north present in the Canadian consciousness"?

Could we not give Canadian content credits of 150 per cent to 200 per cent for broadcasters who produce and/or schedule Native programs? Could not the CAN-COM "super stations" each schedule in the "primary markets," 2.5 hours per week of Native programmes – i.e., news, public affairs, children's and "How-To" programmes. That is TRUE access. To say that up to 10 hours weekly to be uplinked is "available access" and stop at that, is tantamount to saying "we've built you a sand box all your own. ... now bring your own toys." ...

Southern Canada is a highly wired community. We now have cable distribution systems throughout most of this country. Access can and should be made available for a dedicated channel on cable FM radio as well as a full or shared cable television channel. Access of this magnitude is what is needed for the NNBAP to broadcast their creative endeavors, and access for Canadians in the south to hear and see what the Canadians in the north are like, what they think about themselves and about us, what they think and hope to do about the ecology, the environment, the Canadian life-style, oil exploration, self-government and world peace. (5–6)

Support for multidirectional broadcasting access is then taken to another stage as the author argues that reception in the South of Northern-originated programming would make for a more inclusive "multicultural" environment within Canada (again fuelling the confusion about whether or not aboriginal peoples are to be subsumed in multiculturalism policies):

It is common knowledge that like most French-Canadians, Native peoples, because of their special status, find it difficult to see themselves in and part of the Canadian Multicultural Society. But, none-the-less, by reversing the flow of communications we would all be increasing our understanding, an important factor in realizing our multicultural identity. In fact, the weakest fibre in our multicultural fabric in Canada could well be how little we know of this part of ourselves.

If we are to overcome those with "ghetto mentalities" in order for the objectives of multiculturalism to be achieved, then surely we must also overcome those with "reservation mentalities" if the objectives and aspirations of Native peoples in broadcasting are to be met. (6)

In both of its incarnations, *Ikarut Silakkut* generated theoretical interest. However, according to Chiasson whom I interviewed in 1992, neither

Putalik Illisituk from Salluit was the first Inuk television producer to visit Nain, Labrador, in 1982. Used with permission of Tom Axtell.

appearance coincided with a historically appropriate moment to enact its agenda. Because of conflicting political and economic ideologies, cooperation between the circumpolar states could not be counted on to be forthcoming: the Cold War between the Soviet Union and the United States was still escalating; the Inuit Circumpolar Conference[2] was not yet strong enough to construct cross-border broadcasting infrastructure relationships; and the general Northern public was waiting for "adequate services" to be installed within its own regions before contemplating building bridges across state jurisdictions.

This is not to say, however, that there were no early native initiatives in this regard. As noted in previous chapters, the Inuit Tapirisat of Canada, Taqramiut Nipingat Incorporated, and several other Native Communications Societies had already taken advantage of two-way "experimental" satellite-access projects and, in so doing, had seized opportunities to develop community knowledge and facilities through lateral broadcasting methods. Furthermore, a technically sophisticated version of the Kenney model for local and regional access had been put in place as part of the standard broadcasting infrastructure. The termination of scheduled lateral broadcasting between and among local communities and regions in the North before the establishment of TVNC was not due to lack of interest but rather to scarcity of funds to cover the prohibitive uplinking and downlinking costs. Because of these high fees, very little interregional Northern broadcasting was financially viable within Canada at the time. But the idea of crossing bridges would inevitably arise again in a country with such vast and isolated regions.

EARLY NORTH/SOUTH OUTREACH INITIATIVES

"It used to take two weeks for me to get 110 miles to Carmacks. Now it takes 20 seconds for me to get across Canada."
Ken Kane, president of NNBY's board of directors, 23 July 1990

Until the 1990s, Native Communications Societies were mandated to produce programming in accordance with the federal policy objectives of native language reinforcement, of affirmation of cultural identities, and of the presentation of a native perspective on issues important to their own regional communities. The fact that non-native people and those from other aboriginal nations living in the region could see and hear this programming was secondary to their official purpose.

In the mid-1980s, several of the Societies initiated private contract arrangements to produce programming for Southern viewers as well. Partially to counter anticipated funding cutbacks, and partly in an effort to reach a broader audience, NCSs began working out ways to bypass their interlocking dependency on the federal government. Though some – like the Inuit Broadcasting Corporation and WaWaTay Native Communication Society – initially operated on an occasional-contract basis, others began planning and organizing pan-Northern distribution possibilities, seeing this as a way to secure long-term commitments from funders. In the meantime, the Northern Native Broadcasting, Yukon (NNBY) had taken another route in an attempt to both challenge and go beyond what it considered to be its regional development constraints. In 1989, just after CBC Newsworld had commenced its national news service, NNBY's board made a decision to produce Southern-targeted programming on a long-term basis. With the assistance of *Why Not? Productions* in Toronto, NNBY began to create a weekly national version

NNBY crew shooting cultural programming for their flagship program, *Nedaa*.
Photographer: Robin Armour. Used with permission of NNBY.

of its regional show *Nedaa* (Your Eye on the Yukon), which CBC Newsworld agreed to broadcast twice a week and for which NNBY received $500 per program.

Yukoners' responses to the CBC Newsworld/NNBY relationship were both negative and positive. Criticisms were mainly based on the fact that NNBY was receiving federal money to produce regional programming targeted at aboriginal audiences. The secondary, non-native viewer was considered outside federal criteria for the Northern Native Broadcast Access Program. It was suggested that NNBY had betrayed regional goals of self-development and cultural/linguistic preservation. At a more serious level, NNBY was accused by some of having misdirected public monies.

Even members of its production team expressed concern over the apparent *watering down* of cultural and language development objectives as a result of attempting to attract two very different audiences. Team members, and others, were asking critical questions regarding the board's decision. How would being on Newsworld change the organization's priorities of self-development? How would national channel access reshape NNBY's programming content, formats, and perspectives? Would it result in native-language users (already as low as 12 percent of the Yukon's total population) feeling compelled to speak in English only? Would producing a weekly national program entice the organization to hire more non-native, professional producers, thus eliminating employment possibilities for native residents in the area? Would it put pressure on the organization to professionalize and standardize its approach to native perspective and content? Would local norms of video-shooting techniques vanish? Would NNBY create a native televisual aesthetic, or would local producers' distinctive styles be lost in the push to conform to Southern broadcasting standards?

Indeed, NNBY's board members were well aware of the pressure being put on them to conform to Southern broadcasting norms. However, in their collective opinion this was something they were willing to endure if it meant that aboriginal and Northern viewpoints would begin to reach a national audience. Their logic was that, once a primary native Yukon service was in place and functioning well, the next step would be to integrate their programming into a national network such as Newsworld. Furthermore, they considered their contractual arrangement with CBC to be highly valuable and significant in that it crossed over social, racial, territorial, and cultural borders. *Nedaa*'s presence within the Canadian mainstream exposed Southern viewers to images, voices, and information that they had never had the opportunity to see or hear before; it also opened up a mainstream space in which aboriginals could address their own issues. Insisting that their Northern regional show *did* fulfill NNBAP criteria, NNBY's board members maintained that *Nedaa*'s Newsworld slot was a slightly modified version (a derivative and extension) of the original production, albeit adapted for Southern viewers. Finally, they felt that their contractual arrangement with Newsworld would enable them to lean less on the federal government for financial support and move them closer to becoming independent producers.

In fact, this shift to national media status disrupted the broadcasting development paradigm into which the federal and territorial governments had originally placed the NNBY. It gave the NNBY the latitude to refocus its program themes – on Newsworld, for instance, NNBY could broadcast material that revolved around serious political and social issues in the North. Interestingly enough, this shift coincided with CRTC policy changes (1989–90) that recast aboriginal broadcasting in definitional terms that privileged "native perspective" and "organizational control" over the older categories of "language" and "culture."

NNBY on Newsworld attracted a small but loyal following in the South, despite being broadcast at inconvenient times (midnight on Fridays and noon on Saturdays. Those who discovered *Nedaa* by chance through channel grazing often became regular viewers – taping it if they could not catch it at the time it aired.

Unfortunately, there is no quantitative audience survey data to tell us who actually watched *Nedaa* on Newsworld. This is because whatever NNBAP monies were allocated to the NNBY NCS for survey research had to be used to measure *Northern* regional audiences' viewing patterns exclusively. Nor could CBC Newsworld afford to pay Nielsen the prohibitively expensive "special project" fee required to attain ratings figures for small audiences. Consequently, NNBY and Newsworld could only get a sense of their audience through informal channels like letters and casual conversations conducted either in person or by phone. Though NNBY received quite a lot of written feedback, which was kept in a "support" file, this information was never formalized into a document and circulated. The latter might have come in handy when the need arose to provide evidence of NNBY's success on Newsworld.

As a phenomenon, the NNBY/Newsworld arrangement provoked interesting discussions in the North regarding how one goes about building cross-cultural alignments. George Henry, a member of the NNBY board of directors and a key negotiator for the NNBY/Newsworld deal, felt very strongly about this aspect of their undertaking. It was more than a project – projects have terminating points, which he refused to recognize in this context. This was a long-term commitment.

We have to have the ability to give our messages a modern-day voice ... in order to promote and effect social change, such as [changing] the misconceptions that Canadians have about the aboriginal people in terms of their languages, cultures, and customs.

If you look at the last ten years, Indian people have been fighting to change the minds of the Canadian middle class or the middle ground. They're not really dealing with the politicians. They're not really dealing with the ethnic communities. They're trying to change the views of the majority in Canadian society. They've carved out their allies and that's where communications comes in. The more understanding and education you give people, the more tolerant a society you have. (Henry, personal interview, 1990)

Henry also referred to the potential of using media as a persuasive or lobbying tool:

We are now making non-native audiences aware of what's going on in the native communities in the Yukon: not so much for approval, but as a way of trying to get support in principle for our ends – controlled and sustained development.

We need to convince the Southern majority that aboriginal rights, title, and interest in terms of land management, fishing and wildlife, are no different than theirs. In the past, because they've always looked at Indians as on the periphery, they've neglected to listen to [Indian] concerns. Whereas, now, people are finally coming around to see that Indians are not reactionary politicians and they're not absolute environmentalists.

I think that it's the middle ground that will cut the deal for what the new relationship will be for Indians and non-Indians in Canada. (Ibid.)

Henry's perspective falls into line with those who endorse the notion of a "conflictual" public sphere in which a range of First Peoples' constituency groups argue for self-representation of their issues (Armitage 1992a,b; Jhappan 1990, 1992) and consider that non-native public opinion is critical to the formation of state policy affecting their communities' issues (Wartenberg

1992). Henry speaks equally to the fact that outside of the regional Native Communications Societies and local community radio stations, First Peoples have had to be dependent on external media to cover their issues. This arrangement has not been particularly successful at informing politically relevant publics about native concerns. My own research on the Kanehsatake and Kahnawake confrontations with the federal and provincial governments in 1990 concludes that few mainstream journalists have the necessary ethnographic training to understand the inside stories and conflicts they are assigned to cover (Roth 1992). This means that, beyond the "media campaign," the "crisis," and the "conflict over resources" stories that make it into the news, there is little "informed" coverage of First Peoples and their issues in mainstream Southern media. And rare indeed are the programs that represent them as developing nations of "special status" within Canadian society.

In order to take their place in the Southern mainstream, First Peoples' leaders have had to learn to speak "media language." They have learned how to talk in sound bytes when interviewed, how to use the rules of techno-rational discourse to their own advantage, and how to use the tactics of embarrassment and shame to expose problematic government officials and policies. But these initiatives are not, in themselves, adequate. What First Peoples want is acceptance as equal members of Canadian society. They want native-produced primary and secondary services. Of top priority are basic community and regional broadcasting services. Of secondary priority, First Peoples broadcasters want their programming to get broader and more regular exposure in the mainstream media. These objectives have been explicit in all Northern First Peoples' interventions at the CRTC and at other public agencies since the 1970s. They want their media to be foundational – a routine service recognizing their active participation in Canadian society as "normal." To do this, they have needed to situate themselves within the political vernacular of both the native and non-native publics in the South by speaking directly to "the other side of empire" (Valaskakis 1981, 180) as well as to themselves.

This has not been an easy process, given the diversity of communities represented in the First Peoples' world and in Canadian society, and given that each of the thirteen Native Communication Societies has moved at its own pace to meet its regional needs. Though directly addressing the non-native public would eventually become a common goal of all television-producing NCSs, this did not happen until a primary native-language service with firm funding commitments was solidly in place.

NNBY became the first NCS to consistently move across the territorial borderlines. This, in part, was because its programming used English as its lingua franca. Equally important, however, was that its management was confident that the economy in Whitehorse could support an aboriginal television service through private advertising should federal funding be discontinued.

In relation to the broader social field, NNBY management felt that its specific set of broadcasting practices would become a central core around which different constituency groups in the South could align themselves. In effect, NNBY saw its programming as a central native-oriented mediaspace. Knowing that social and political alignments come into existence for limited amounts of time and in relation to particular issues, George Henry and Ken Kane (president of the NNBY board for several years) wanted to make sure that NNBY was present on the national airwaves in the event that an issue arise over which Yukoners or First Peoples might find it useful to solicit public support.

Henry, Kane, and the NNBY staff expressed a strong belief that the non-native public could play a role in the constitution of power relations between First Peoples and the federal government. If it were possible for native broadcasters to construct political, economic, social and cross-cultural alignments across Canada's North and South, and if these alignments resulted in a public opinion shift in favour of their political agendas, First Peoples would benefit. NNBY considered itself the test case towards meeting this objective.

In summary, Henry and others in the NNBY management saw their ongoing public presence on national television as having several important consequences: a) it allowed for the possibility of cross-cultural education through consciousness-raising; b) it triggered NCS and federal government management across the country to rethink the constitutive elements that differentiated native from non-native and ethnic program structures and contents, which was a useful conceptual exercise; c) it encouraged the building of non-native constituency group support for native issues such as land claims, self-government, and environmental issues; and d) unlike special media campaigns about specific controversial issues (such as the James Bay Cree opposition to hydro-electric development), the weekly broadcast of *Nedaa* could become integral to the routine programming infrastructure of Newsworld – thus contributing to the normalization of native perspectives and Northern information access for Southern audiences.

While NNBY's directors lauded *Nedaa*'s presence on Canada-wide television, they were not naive and realized the complexity of Newsworld's commitment. They were concerned that Newsworld's relationship with NNBY might lead to Newsworld's management feeling that it had taken care of its obligations to represent "native life" and hence discourage it from actively recruiting a diversity of native talent and programming for *other* time slots on the Newsworld schedule. In light of these concerns, the 1991 Broadcasting Act actually supported NNBY's extension into the South by concretely building the necessary presence of aboriginals in the national communications infrastructure into the broadcasting mandate. In the words of George Henry, this move "completed the national broadcasting mandate" (Henry 1990).

In retrospect, NNBY played a significant role in the introduction and ongoing acceptance of native productions on mainstream television. As far as CBC Newsworld was concerned, there had emerged a convergence of objectives between itself and NNBY, so it was easy for CBC to integrate NNBY on its programming grid. Joan Donaldson, then head of Newsworld, saw *Nedaa* as fulfilling her regionally inclusive vision for the network. NNBY saw it as a venue in which to facilitate cross-cultural relations through public media education. Eventually, the availability of *Nedaa* programming outside of the Yukon came to be seen by most as an acceptance of a regional aboriginal voice within the national broadcasting spectrum.

NNBY's pioneering step onto the Newsworld schedule was visionary and helped plant the seeds for thinking about First Peoples' Television programming that extended beyond enclosed audiences within a given region. To what extent would it be possible for all Native Communications Societies in the North to have access to mainstream networks originating in the South? Would this be the best window for their programming, or would this be jumping too quickly into mainstream infrastructures without the public recognition of First Peoples' uniqueness within a separate dedicated service? A bold initiative in its own terms, NNBY's national project reframed native broadcasting in some ways but did little to solve the pan-Northern challenges of distribution for the other Native Communication Societies.

Other NCSs did not quickly follow the route travelled by NNBY, but watched carefully to see how its place on Newsworld would evolve, and what it could tell them about public media strategy for their own organizational futures. At first, they remained focused on their own regional services. When they became exceptionally aggravated by their dependency on the good will of Cancom and CBC Northern Service for carriage of their native-language programs, they began to lobby individually and collectively for a dedicated Northern transponder to establish a pan-Northern service. Collectively, they formed the National Aboriginal Communications Society (NACS), a lobby group dedicated to representing the NCSs in negotiations with key players involved in policy matters. It would take time, experience, and cooperation from multiple players before a national service would evolve, but support activities and interventions organized by NACS helped to prepare them. In the early 1990s, the NCSs were ready to mount the challenge for a pan-Northern service as a preliminary step in this direction.

7 Television Northern Canada: The Dream of a Northern Dedicated Transporder Becomes a Reality

In January 1987, aboriginal and Northern broadcasters met in Yellowknife to form a consortium with the goal of establishing a pan-Northern distribution service. The expectation – built into the NNBAP – that CBC Northern Service and Cancom would be the primary carriers for Northern native programming had proven too complex and frustrating. National programming such as "Hockey Night in Canada" had often preempted NCS programming on the CBC. Even coverage of the *first* plebiscite to determine whether or not the Northwest Territories would be divided into Nunavut (Inuit territory) and Denendeh (all other territories of the former NWT) had been cancelled because of national preemption. Logic pointed to the need for a Northern-dedicated satellite transponder.

In 1988, the federal government's Department of Communications approved research and development monies, in principle, to explore the feasibility of a separate Northern channel. Satisfied that such a channel would fulfill Northern distribution needs, the Department of Communications granted $10 million funding to establish the infrastructure for Television Northern Canada. Systematic organization of TVNC began at this point and continued until 1991, the year in which aboriginal broadcasting was enshrined in the revised Broadcasting Act. This would prove to be the critical policy principle needed to move the aboriginal communications' agenda forward.

On 28 October 1991, following a public hearing in Hull, the CRTC approved the TVNC application for a native television network license to serve Northern Canada "for the purpose of broadcasting cultural, social, political and educational programming for the primary benefit of aboriginal people in the North" (CRTC 1991). By granting the license to TVNC, the Commission recognized the importance of Northern-based control over the distribution

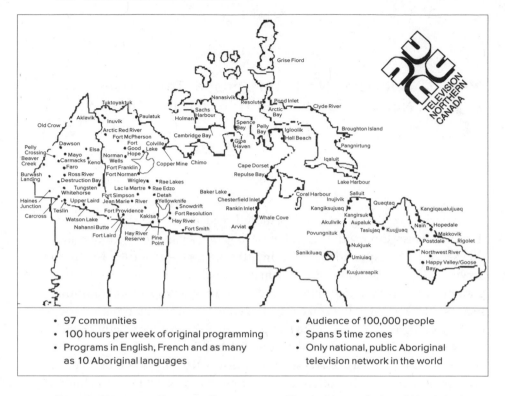

- 97 communities
- 100 hours per week of original programming
- Programs in English, French and as many as 10 Aboriginal languages

- Audience of 100,000 people
- Spans 5 time zones
- Only national, public Aboriginal television network in the world

Communities served by TVNC. Source: TVNC. Used with permission of Aboriginal Peoples Television Network (APTN).

of native and Northern programming. TVNC was to become the vehicle through which First Peoples would be able to represent themselves and their concerns to the entire North. Their efforts at local or regional self-representation and identity building would no longer be restricted by geography or by the limits of antiquated technology. In this respect, TVNC constituted a de facto recognition of the legislated communication rights of the First Peoples in the North.

TVNC's network members consisted of the Inuit Broadcasting Corporation (Ottawa, Iqaluit), the Inuvialuit Communications Society (Inuvik), Northern Native Broadcasting, Yukon (Whitehorse), the OKalaKatiget Society (Labrador), Taqramiut Nipingat Incorporated (Northern Quebec), the Native Communications Society of the Western NWT (Yellowknife), the Government of the Northwest Territories, Yukon College, and the National Aborigi-

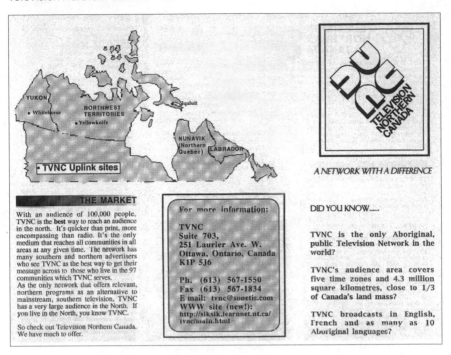

TVNC uplink sites. Source: TVNC Pamphlet . Used with permission of Aboriginal Peoples Television Network (APTN).

nal Communications Society. Associate Members included CBC Northern Service, Kativik School Board (Quebec), Labrador Community College, Northern Native Broadcasting, Terrace, Telesat Canada, and Wawatay Native Communications Society (Sioux Lookout).

The organization's mission statement elaborated its goals: "Television Northern Canada shall be (is) a dedicated northern satellite distribution system, for the primary benefit of aboriginal people in the North, by which residents of communities across northern Canada may distribute television programming of cultural, social, political and educational importance to each other, increasing communications access and promoting dialogue in their remote and under-served homelands" (TVNC 1993, 3).

TVNC began broadcasting at a primary level of service on 21 January 1992. Spanning five time zones and covering an area of over 4.3 million kilometers, TVNC network members broadcast approximately one hundred hours per week to ninety-four communities (in English and multiple native

Fall/Winter 1998 Schedule

TELEVISION   NORTHERN CANADA

Eastern	MONDAY	TUESDAY	WEDNESDAY	THURSDAY	FRIDAY	SATURDAY	SUNDAY
12:00PM	Environment Canada	Environment Canada	Environment Canada	Environment Canada	Environment Canada		
12:30PM	Labradorimiut	Suangaan (R)	TNI Presents (R)	Nunavimiut (R)	KSB Presents (R)		
1:00 PM	Best of Takuginai	Metawetan	Best of Takuginai	Takuginai (R)	Best of Takuginai	Environment Canada	Environment Canada
1:30 PM	Tell-A-Tale Town	Tell-A-Tale Town	Tell-A-Tale Town	Tell-A-Tale Town	Tell-A-Tale Town	Takuginai	Metawetan (R)
2:00 PM	Intro to Business	Qimaivvik (R)	Heartbeat Alaska (R)	Qaujisaut (R)	GNWT Presents (R)	Tell-A-Tale Town	Frame by Frame (R)
2:30 PM	Intro to Business cont...	Dene Weekly...(R)	Spirit of Denendeh (R)	Extreme Sports (R)	GNWT Presents cont..	No Name Youth Show	Frame by Frame cont
3:00 PM	Environment Canada	Environment Canada	Environment Canada	Environment Canada	Environment Canada	Lebret Eagles	Labradorimiut (R)
3:30 PM	Environment Canada	Environment Canada	Environment Canada	Environment Canada	Environment Canada	Lebret Eagles cont..	KSB Presents (R)
4:00 PM	Dotto's Data... (R)	Frame by Frame (R)	Intro to Business (R)	KSB Presents: ITN	NFB Presents (R)	Lebret Eagles cont..	Nunavimiut (R)
4:30 PM	GNWT Presents (R)	Frame by Frame cont.	Intro to Business cont..	KSB Presents: ITN	NFB Presents cont..	Lebret Eagles cont..	TNI Presents (R)
5:00 PM	GNWT Presents (R)	Indigenous Circle (R)	Sharing Circle (R)	KSB Presents: ITN	ICSL Phone-In (R)	Lebret Eagles cont..	Qimaivvik (R)
5:30 PM	Takuginai (R)	Maamuitaau (R)	Wawatay Presents (R)	KSB Presents: ITN	ICSL Phone-In cont..	Lebret Eagles cont..	Qaggiq (R)
6:00 PM	Igalaaq	Igalaaq	Igalaaq	Igalaaq	Igalaaq	Wawatay Presents (R)	Netsilik (R) followed by
6:30 PM	Qaujisaut (R)	TNI Presents	Nunavimiut	Kippinguijautiit (R)	Labradorimiut (R)	Qanuq Isumavit (R)	The Way We Were (R)
7:00 PM	No Name Youth Show (R	The Way We Were	ICSL Phone-In	Netsilik followed by	Frame by Frame	Qanuq Isumavit cont	Dotto's Data... (R)
7:30 PM	Wawatay Presents	KSB Presents	ICSL Phone-In cont..	Metawetan (R)	Frame by Frame cont.	Qanuq Isumavit cont	Extreme Sports (R)
8:00 PM	Tamapta's Past (R)	Qanuq Isumavit	Qimaivvik	Modern Day Grandparents	Dene Weekly	IBC Vintage (R)	Indigenous Cirlce (R)
8:30 PM	Kippinguijautiit	Qanuq Isumavit	Qaujisaut	Qaggiq	No Name Youth Show	NFB Presents	Sharing Circle (R)
9:00 PM	Qaggiq (R)	Qanuq Isumavit	GNWT Presents (O)	Nedaa (R)	Suangaan	NFB Presents cont..	Dene Weekly... (R)
9:30 PM	Spirit of Denendeh	IBC Vintage	GNWT Presents cont..	Vintage Nedaa (R)	Tamapta's Past (O)	Qaujisaut (R)	Maamuitaau (R)
10:00PM	Extreme Sports	Dotto's Data...	No Name Youth Show	Spirit of Denendeh (R)	Kippinguijautiit (R)	Heartbeat Alaska (R)	GNWT Presents (R)
10:30PM	Nedaa	NFB Presents (R)	Tamapta's Past (R)	Haa Shagoon (R)	Extreme Sports (R)	Haa Shagoon (R)	Spirit of Denendeh (R)
11:00PM	Vintage Nedaa	NFB Presents cont..	Modern Day Grandparents R	The Way We Were (R)	Wawatay Presents (R)	Nedaa (R)	Spirit of Denendeh (R)
11:30PM	Haa Shagoon	Heartbeat Alaska	Indigenous Circle (O)	Sharing Circle (O)	Maamuitaau	Vintage Nedaa (R)	Suangaan (R)
12:00AM	Northbeat	Northbeat	Northbeat (O)	Northbeat (O)	Northbeat	Environment Canada	Environment Canada
12:30AM	Nedaa (R)	Environment Canada	Environment Canada	Environment Canada	Environment Canada		
1:00 AM	Environment Canada						

Effective: October 12, 1998

TVNC sample schedule, eastern time zone, fall/winter 1998. Source: TVNC. Used with permission of Aboriginal Peoples Television Network (APTN).

languages). TVNC was not a program producer but rather a distributor of its Northern consortium members' productions. Initial programming consisted of a variety of programs from members, as well as acquisitions such as old NFB ethnographic films and videos. One of these – *Heartbeat Alaska* – had been the first international indigenous program to be broadcast across the North several times a week. Times for programming were apportioned in the following manner: thirty-eight hours per week of aboriginal language and cultural programming; twenty-three hours per week of formal and informal educational programming; twelve hours per week of produced and acquired children's programming, over half of which were in aboriginal languages (TVNC 1993, 4).

These figures only add up to seventy-three hours per week. The remainder of the one hundred hours per week consisted of reruns, wraparound news text by Broadcast News, and Environment Canada iconic weather reports and forecasts.

TVNC was designed as an infrastructure to broadcast the same schedule throughout the North, yet it was also organized with a narrowcasting strategy as a way of designing and targeting programs for a particular regional and linguistic audience without the use of subtitles. To address the objectives of these two different approaches to programming – one aimed at a mass, undifferentiated Northern audience, the other at very specific cultural and linguistic viewerships – TVNC members had to balance complex scheduling options. That linguistic *narrow*casting and cultural *broad*casting were equally integral to its mandate presented TVNC with an interesting challenge in terms of its broader objectives. The ways in which Northern producers and viewers thought about broadcasting services began to shift. TVNC took on the challenge of trying to figure out ways to encourage its audiences to think along pan-Northern lines – beyond the local and regional to a more global perspective. The fact that TVNC covered multiple time zones also necessitated that decisions be made regarding the structure and promotion of its schedule so that viewers, rather than randomly searching for specific programs, could easily plan out and then tune in to what they wanted to see.

In response to these prerogatives and needs, TVNC considered two scheduling options – vertical and horizontal block-programming – each of which had its assets and its liabilities. Vertical block-programming meant that substantial blocks of time would be devoted to one language, one type of program, or one region's programming on any given evening. The main problem here was that viewers risked being excluded from programming for significant periods of time – creating possible resentment and a sense that TVNC was a network "for the *other* regions." It was felt that promoting vertical block-programming within the regions would work well given that specific audiences would be able to tune in regularly to their region's programming without having to browse, and operators would be able to uplink programming a few hours at a time. However, this first option would be more difficult to promote at the pan-Northern network level.

The second option, horizontal block-scheduling, meant that programs carrying similar content – a hunting show, for instance – would be slotted in at the same time each day. Alternatively, programs might be chosen to fill particular time slots on the basis of language. In short, clear and predictable programming patterns as assured by horizontal block-scheduling would, in addition to allowing viewers to tune in and out according to their interests and language, would make life easier for TVNC both technically and logistically (TVNC 1993, 3–4).

Eventually, a compromise was reached. TVNC went for both the horizontal and the vertical options and a schedule was devised according to the following principles: horizontally, a certain kind of program would begin Monday to Friday at the same time, so that people would learn when to tune in; vertically, a certain language would run for two to two and a half hours, so that people could continue to watch once they had tuned in; concerning uplinking, the day would be divided into three or four uplink shifts.

However, a problem arose when it became apparent that each of the Native Communications Societies wanted their programming to be shown in the prime time slots of *their* region. How could this be factored into TVNC programmers' plans? TVNC would have to take into account the time zones (between 9:00 p.m. EST and 11:00 p.m. EST, for example) that hit "prime time" for all the communities across the North. TVNC's challenge, then, was to schedule programs in this two-hour block that excluded the least number of viewers. Deeming these blocks "accessible" time slots, the idea was to fill them with programming of interest to the most number of people, in a format accessible to the most number of people. This meant that if, for instance, "an aboriginal language program was to be scheduled in this time period, it should be subtitled, as it would then exclude fewer people, and be of interest right across the north" (TVNC 1993, 4).[1]

Once scheduling decisions were made, TVNC began to publicize its programming on the TVNC publicity roll, in cable-TV listings, in newspapers, in magazines, in post offices, and on posters around the communities. It also sent out schedules and a guide for improving the reception of TVNC's signal to all the households across the network service region.

As previously noted, there was more airtime available than programmers could fill, but program recycling was received surprisingly well. Early TVNC feedback indicated that "people either liked reruns (because it gave them a second chance to see a show they missed or wanted to see again), or they accepted them as a fact of television life" (TVNC 1993, 10). Public opinion further indicated that "it was okay to re-run the same program in the same week at different time slots," but "it was bad if the same show was run week after week in the same time slot" (TVNC 1993, 10). Viewing patterns, in other words, were beginning to emerge but, once again, could not be quantified or even identified in any systematic way due to a lack of available funding; nor could the individual NCSs continue to keep tabs on their audiences, given that the NNBAP had eliminated survey funding from its earmarked sponsorship of the NCSs in 1992. In other words, it was an *imagined* audience response that guided producers and team members in their decisions over content development, program aesthetics, and scheduling priorities.

Kevin Gargan. Photographer: Kelly Reinhardt. Used with permission of the Native Communications Society of the Western NWT.

ABORIGINAL PROGRAMMING: CONSIDERATIONS AND DILEMMAS

Narrowcast programming – though it risked alienating non-targeted audiences during a given time period – became routine throughout the North during the tenure of TVNC. Native Communications Societies and their respective audiences regularly viewed programs from other regions, which meant that they were exposed to multiple languages and formats, as well as to a variety of Northern perspectives. For most audience members, this was something new. They had worked together politically and organizationally to create a viable aboriginal television service, but this was the first time that they could actually see each others' productions. Gradually, they became aware of the diversity of aboriginal content, the range of production values and ethical concerns, and the wide variety of innovative techniques used by NCSs outside of their regions.

Programs about traditional hunting and cultural practices were shown, as were shows about the daily lives of Northerners and their relationship to animals and the environment. Educational programs for children (*Takugi-*

Sarah Abel, TV Producer at OKalaKatiget. Photographer: Primrose Bishop. Used with permission of OKalaKatiget Native Communications Society.

nai, IBC) and teen programs (*The Tube*, GNWT) were very popular: often shown in the classrooms of Northern schools, they had "cool" hosts who talked about popular culture and music, as well as about more serious issues directly affecting children and youths. For those interested in news and current affairs, CBC Northern Service produced two programs: *Focus North* – in English with some Dené-language content – with its emphasis on NWT politics; and *Igalaaq* – in Inuktitut – which focused on the Eastern Arctic region. Each of these programs were initially seen twice a week. As for *Nedaa*, its Northern version differed from the one NNBY had shown on Newsworld in that it focused exclusively on political, social, and cultural issues unfolding in the Yukon.[2]

IBC's programming reflected a wide range of interests, covering topics such as substance abuse, violence against women, and the formation of Nunavut. Over the years, IBC also experimented with multiple formats – everything from documentary and current affairs programs to dramatic productions. As a result of a contractual arrangement with the GNWT, IBC produced a series of one-minute AIDS commercials in 1988 that were broadcast as NWT Public Service Announcements, first on CBC Northern Service, then on TVNC. These were excellent examples of how, by localizing the universal, a widespread health issue like AIDS could be rendered culturally relevant to the Inuit, while simultaneously rendering the Inuit way of dealing with it applicable to the rest of the world. Such reciprocity is evident in one of these ads, which opens with an Inuit hunter with a broken snowmobile out on the tundra greeting another hunter who has obviously arrived to help. The accompanying voice-over speaks of the Inuit tradition of helping others out, urging anyone who knows someone with AIDS to lend them a hand in accordance with this Inuit tradition. The ad then goes on to provide practical details about AIDS and its transmission. It finishes by flashing the phone number of the NWT Health Services to obtain further information.[3] These groundbreaking ads were unique in that they cushioned a very modern epidemic within a highly traditional cultural context. The fact that they went on to become "collector's items" attests to their popularity and, one would hope, their effectiveness.

TVNC's most ambitious project satellite-linked communities across the North with several cities in the South and with indigenous communities in Torres Strait, Australia. Called *Connecting the North*, this 1994–95 venture consisted of setting up a virtual conference in which the "information highway" and what it meant to aboriginal peoples in the Northern and Southern hemispheres were discussed. Experiences were shared, expectations, objectives, obstacles, and concerns with regard to World Wide Web access, use, and cost were debated. *Connecting the North* generated a lot of discussion before and after the actual event; it facilitated First Peoples' informed entry into the electronic commons.

Interactive projects like this were often followed by phone-in shows. Particularly in light of not having budgets for audience research, this became the chosen method by which TVNC established contact with viewers and gained some awareness of how people were reacting to programs.

As for ethical questions relating to the amount of information that nations should publicly disclose about themselves, or whether broadcasters should use the name or show the image of a dead person on air, these were left up to each of the thirteen Native Communications Societies to resolve on their own. The dissemination of TVNC and phone-in shows provided them with the opportunity to see and hear how others responded to these critical representational issues. The NCSs proved highly interested in comparing their own hunting, shooting, food preparation, and sewing techniques with those from elsewhere, and the difference between regional video-makers' shooting and editing styles were extensively discussed. For example, it was recognized that people in the Western Arctic used quick edits to depict only the key aspects of the process of hunting and skinning an animal. Eastern Arctic video producers, on the other hand, devoted more time to procedural details including lengthy shots depicting real-time bleeding of animals. Western Arctic Inuit actively criticized the Eastern Arctic image-makers, and vice versa.

The issue of "aboriginality" was also one with which the NCSs were left to grapple, particularly because of the ways in which the notion of "culture" had initially been circumscribed by the federal government's Northern Broadcasting Policies. The question of what should be considered as "authentically aboriginal" was often raised, as Lorraine Thomas – one of TVNC's organizational consultants at the time – suggests in her discussion of a scene shown originally on TVNC:

Picture this: a sixteen-year-old girl is out on a polar bear hunt. She has just shot her first polar bear. She is a very Inuk young woman, wearing a traditional parka and talking about her feelings after having killed her first polar bear. She has a punk haircut with one blonde streak down the middle of her head. She is wearing a bunch of earrings on one ear. This is a perspective people never see even in their wildest imagination: a sixteen-year-old Inuk woman shooting her first polar bear and looking like a punk rocker. This is a real cross-cultural mix. That one portrait of a young woman is a mosaic of impressionistic images of what the North is all about. And this image was videotaped by kids for a show called *The Tube* (personal interview with Lorraine Thomas, 13 November 1992).

Such a syncretic blend of the traditional and modern might well strike an elder as offensive: the imagery being seen as disrespectful to the animal, perhaps, or to the notion of how one is supposed to dress when going hunting. Others, however, might find it refreshing to see young people combining and simultaneously inhabiting the old and the new. Given the diversity of lifestyles, customs, and fashions coexisting in the North, and given that there is no Northern aboriginal consensus on what counts as "authentic," showing a range of images of people in a variety of settings seemed the most appropriate representational strategy for TVNC to adopt. It goes without saying that these kinds of questions continued to preoccupy TVNC, particularly when

Location Shooting at Terrace, BC. Used with permission of Art King, NNBAP, Department of Canadian Heritage.

management began to take steps towards being picked up by cable operators in the South, or pushed to become Canada's third national network.

NORTH-NORTH AND NORTH-SOUTH BROADCASTING

In addition to trying to work out which kinds of cultural broadcasts would meet the information and entertainment needs of both native/non-native Northerners and Southerners, TVNC recognized the complex sensitivity of programming that – when removed from its intracultural context – might generate controversy. For example, how might members of animal rights organizations like Greenpeace respond to those Eastern Arctic productions in which minute details of animal killings were central? If these were the kinds of programming considerations that TVNC would have to address when negotiating a broadcasting arrangement with the South, there was, however, a more pressing administrative issue that had to be dealt with first. This concerned the acquisition of rights for broadcasting in the South.

Up until the time that TVNC's extension to the South began to be seriously considered, Northern acquisition rights were extremely economical because TVNC was recognized as a non-profit, public broadcasting distribution organization. Indeed, program distributors – acknowledging that TVNC's special financial conditions prohibited its ability to purchase expensive programming – virtually subsidized acquisition rights. Were TVNC to be picked up in the South under different circumstances, however, acquisition costs for these same rights would increase considerably. Such a move, in other words, would not only restrict TVNC to showing its own – as opposed to any acquired – programming, but lead to a further reduction of its already limited on-air time.

Despite these constraints, however, TVNC went ahead with its plans to become a third national broadcasting service. From the conversations I had with staff at the time, it was clear that TVNC organizers felt that their long-term mandate was to reach out to *both* North-North and North-South audiences. As a supporter of the strategy to extend programming to national aboriginal and non-aboriginal publics, Lorraine Thomas described TVNC's programming as "sociocultural mediation." Speaking for herself (as opposed to in her capacity as a TVNC organizational consultant), Thomas stated: "TV can be a tool for mediating social and racial relations. We need volume though. Our programming does not draw lines – it promotes cross-cultural relations" (personal interview with Lorraine Thomas, 1992).

When asked if she thought Southern audiences would be interested in receiving TVNC's programming, Thomas elaborated:

If you look at the recent Stats Canada figures, there are a significant number of aboriginals living in cities – 1.5 million, to be exact.[4] Well, here we are with fifty thousand people up North who are producing one hundred hours of aboriginal programming [*sic*]. And there is hardly any programming down South. People would be fascinated to see our programming – to see what the North is like.

There is a public interest demonstrated in the polls. Aboriginal issues are still high on the list of preoccupations of non-natives, even after the constitutional talks ceased. They are interested in aboriginal affairs – they support land claims. (personal interview, 1992)

Thomas noted that there were other reasons that justified broadcasting to the South:

We would like to inform the Canadian public about health problems, cost of food, and other difficulties specific to living up North. This would give them a more balanced picture of Canada ... The Southern media still promote big clichés. They either deal with the drum dance or with Davis Inlet – the two extreme clichés. People get a very skewed picture of the North, which falls somewhere in between the two perspectives. TVNC in the South would provide 100 hours of contextual programming. Sure, it's still selected images by aboriginal and educational broadcasters for their audiences. But it provides a better, more balanced impression. (Ibid.)

She then went on to describe the interest expressed by letters from Southerners who were already picking up TVNC's Northern signal from their satellite dishes: "We could definitely benefit by sending regular streams of images from the North to the South. We get lots of requests from the US ... For example, the Navajo people in Florida who own satellite dishes. They write us asking for our listings. They're fascinated. It's interesting that we have a following in the US of people who watch us regularly" (personal interview, 1992).

On a more formal basis, a 1 March 1993 submission to the CRTC outlined TVNC's next planned stage of development:

We now stand poised to take the next step – maintaining our role as a primary service in the North, while at the same time expanding our audience to include aboriginal and non-aboriginal viewers in southern Canada (CRTC 1993, 1).

... By identifying TVNC and aboriginal broadcasting as a basic service on a re-structured cable distribution system (as channel availability permits), the Commission will ensure that people in southern Canada will have the opportunity to acquire an understanding of the North, and the people who live there. This will only serve to further the struggle for Canadian unity, and develop more understanding between peoples in all regions of this country. (CRTC 1993, 8)

At the time, it was felt that if TVNC were to be picked up in Southern Canada by cable operators, it would help to inform Southern audiences that a rich and vigourous life was going on North of the fifty-fifth parallel. At worst, it might serve to fuel the controversy surrounding animal rights. However, even this possible outcome might end up facilitating a productive intercultural dialogue between First Peoples and non-natives within Canada. As had been the case with *Nedaa*, it was felt that the broadcasting of TVNC throughout Canada would help First Peoples accumulate influence in the South. Possible coalitions to grow out of these exchanges might prove useful when lobbying the various levels of the federal, provincial, and territorial bureaucracies over complex, high-stake issues like aboriginal self-government.

Though the CRTC eventually permitted TVNC to be listed as an eligible service for cable companies to broadcast, very few seized upon this opportunity, and little came of TVNC's dreams of being picked up by cable operators in the South. For TVNC administrators, going the voluntary cable route would not turn out to be a fruitful way to extend service to the South. Rather, they would have to insist upon the federal government making carriage of the service mandatory.

8 | The Aboriginal Peoples Television Network (APTN) – Going National

There are some six hundred ... First Nations. We are always fighting for this right or that right. But we are one people. This [channel] would bring us together. I am very excited by the opportunity the aboriginal people of Canada have been given. This historic decision will be a major step in building bridges of understanding between aboriginal and non-aboriginal people in Canada.

Abraham Tagalik (APTN chairman at the time, quoted in TVNC Newsletter, March 1999, 1)

TVNC's pan-Northern successes convinced its board of directors and staff to pursue the establishment of a nationwide network. After a vote in June 1997, steps were initiated to make this dream into reality. First, TVNC representatives attended the Assembly of First Nations' (AFN) annual general assembly in 1997 at which the AFN passed a resolution supporting TVNC's attempts to develop a national service. This was followed by similar presentations to other national aboriginal organizations. Henceforth, submissions to the CRTC became a regular occurrence (Explore North 1999).

In January 1998, TVNC hired Angus Reid (a public opinion consulting firm) to conduct an audience survey among a representative cross-section of 1,510 adult Canadians regarding the desirability of establishing a national aboriginal broadcasting service. Results indicated that 79 percent of Canadians supported the idea of a national aboriginal TV network, even if this would mean displacing a service already being offered (ibid.).

In February 1998, the CRTC responded positively with Public Notice 1998-8, thereby opening the doors for TVNC to go national:

The Commission recognizes that TVNC is a unique and significant undertaking serving the public interest and the objectives of the *Broadcasting Act*, especially those objectives that relate to the special place of aboriginal peoples within Canadian society. Such a service should be widely available throughout Canada in order to serve the diverse needs of the various Aboriginal communities, as well as other Canadians. The Commission will consider any application by TVNC designed to achieve these objectives.

The Commission expects any application by TVNC to demonstrate how it will adapt its programming service to reflect the diversity of the needs and interests of aboriginal peoples throughout Canada (TVNC, March 1998, 1).

Responding to the commission's formal recognition of the importance of a national aboriginal channel, TVNC submitted a license application for the Aboriginal Peoples Television Network in June 1998. To be economically viable, it would have to be a mandatory service available to the nearly eight million Canadian households served by cable, as well as to those households with direct-to-home and wireless service providers such as ExpressVu, Star Choice, and Look TV. To assure consistent and secure funding over the long term, TVNC requested that the CRTC insist that cable providers charge each subscriber household $0.15 per month. This would amount to $15 million – money that APTN would use to support production of indigenous programming – with APTN administration projecting an increase in incoming monies as a result of anticipated advertising revenues. In exchange for this small charge, subscribers would receive a service aimed at both aboriginal and non-aboriginal audiences and covering a wide range of interests: children's cartoons and shows aimed at young people; cultural and traditional programming in the realms of music, drama, food, comedy, and dance; news and current affairs programs; live coverage of special events; and interactive programming. Initially promising 90 percent Canadian content with the remaining 10 percent devoted to indigenous programming from around the world, including the US, Australia, New Zealand, and Central and South America (APTN 1999, APTN Fact Sheet, 2), APTN has since lowered its Canadian content percentages to "no less than 70 percent" in recognition of how difficult it is to sustain this unusually high level (Whiteduck Resources Inc./Consilium 2003, 40).

The CRTC received approximately three hundred letters from the general public urging the commission to go ahead and license the channel. Though support for the network was fairly consistent among existing Native Communications Societies in the North, it was challenged on a number of organizational and control issues during the transition from a Northern to a national network. One such challenge came from Northern Native Broadcasting, Yukon over the question of Northern representation on the board of directors. NNBY's position was clear. Given that TVNC was the distribution service for television programming produced by the original thirteen Native Communications Societies, NNBY worried about the potential loss of its and other NCSs' authority on a national board and argued for guaranteed representation for existing board members. NNBY's conditions for full endorsement of APTN's application were explicitly stated: "NNBY can support this application only if APTN guarantees continued Northern ownership and control of the network, that majority control will remain with its founding Northern members, and that decision-making will continue to require a majority of TVNC's founding members' support to proceed. In addition, NNBY can support this application only if ... the board remains entirely Aboriginal" (NNBY, 19 October 1998, 5).

Though troubled by certain technical and administrative details of the new arrangement, NNBY's other main concern was that the interests of aboriginal peoples of the North not be forgotten. With this in mind, NNBY also demanded the "unrestricted right of continued distribution of their programs to support their languages, dialects, and cultures" (6). TVNC eventually assured NNBY in writing that these conditions would be met. In response to NNBY's concerns over the makeup and powers of the board, TVNC explained that a professional workshop, in which fair and equitable board structures and regional board-member selection processes would be the central focus, was being planned. (TVNC, 30 October 1998, 11). This conflict was temporarily resolved when a twenty-one-member aboriginal board of directors was set up with representation from all regions of Canada. (For further information about APTN's current bylaws and criteria for its board of directors, see APTN's website at aptn.ca/home/home_html.)

Given the publicity that Northern broadcasters' responses to the possibility of losing some of their control at the board level attracted, Southern cable operators – whose services would be most impacted by the APTN license decision – became even more vocal about their dissatisfaction. Framing the decision as anti-democratic, the cable operators began to articulate strong resistance to the idea of a mandatory *national* channel. There were some exceptions (Cancom, WETV, among others), but most cable operators expressed preference for APTN to be licensed on the same optional distribution basis as all other fee-based Canadian services. In their view, TVNC/APTN should be a specialty pay-TV service that targeted a specific niche audience. TVNC/APTN responded to this by insisting that they were *not* a specialty service, but rather a service with *special status* as a result of being one of the three Founding Nations of Canada. Here, of course, they were touching on a highly contentious and conflictual issue in Canada and Quebec. Most English and French Canadians operate on the assumption that theirs are the only two Founding Nations. Among other things, APTN's argument for mandatory carriage as a parallel service to that of the Canadian Broadcasting Corporation and Radio Canada (Canada's two national public broadcasting services) raised the political/historical stakes in Canada's national debate about confederacy.

The position adopted by the Canadian Cable Television Association (CCTA, Canada's largest cable industry lobby group) revolved around notions of open competition and greater customer choice. It was again based on the assumption that APTN should be a specialty, pay-TV service. To this end, the CCTA argued that the signal would be seen to have been forced upon cable subscribers if they had to pay $0.15 a month for a service they had not requested. In addition to the monthly subscriber fee, the CCTA was also concerned about the one-time costs associated with coercing people to take a service on the basic tier. These included "expenses related to informing customers of the change in the line-up through channel line-up stickers and explanatory letters, and in order to receive the signal, additions to head-end equipment" (CCTA 1998, 3). The CCTA estimated that the cost would be nearly "$4.8 million dollars with line-up sticker costs at 40 cents per subscriber and head-end expenses at $3,500 each, for 500 head-ends" (3-4). Finally, the CCTA insisted that it would be expensive to shift around channel allocations, to no longer offer existing channels – as in the case of the weather channel in Winnipeg – or to bump up channels from one of the basic tiers to a more expensive premium package (Cobb 1999, F-5).

In short, most cable operators did not accept the argument that First Peoples, amounting as they do to under 3 percent of the national population, should have either a special status or a mandatory national channel in Canada. The CCTA said that it "supported the concept of the network but not the insistence that it be offered as part of the basic cable service" (F-5). In other words, cable operators regarded APTN as they would any other specialty channel.

For the most part, it is difficult to disentangle the cable operators' basic preoccupation with cost recovery from their politics, and one might well ask whether economic rationales were not used by cable operators to mask their

A NATIVE NORTH AMERICAN NEWS MAGAZINE   OCTOBER / NOVEMBER 1999
WWW.ABORIGINALVOICES.COM

Everett Soop
Reflections on the
life and times of
Native journalism's
reluctant hero

Show Me the
Money!
A look at the financial
challenges faced by
Native filmmakers

Please Adjust the
COLOUR
On Your Set

Abraham Tagalik and the Aboriginal Peoples
Television Network are giving Canadian TV a
whole new look this fall

Vol. 6, No.5 $5.95

HEAR YOUR WRITTEN WORDS SPOKEN • P.60

"Please Adjust the Colour On Your Set Announces the Arrival of Indigenous 'Colour TV' in Canada." Source: *Aboriginal Voices*, vol. 6, no. 5, October/November 1999. Front cover. Courtesy of *Aboriginal Voices* magazine, Gary Farmer, publisher.

political opposition to the acknowledgement of First Peoples' special and unique national status. What is clear is that neither cross-cultural considerations nor notions of fair resource distribution to minority peoples seemed to be critical factors for most cable operators – although these clearly were concerns for members of the Commission.

On 22 February 1999, the CRTC approved TVNC/APTN's application and granted its mandatory carriage on basic cable throughout Canada with a $0.15 monthly subscription fee in the South. In the North, residents of the ninety-six communities would continue to receive the service free of charge (TVNC, March 1999, 1). To provide continuity of service to Northerners, a separate Northern feed was to be established to ensure that special Northern programming, including legislative coverage and special events, would be broadcast in the North on an ongoing basis.

The time between the date on which the license was granted and APTN's actual launch was unusually short – just a few days over six months, to be exact. This was no doubt stressful for the organization but necessary, according to representatives at APTN, given that they wanted to go on air at the same time as several specialty services that had been licensed in 1996. Doing this would mean that APTN expenses could be included within the one-time costs for publicity and head-end equipment incurred by the other service launches.

APTN began broadcasting, as planned, on 1 September 1999. Until production surpluses could be created, programming was repeated three times daily, or once every six hours. 60 percent of the programming was broadcast in English, 15 percent in French, and 25 percent in a variety of aboriginal languages. News and live programming began in the early part of 2000.[1]

INITIAL IMPACT OF THE ABORIGINAL PEOPLES TELEVISION NETWORK

"The Canadian track record with respect to its own original peoples has been spotty at best. One of the issues that continues to visit us is one of territoriality, and land rights. In our electronic age, we should provide the necessary mechanism for ownership in a national space to express Aboriginal viewpoints in a full, fair, and balanced fashion to reflect native diverse perspectives and to ensure that this reflection is a part of the diversity to be reflected in the public interest." (WETV intervention at CRTC hearing, 12 November 1998, 3)

For a few days after APTN was licensed and for about a week before and after it actually went on air, APTN generated a large amount of editorial commentary in the Canadian press. This revolved primarily around it being "the first in the world" and around the sociocultural and political contexts surrounding the CRTC decision.

On the day after the CRTC licensing decision was announced, for instance, the *National Post* – one of Canada's two national newspapers – published a single article on the subject that presented the opinions of the majority of cable operators. The article's headline read: "COMING SOON TO YOUR LIVING ROOM: The CRTC is forcing a new aboriginal TV channel – and its cost – on most Canadian cable viewers." The article then proceeded to lay out the arguments of the cable industry in some detail, noting briefly the CRTC's view of APTN as being in the "best interests of Canadians" and running one comment by the chairman of the Television Northern Canada Board, Abraham Tagalik, that stressed the importance of the mandatory status of the channel in terms of its recognition of aboriginal peoples' special place in Canadian society (Chwialkowska 1999, A3). Despite the attempt to *look* balanced, the overall impression was that the *National Post* supported the negative opinions of the cable operators.

The Globe and Mail, however – Canada's other national newspaper – presented a quite different perspective in a 24 February 1999 editorial, going out of its way to stress how important it would be for non-native audiences to have access to television produced by indigenous peoples. Certainly the most favourable print editorial that I was able to find in APTN's extensive clipping collection, it is worth quoting in its entirety as it succinctly explains APTN's sociocultural significance within Canadian society:

Television is so confusing. At the same time that it *isn't* reality, it *is* authenticity. Just to be seen on TV makes people genuine in a way that almost nothing else in 20th-century culture does.

This is the psychological underpinning for the CRTC's recent decision to grant a license for an aboriginal television network. Not only will the Aboriginal Peoples Television Network be a place for native people to present themselves to one another in English, French and 15 native languages, but it will be an electronic arena in which many Canadians will encounter aboriginals in ways they might never do otherwise. Native cooking, native children's programs and native talk shows must make native existence both wider and more authentic.

That's why we support the CRTC's decision to make this channel a part of the basic cable package. Not only will it provide a secure source of funding for the APTN's programs, but it will make the network something people will chance upon as they click their way along the TV dial. Aboriginal television will be inescapable. And that inescapability will express something that the isolation and marginality of many native people's lives often obscures.

Their relation to other Canadians isn't tangential; it is inevitable. (Editorial, "The Native Media," *The Globe and Mail*, 24 February 1999, A14; reprinted with permission of *The Globe and Mail*.)

The Globe and Mail editorial raises key points about the relationship between absence and presence as it plays itself out in an important national community in Canada and about issues surrounding (in)visibility and (in)audibility. If it is relatively easy to circulate a liberal discourse of tolerance and multiculturalism in our politically correct era, this editorial highlights how it is even easier to pretend liberal tolerance when a subject/ person/community is absent from our visible and conscious landscape and when what is outside of the purview of our senses can be faded out of our world of social relations. However, when an "unpopular" constituency group evolves into a notable presence within our everyday mediascape, the issue of intolerance becomes more difficult to mask. Coming face to face via our TV screen with a constituency group whose values and programming qualities are significantly different from those of mainstream Canadian television can strongly challenge the silent kind of racism that festers away in living rooms across the country. At the very least, it forces audiences to acknowledge that First Peoples are integral citizens of both the country and the airwaves that we all, according to the law, share.

The launch of the Aboriginal Peoples Television Network service took place at 8:00 p.m. on 1 September 1999. The first live broadcast wove together a broad cross-section of commentators, members of Native Communications Societies that had been involved in television production since at least 1983, entertainers (singers, dancers, drummers, and other musicians), clips of key events in First Peoples history, and landscape images. It was a celebration of the opening up of mainstream Canada to the lives of First Peoples *and* of the opening of First Peoples cultural windows to mainstream Canadians. In this sense, it was of great symbolic importance. Regular scheduled programming commenced at 11:00 p.m. on that night and has since become an important source of information and entertainment for First Peoples and for those interested in acquainting themselves with native perspectives on the world. It has also attracted its fair share of detractors and champions.

On 2 September 1999, for instance, an editorial entitled "Consumers Should Decide What They Want to Watch" ran in *The Vancouver Province*. The following excerpt is illustrative of a common perspective that circulated after the first night of programming: "The CRTC decision was another in a long line of loopy broadcast regulations that amounts to political correctness disguised as social engineering ... We wish APTN the best of luck. But, while Ottawa can make consumers pay for the new channel, it can't make them watch it. It's a good job APTN won't have to rely on Vancouver ratings to pay its way" (Editorial, A-36).

A few days later, in the *Winnipeg Free Press*, a more evaluative look at how other newspapers had been covering APTN's new media status was taken. Summing up "the tenor of commentary in the white man's press surrounding the fledgling aboriginal cable TV channel" as "skeptical, if not outright hostile," arts commentator Morley Walker – in his article "Aboriginal TV deserves better spot on dial" – is clearly critical of those opposed to the licensing of

APTN as a mandatory service. As he goes on to elaborate: "Fifteen cents a month today is a small price to pay as a cable subscriber to support a voice that is both indigenous to our country and vital to offering role models for a dispossessed minority ... It seems to me that a first nations TV channel is an excellent addition to the Canadian television landscape" (Walker 1999, B7).

Disturbed by the conservative press's framing of APTN as "a project of social engineering" and frustrated by how it kept misleadingly pointing out how "only 300 Canadians asked the CRTC for the channel," Walker also raised the issue of APTN's remote location on the channel grid - an issue that is, in many ways, symbolic of First Peoples' sociopolitical placement as always slightly outside the center of things.

APTN – ON THE MARGINS OF MAINSTREAM TELEVISION

Since APTN has been on the air, it has competed with a rather sophisti-cated technological and broadcasting infrastructure put in place in Canada in the 1950s. Although it benefits from these assets, APTN's underfunding and lack of national experience does have consequences in terms of its need for a lengthy transitional period in which to build human resource capac-ity, program surpluses, financial stability, and broad public support from cross-cultural audiences. It is too soon to judge its overall quality, but it should be given a fair amount of latitude in its program development process and a moderate amount of positive publicity to allow it time to improve its programming and to expand its audiences. It has still to become part of the conventional range of television channels – people have to find it, watch it, and give it a chance to demonstrate its professional standards, its diversity of subject matter, and its uniqueness.

In 1999 – before the increasing proliferation of digital cable and satellite services with their hundreds of channels – a key technical issue that margin-alized APTN and relegated it to the equivalent of a "media reservation" was its geographical location on the majority of cable systems' analog channel grids. Due to considerations of existing industry tier structures in Canada, as well as cable providers' expressed concerns in regard to the shifting of cur-rent channel locations, APTN was allocated to the high end of the analog channel grid in most communities. For instance, in Montreal it was received on channel 68 in the west end, channel 58 in the east. In Ottawa, it was received on channel 75. In most other places, too, it was way up there beyond the usual stomping ground of channel grazers.[2] Of course, committed viewers did not care where the channel was located. They could find it in the same way that they found *Nedaa* on CBC's Newsworld.

Another practical challenge that faced APTN in the early days, and impacted its outreach, concerned television guides in newspapers across the country, and their slowness in changing templates to include APTN on their daily channel listings. For instance, in Montreal where I live, it took two years for the main English-language daily, *The Gazette*, to begin consistently publicizing APTN's channel numbers on its weekly schedule grid. Not only was this done somewhat sporadically over the first two years, but the information provided also tended to be incomplete: APTN would be listed, but the channel number would be missing – leaving it up to the prospective viewer to work out where it was located on the grid. What message did this send APTN, not to mention its potential and actual audiences? In other words, not specifying APTN's channel locations on daily TV programming grids no doubt contributed to the perception held by some that the network was a channel that did not warrant a look-in, regardless of the real reasons for this problem.[3]

Small routine details like these – ones that tend to go largely unnoticed – can have unquestioned and long-lasting impacts on public perception, opinion, and viewing habits.

APTN'S CURRENT PROGRAMMING AND AUDIENCES

APTN's programming has expanded its range and improved considerably since its launch. In 2000, under the direction of Dan David, APTN introduced live news and current affairs programming that gave Canadians the chance to see news and public affairs through an aboriginal lens. Concurrently, he initiated a crew-training process and began experimenting with a range of news and current affairs formats. When David left in 2003, Rita Shelton-Deverill moved to APTN from Vision Television (a multi-faith network) to take over his position. These two producer/directors have transformed APTN's news and current affairs programming by opening up multiperspectival approaches to critical issues common to both native and non-native constituency groups in Canada, but of interest to international communities as well.

For example, one of the network's most popular programs is *Contact*, a phone-in current affairs show hosted by Rick Harper. An informal version of CNN's *Larry King Live*, *Contact* is a national show with a local feel that combines live interviews with a phone-in component. The casualness of dress and of interviewing style, not to mention the "ordinariness" of the people being interviewed, give the show an at-home feeling – almost as if the participants were sitting in your own living room.

On a memorable episode about two-spirited people – a concept close to that of homosexuality in the non-aboriginal world – the host conducted a candid interview with a couple of two-spirited men, one much older than the other. They explored the distinctness of the concept, as well as how it relates to Western perspectives on being gay or lesbian. They talked about elders, youth, and middle-aged homosexuals in First Peoples communities. They talked about its taboo-ness and how hard it is to come out. The mood was relaxed, and the subject matter entirely rivetting. It became rivetting in quite a different way when, during the phone-in response, host Rick Harper was rendered utterly silent by a female caller who launched into a long-winded monologue on her personal encounters with two-spiritedness. Throughout, she remained completely oblivious to his attempts to cut her off and go on to the next caller. What is interesting here is how a program with such a home-town feel to it – so hometown, in fact, that it can be taken over by an overly chatty audience member – also fulfills the role of transmitting important and cutting-edge cultural information to a broad spectrum of cross-cultural viewers.

In addition to introducing new programs like the one described above, APTN continues to broadcast cultural programming from the Regional Native Communications Societies, as well as dramas, variety shows, and children's programs. Comedy also has a place on APTN. The well-known Yukon elders Sarah and Suzie, for instance, perform hysterically funny routines that are reminiscent of *Codco*, but with specifically Northern native content. APTN also screens films on *Reel Insight* and on its most popular program of the week, *Bingo and a Movie* (BAAM). In this latter program, a host interviews a guest or guests who may or may not address the subject being covered in the film. The film itself is shown in fifteen- to twenty-minute segments slotted sporadically throughout the interview. An ongoing bingo game also breaks up the interview. The program is, in effect, uniquely aboriginal in tone and approach. To recruit an audience, it exploits the popularity of bingo in aboriginal communities; it features a guest and covers an issue of social interest; and it entertains – all within the same three-hour time slot on a Friday night. Moreover, in the actual breaking up and interweaving of diverse tele-visual genres, it offers the viewer a specifically aboriginal approach to "prime time" management of the airwaves.[4]

As for getting the word out there with regard to all these programs, APTN is currently engaging in an interesting promotion of itself. Like many other channels, APTN displays its logo between program segments. However, there is an important difference. Whereas on most channels well-known television personalities from flagship series pop onto the screen and interact with the logo, APTN features ordinary local citizens from territories across the country. In these cameos, people come on to the screen with their children, friends, and family. They look out at the television audience in a casual manner and are then framed by the APTN logo while a voice-over states: "APTN – Sharing our stories with all Canadians." Its impact is powerful. Here, in front of our eyes, are the First Peoples of Canada who have for far too long been lumped into a monolithic aboriginal stereotype. APTN makes them flesh and blood and gives them individual lives. We see before us those peoples whose stories are actually being told. As for those on the receiving end of these stories, not much systematic audience research has been done to date. However, preliminary forays into this area indicate that APTN has a loyal and committed audience that is supportive of its service, in spite of some technical inconsistencies. Recent aboriginal viewing research (2003) done on behalf of APTN indicates that its broadcasting services are viewed twenty-two hours per week per aboriginal person in the North and 18.5 hours per week by aboriginal residents in the South. This compares with the general population's average of fifteen hours of television per week (www.pch.gc.ca/progs/emcr/eval/2003/2003_05/6_e.cfm, 11/11/03, 4). Given APTN's relative newness on the air, these figures are reasonably good – especially when one considers some of the financial challenges and technical difficulties facing APTN when it comes to distribution.

Here, the major problem is not so much *maintaining* audiences but rather *figuring out* a way to reach that portion of aboriginal reserves (mostly in the mid-North) that still does not have cable or digital satellite access. A significant portion of the approximately 35 percent of the aboriginal populations that live on reserves is not yet receiving APTN programming. In addition, equipment failures in eleven Northern communities have made it impossible for these audience members to receive APTN (Whiteduck Resources Inc./Consilium 2003, 76). Such distribution-related problems still need to be addressed and resolved if APTN's national mandate is to be fulfilled.

APTN pamphlet:
Television with a View.
Used with permission of
APTN.

THE SYMBOLIC SIGNIFICANCE OF THE ABORIGINAL PEOPLES TELEVISION NETWORK

Despite resistances and challenges, the case of aboriginal broadcasting in Canada can be seen as a prototype for other states within which diverse constituency groups compete for service access that will allow them to address and construct alignments across race, social, economic, and territorial lines. Over the years, First Peoples have fought for, and been granted, political opportunities to build a nationwide mediaspace to heal the historical communication ruptures within their societies and between their communities and others living within Canada. As a result of the convergence of a strong political will on the part of the federal government and the CRTC, of amiable negotiations among all key parties, and of First Peoples' policy savvy and their demonstration of the skills needed to develop and manage distinctively Northern

APTN logo. Used with
permission of APTN.

broadcasting infrastructures, APTN has evolved from an idea to a fully operational television broadcasting undertaking. The network is relatively secure
in terms of its funding and distribution, and, most importantly, its existence
is enshrined in national legislation. The Northern Native Communications
Societies, which provide APTN with much of its Northern programming,
are also fairly stable. Basic NNBAP funding pays for production costs, which
is fine as long as the Native Communications Societies' analog equipment
holds out. However, APTN's technical standard is digital, and neither APTN
nor the NCSs have the budget to do program transfers professionally. Consequently, the current priority with the NCSs is to upgrade their equipment to
the digital standard so that they can continue to be carried on APTN. Thus,
the NCSs are involved in several struggles at present: the first is to figure out
who will carry the financial burden of maintaining their analog equipment
when it breaks down[5]; the second is to determine who will foot the bill for
going digital; the third concerns the six NCSs that are still not subsidized to
produce television programming (see appendix C).

As regards the latter, these six absent NCSs create regional vacuums in
APTN's programming. Currently limited to regional radio services, they
have all stated that they are ready and willing to produce television programming, if only federal or private funds could be made available to them. The

Missinipi Broadcasting Corporation and the NCS of the Northwest Territories, it seems, have developed television units on their own, using funds
raised within their organizations. However, the others – Aboriginal Multi
Media Society of Alberta, James Bay Cree Communications Society, Northern
Native Broadcasting, Terrace, and Société de communication Atikamekw-
Montagnais – have not had the capacity to undertake such an initiative, thus
leaving their perspectives out of APTN's programming (personal interview
with Art King, 17 November 2003). For reasons of equity, this absence should
be addressed as soon as possible.

Despite these kinds of financial challenges and inclusivity/exclusivity
issues, APTN has enabled many indigenous messages to be heard by constituency groups that, otherwise, might never have had access to a live person of
aboriginal descent. In this way, it provides an opportunity to share imagery
and histories, to build bridges of understanding across cultural borders, and
to disrupt and interrogate the conventional and traditional distorted views
about First Peoples. This is not to say that this will always be the case. Viewers who already have a negative view of First Peoples will undoubtedly find
programming content on the channel that will serve to reinforce their own
prejudices, negative stereotypes, and possible racism. The important point,
though, is that APTN exists, that it can vie with other services for audience
attention, and that it is now a performer on the electronic power grid. It is
"something new in the air" to stimulate audiences and to provide them with
innovative perspectives that implicitly challenge those offered on other Canadian television channels.

The configuration of Canada's airwaves may be perceived as reflecting the
actual political arrangements and social networks into which multicultural
and multiracial constituency groups have been placed within mainstream
society by dominant governing bodies. Given its current disadvantaged
location on the margins of the mainstream, it is clear that APTN still has a
way to go before it can effectively compete for cross-cultural audiences with
central and powerful networks such as those of the Québécois, the English
Canadian, and the US broadcasting services. That the network is now, at least
officially, one of the mainstream players opens the door to a consolidation
of new power relationships with Canadian media institutions, policy bodies,
and audiences – and this is no small accomplishment, considering how far a
distance APTN has had to travel to get to this place.

APTN as a national public television network is unique on the international airwaves. There is nothing like it anywhere in the world, both from

the programming perspective and in the way it is financed both through advertising and as a social cost to the cable providers. Essentially, it is a new economic prototype for assuring the sponsorship and sustenance of public service programming that might be otherwise unaffordable.

In a sense, APTN is a hybrid between what has traditionally been defined as "public" and "private" broadcasting. It carries advertising yet models itself on public service television, addressing issues of concern to Canadian national publics and niche audiences. Its content and production staff and management are multilinguistic, multicultural, and multiracial. It attempts to be both local and global. It does very little original production of its own but rather distributes local and regional cultural programming to national audiences. That APTN is already integrating international programming into its scheduling and is considering the possibility of expanding to become an international First Peoples television network demonstrates its global objective of constituency group-building across national borders. What all of this shows is that APTN does not easily fit into existing categories of public service broadcasting.

The *look* of APTN is much like the *look* of public access television in the United States or like that of community television in Canada. Its quality is still uneven, though it has improved tremendously since its inception. It doesn't replay the same programs as often as it did in the beginning, but the repetitions remain an irritant to some audience members (albeit a lucky convenience for those with busy schedules). Its mandate to serve all aboriginal communities North and South, as well as the rest of the Canadian population, is extremely complex and difficult to manage.

Despite all these constraints, gaps, and challenges, APTN has served Canadian constituency groups well insofar as it has Northernized and indigenized television programming, enriching it with a diversity that has, so far, only been manifest in policy discourse. It has delivered distinct voices and imagery from coast to coast to coast with multiple perspectives that express what it is like to "live the difference" – an idea that is extensively discussed in various ethnocultural literatures. First Peoples are, indeed, "sharing their stories with all Canadians," as APTN so often informs us between programs. As a minority constituency group, aboriginal peoples have more than symbolically gained their broadcasting rights.

In the current age of the five-hundred-channel universe and the World Wide Web, APTN represents a distinct opportunity for all viewers to become informed about and to reflect upon the recognized "special status" of First Peoples, their cultures, and their priorities.

TOWARDS THE FUTURE: AN INTERNATIONAL TURN

So far, TVNC and APTN have been the only aboriginal television networks in the world to broadcast such a high volume of programming from indigenous sources. CAAMA (the Central Australian Aboriginal Media Association) has had a remote commercial television service license since 1987. However, its service, Imparja, broadcasts to mostly non-aboriginal viewers. Consequently, its programming tends to be fairly European-oriented (Browne 1996, 38). Apart from the fact that both APTN and CAAMA are indigenous-controlled, they have little in common.[6]

At least theoretically, TVNC/APTN have been in the interesting position of being able to forge video connections with Inuit and aboriginal groups in other countries through program exchanges and uplink/downlink satellite arrangements. In reality, however, TVNC was unable to do much of this in the 1990s because of technical (different broadcast standards) and financial (prohibitive costs) barriers. What it *was* able to do was offer Northern viewers limited access to programming about the activities of indigenous people from around the globe. For example, in the mid-1990s, the network aired a half-hour weekly current affairs program called *Heartbeat Alaska*, which originated in Anchorage, Alaska, and was supplied to TVNC for the cost of one-way shipping.

Also in the 1990s, IBC and Greenland's Kalaallit Nunaata Radioa-TV (KNR-TV) briefly developed a television program exchange with TVNC. Unfortunately, the project came to an abrupt halt due to technical difficulties (the 3/4 inch VCR machine, given to KNR-TV by IBC, broke, and neither group could afford the repair costs). Because the video and electrical standards between North America and much of the rest of the world are incompatible (for video, PAL vs NTSC), international or circumpolar electronic exchanges have been somewhat hindered. Sometimes, as in the case of Siberia, political barriers to such exchanges have also existed.

APTN, active in an era of new and expanding technologies, has taken up this challenge and is currently broadcasting several hours a week of international programming. Technological convergence, cross-cultural interest, and the will to reach out to others in parallel political positions have made this begin to happen on a more systematic basis. This recent coupling of a willingness to carry international programming with unlimited possibilities to both send and receive multiformat video materials beyond the borders of North America has meant that APTN is pioneering a sixth phase in indigenous broadcasting – and taking an international turn.

As APTN becomes more widely known, I believe that it will attract and engage in exchanges with dedicated niche audiences who will want to be in touch with indigenous peoples in other parts of the world. In an expanded version of Rod Chiasson's early cross-cultural perspective, APTN staff envision a multicultural/multiracial, multilingual, international indigenous, or Fourth World television broadcasting undertaking in which they will play a central coordinating role.

This is not such a far-fetched idea. In fact, it is actually quite timely given the current international recognition that Canada is receiving for its leading position in the aerospace industry and its demonstrated good will in legislating broadcasting access rights to First Peoples. As already noted, it was years ago that the Canadian Commission for UNESCO acknowledged the important role that the Canadian North had played in media and development (see Stiles and Litwack 1988). Australian Aboriginal representatives have already visited the Canadian Arctic several times since 1986 and are clearly looking at Canada as an exemplar for their own cultural broadcasting plans. The Ainu of Japan, the Chinese, the Thai, the Waiapi of Brazil, indigenous representatives of Bolivia, the Greenlandic and Alaskan Inuit communities, the Saami peoples of Finland, North American Indian media representatives from the United States, people from the Caribbean, and the Siberian Inuit have all made contact with Canadian First Peoples in the past fifteen years to request information, to discuss strategies of media development and program exchange, and/or to solicit broadcast training assistance.[7] It is, therefore, reasonable to assume that indigenous nations elsewhere will continue to show the same interest.

In the near future – after its producers are satisfied with its primary Canadian service – I believe that APTN will transform into an international indigenous broadcasting network. Of course, it will take many years of organizational work to put this in place, but, given the demonstrated cultural persistence of First Peoples of Canada and advancements in digital satellite technology, this idea does not seem as unrealistic as it might have ten years ago.

Conclusion

It is only when a multitude of voices is heard that social actors begin to realize that they can do more than respond; they can choose. The diversity and activity of a given public provide indices to the likelihood of its ability to differentiate between the glitz of public relations satisfied with images and competent rhetoric seeking to articulate reality.

Gerard A. Hauser ("Features of the Public Sphere," 443)

This book has situated indigenous broadcasting development within the broader context of contemporary Canadian multicultural society. Through historical analysis of the key phases in indigenous television broadcasting development and, more specifically, through several case studies, I have shown how broadcasting sites have become pivotal tools of expression for First Peoples' cultural, social, and political imaginaries. Furthermore, indigenous broadcasting has opened up frontier audiovisual spaces, improving the information structures, sources, and conditions for the renegotiation of their power relations in Canadian society. First Peoples have become national media citizens in control of their own information services and public intellectual perspectives.

The deliberate and strategic use of media as a tool for self-empowerment in Canada does not originate with First Peoples experiences. It is historically grounded in the approaches of John Grierson (in the 1940s and 50s) and the now defunct *Challenge for Change* Program of the National Film Board (in the 1960s and 70s), both of which perceived the media not only as a cultural product but also as a tool for community development. It is within this tradition that First Peoples, located at the media margins, set themselves the challenge of innovatively using broadcasting in an alterative fashion (Roncagliolo

1991, 207) as a transformative vehicle. Three kinds of transformations have been the subject of this study: first, the evolving ways in which television has been used to reinforce indigenous languages and cultures in order to build and promote stronger cultural and national identities; second, the critical stages through which indigenous peoples have co-moved with other minorities as they have negotiated a "special" national place for aboriginal broadcasting within legislation; and third, the recognition of television as a tool for mediating social relations and building coalitions towards political ends.

In preceding chapters, I have argued for the importance of the role indigenous media activists have played in the enshrinement of collective communication rights. Beyond their immediate successes in this regard, First Peoples' presence on the airwaves has expanded outsiders' perceptions of Canada as a liberal culturally diverse state.

I have further pointed out that key participatory development processes and their accompanying discourses in Canada have emerged at the territorial and racial peripheries of society. As demonstrated by First Peoples, when minorities gain communication rights and can produce, control, and transmit their own messages in their own and others' languages, media can play a significant role in tearing down antiquated power relations, as well as in clearing new grounds for political and discursive engagement among constituency groups and governments. The accomplishments of First Peoples' broadcasters are no small achievement. They confirm that shifts in power configurations can be initiated from any location in Canada, not *just* from urban centres. Thus, it is a finding of my research that creative and unpredictable, even serendipitous, foundations for new media politics, policies, discourses, and practices can be discovered in the most remote hinterlands and among previously disempowered members of Canadian society.

Beyond this, the case of First Peoples' broadcasting can highlight several questions – even when definite answers have yet to be found. I would like to conclude my reflections by considering three questions raised at the beginning of this study. (1) What role might indigenous broadcasting play in mediating social and race relations between First Peoples and non-aboriginals who have never had direct contact with one another? (2) What can the First Peoples' broadcasting case tell us about the policy-making process in Canada? (3) How can indigenous media be understood in light of the existing crisis in communications development theory and what can it contribute to its revision?

INDIGENOUS BROADCASTING AND THE MEDIATION OF SOCIAL RELATIONS

Television and other media have played a key role in development and modernization processes in the North. When first introduced in the 1960s and 70s, television temporarily stalled indigenous self-development by introducing yet another Southern medium devoid of First Peoples' images, voices, and cultural activities. However, as shown in this book, it didn't take much exposure for First Peoples to recognize that the media could also be used for sociocultural, linguistic, and political empowerment. Consequently, Native Communication Societies and TVNC programmers did not adapt mainstream programming formats and content to their audiences. What they did, rather, was experiment with formats, paces, and genres until they found those that provided them with the best cultural fit. When they went national with APTN, producers took local indigenous models – originally designed for *narrow*casting in the North only – and *broad*cast them outside of their original target audience regions. To these, they added programming acquired from independent producers, material purchased from other media organizations, in-house news and current affairs, and cameo appearances by ordinary aboriginal community members.

Broadcasting an indigenous channel across the country raises an array of questions about how to do intercultural programming and the specificities of audience reach. How much of aboriginal culture should be exposed on television? What about cultural privacy? What about the stakes involved in showing a program in which animals are hunted and skinned? Who should APTN's target audiences be? Who's to say that APTN's intended messages are those received by non-aboriginal viewers? – and, if not, does it matter? How might APTN expand its Southern reach without alienating their Northern and native viewers? These are some of the many challenging questions with which APTN continues to grapple.

As nations located on the territorial and social peripheries of mainstream society, First Peoples have become unique competitors for a place in the Canadian national media. Though not yet systematically verified by quantitative audience research, it appears strategically feasible for First Peoples to build alignments with constituency groups across large electronic spaces once they have access to national mediation possibilities. On the other hand, North/North and North/South programming may have little effect in the long run, given its lack of money to pay for the publicity, training, program solicitation, and upgrading of equipment required to meet current broadcasting standards.

Much research is needed to document the relationship between changes in public opinion and exposure to programming by and about aboriginal peoples. The conditions that must be met for indigenous broadcasting to achieve a position of influence throughout Canada must still be identified. In analyzing these conditions, we must be cautious and not assume that APTN will be influential simply because it is present on the airwaves.

Longitudinal audience research might shed light on the kind of programming that would best meet all of APTN's potential audience interests and also win over what George Henry (formerly of NNBY) has called the "middle ground" (or, the mainstream population) to First Peoples' "development" priorities. Before we embark on audience research, however, we should seriously consider whether or not First Peoples' public-oriented broadcasting should be subjected to the logic and dictatorship of commercial ratings, and comparisons to them, in the first place. Pierre Bourdieu has warned us to be skeptical about public opinion. He argues that we should challenge the taken-for-granted assumption that all opinions have the same value and suggests that we be cautious about the way that we formulate questions. There is not always a consensus about which questions are worth asking, and we should take heed of his cautious words in regard to First Peoples television programming (Bourdieu 1979).

Reception studies on APTN need to precisely identify the audiences of the different programs and to evaluate their impact on viewers. The difficulties involved with having different Native Communications Societies, each representing a unique culture and region, on the same channel also merits further study.[1] Fruitful comparisons could be made to other "collaborative" channels, such as la Francophonie's TV-5 or Ontario's Multiculturalism Television (Channel 47). An in-depth analysis of APTN's international broadcasts could also help us figure out the constituent elements of programming designed to mediate cross-cultural relations between groups of common-language audiences living in different regions and states.

Each distinct native mediated public sphere (the Native Communications Societies, for example) also requires further study. Can the NCSs be considered both exhibitionary and pedagogical sites, causing disruptions in the routine practices of race relations among viewers (North and South), while at the same time providing entertainment and information? Many of the arguments used by the NNBY, TVNC, and APTN staff members attest to their underlying belief that exposure of the "middle-ground" audience to the native side of things would have some impact on the reparation of cross-racial tensions. Whether this is true or not should also the subject of further inquiry. We know that the goal of maintaining and developing positive social relations is what guides the ways in which aboriginal media have been used in Canada.

The geographical and infrastructural remoteness of Northern indigenous broadcasters initially meant that their access to the historically reproduced cultural ensemble of media techniques and to social spheres beyond their territory was limited. This, in itself, has not been such a bad thing in that it provided them with the option of creating some refreshing and experimental approaches to production, distribution, and media-mediated social relations. With early interactive projects such as *Naalakvik* and *Inukshuk* in the 1970s and 80s, the current infrastructure of APTN, and cultural crossover programs on mainstream channels (*Nedaa*; *North of 60* on CBC; *Maamuiteau*, a James Bay Cree program originating from CBC Montreal and broadcast early Sunday mornings; and occasional other programs), aboriginal broadcasters with the financial means have employed technology in novel ways that defy the typical sender-receiver and transmission models in that they are miles ahead of most progressive thinking around media organizational alternatives. First Peoples' producers operate on the assumption that their programming and production values are complex, multilayered, and sometimes unpredictable because their cross-cultural perspectives can be so at odds with those of their audiences. There is no simplistic audience theory embedded in their programming: it is assumed that the sender and receiver will not necessarily be, quite literally, on the same wavelength.

As a carry-over from the early experimental period in Northern broadcasting (Naalakvik, Inukshuk experiments) and possibly due also to their geographical proximity to each other, the relationship between director/producer and audience – between senders and receivers – is generally close and informal. Consequently, direct and immediate feedback is often being preferred at the local shopping centre or at the cinema on a Saturday night. This relationship between producers and consumers of indigenous media – not to mention the very nature of aboriginal programming, with its emphasis on social exchange and interactivity – blatantly contradicts the work of Jean Baudrillard, who argues that the media, in their very essence, forbid such a direct response (Baudrillard 1973). Indeed, what aboriginal media show us is that the possibility of response can be restored by subverting some of the normative broadcasting standards that serve to distance audiences. Although its final results can sometimes seem sophomoric, APTN's breaking of conventional televisual codes is refreshing to viewers. With its distinct appearance, tone, format, experimental techniques, and sometimes even its breakdown in communications while on-air, APTN ensures the cultural persistence of heterogeneity and adds much diversity to the Canadian broadcasting system.

It thus indirectly takes up the challenge of Elihu Katz, who in 1977 raised concerns about whether it was possible to use television to express cultural heterogeneity rather than homogeneity. I would argue that First peoples broadcasts of celebratory national events, like a powwow, constitute the very substance of the cultural heterogeneity to which Katz refers. Not only do such broadcasts build pride and self-esteem in First Peoples themselves, they also enhance our understanding of First Peoples contribution to the Canadian collective identity.

But what expectations do aboriginal broadcasters have of their cross-cultural audiences? And can aboriginal broadcasting mediate social relations in Canada? My research over the years suggests that aboriginal broadcasters expect audiences to respond to their programming from the purview of their own cultural premises, perhaps recognizing, in so doing, the complexity of cross-cultural information and entertainment. No one at APTN, for instance, automatically assumes that the intended message will be the one necessarily received. Given the APTN motto – "Sharing Our Stories with All Canadians" – it seems clear that aboriginal program producers, in trying to build bridges of understanding across cultural terrains, are consciously engaging in a social mediation of sorts. First Peoples at APTN have refashioned the Canadian television landscape by indigenizing it – transforming their parcel of electronic space into a catalyst for (cross-)community development and utilizing it to mediate and explore versions of their own historically ruptured pasts and presents.

THE DEMOCRATIZATION OF THE CANADIAN BROADCASTING SYSTEM: POLICY-ING THE NORTH, REVISITED

Democratic publicity requires positive guarantees of opportunities for minorities to convince others that what in the past was not public in the sense of being a matter of common concern should now become so ...

Nancy Fraser 1990, 71.

Gaining control over the production and distribution of their own cultural icons and media products through local and regional venues has involved First Peoples in negotiations with various levels of civil servants, Cabinet ministers, and outsiders with shared interests. Bypassing conventional approaches and bringing with them fresh perspectives, indigenous peoples have introduced an unusual and unforeseen level of cultural complexity to the bureaucratic process. On the one hand, this has had the positive impact of assuring that governmental paradigmatic discourses on cultural and racial pluralism were given serious deliberation in the making and implementation of important native broadcasting decisions taken within institutional and administrative settings; on the other, it has clearly shown the cracks in the coherent appearance of the relations between federal civil servants and Cabinet ministers. The unruliness of policy relations in Canada is evident in the actual aboriginal broadcasting policy-making process and its erratic implementation. Canadian policy-making is "messy" – not that this is atypical in the challenging regulatory environment of the early twenty-first century. However, what the aboriginal broadcasting sector does is make this messiness particularly visible, largely because of its containment within a "special status" dossier.

State bureaucrats have not presented a unified and coherent body of administrative decisions regarding aboriginal media. The implications of this on First Peoples broadcasting are many. The budget cut of 1990, which was announced right after $250,000 had been allocated for a study of native communications needs in the South, is a notable example. Because the study had not yet been widely publicized, the money and the issue disappeared from public purview fairly quickly after the decision had been made to withdraw the funding. From the paper traces of memos, subcontracts, and other minor forms of communications with civil servants at the time, it appears that the minister made this decision unilaterally, without consulting the parties involved. Evidently, there was a lack of consensus and coordination within the federal bureaucracy at the time.

This is not surprising given the paradigm shifts taking place in aboriginal/federal power relations during the last three decades of the twentieth century. In her essay "A New Paradigm in Canadian Indian Policy for the 1990s" (1990), the late anthropologist Sally Weaver offers insight into the turbulence that existed in Canadian policy-making during the 1990s. Weaver points out that coexistent policy paradigms were applied in an ad hoc and sometimes post hoc manner, making it difficult to predict how the government would respond to an aboriginal initiative or program.[2] Consequently, while the more progressive policies were often likely to be followed, their actual application was somewhat more haphazard. As the example of the 1990 budget cuts demonstrates, this could result in the application of a less progressive policy. If we are to read policies as paradigms – that is, as snapshots of the principles and priorities to which government refers when making administrative and financial decisions – then what can we conclude about the processes of First Peoples' broadcasting governance in Canada?

Interestingly, it is precisely because of the turbulence and schisms within the federal state apparatus that First Peoples found pathways into the mainstream corridors of power. By policy-ing the regulators and the policy-makers – i.e., by surveying the players, policing the airwaves, identifying loopholes in existing policies over the years, and building group alignments within and beyond the system's spaces of opportunity – First Peoples were able to successfully negotiate collective cultural "air rights" (Langton 1993, 22).

The Canadian First Peoples case demonstrates how undemocratic the diffusionist model of Northern broadcasting was prior to the period when First Peoples gained participatory rights in its planning, production, and distribution processes. Despite some initial resistance, the Canadian government and broadcast regulators have removed the North/South line of division and opened up new legislative and audiovisual network opportunities. These openings have provided aboriginal television-makers with possibilities to create their own visual and discursive spaces to "contribute to the emergence of a shared, visible, audible, and racially-mixed public Canadian culture" (Roth and Valaskakis 1989, 232–3).

The symbolic enshrinement of aboriginal broadcasting in the 1991 *Broadcasting Act* does not end this policy narrative. It is not enough to simply enshrine communication rights in legislation while leaving aboriginal broadcasters on the technological and socioeconomic peripheries of Canadian society. First Peoples broadcasters have insisted on being integral to the national mainstream media grid. They have requested and received a Canada-wide mandatory aboriginal service, complementary to the French Radio Canada and the English CBC – in short, a national presence subsidized by the Canadian viewing population.

On the political front, there are several other assurances First Peoples wish to acquire. They want guarantees that their broadcasting interests will remain legislatively protected in a changing media environment subject to deregulation and voluntary regulation both over time and through the inevitable revision of the 1991 Broadcasting Act. Second, they see their broadcasting objectives as going beyond a simple redressing of historical imbalances and oppression to something that works towards national self-determination. They are seeking a special place within the confederation of Canada by demanding a new social contract, a reconfiguration of power relations in Canadian society: they want it recognized that that they, too, are founding nations. Steps in this direction, such as the division of the Northwest Territories and the establishment of Nunavut in 1999, have been yoked to the evolution of Northern and indigenous media development and expansion and would likely have evolved at a much slower pace without First Peoples' media. Thus, seeking a national media status in broadcasting has paralleled political movements that work towards aboriginal self-government, as well as territorial and environmental rights. More than merely repairing the damages of colonialism, they have fostered national self-affirmation: ensuring, both in law and through practice, the fundamental recognition of First Peoples' political citizenship and communication rights.

RE-VISIONING THE NOTION OF DEVELOPMENT COMMUNICATIONS

What does all this mean in development terms? How can indigenous broadcasting history inform and reform our understanding of the development process and its explanatory frameworks?

My research suggests that First Peoples are slowly developing new discourses, practices, and explanatory frameworks to account for the specificities of Fourth World communications development. My underlying belief is that societal development is neither a rupture with the past nor an abandonment of supposedly archaic cultures for the sake of achieving the standards of "elsewhere." Indigenous broadcasting history has confirmed that critical social shifts occur when peoples persistently and collaboratively take charge and fashion their destinies in ways that combine their heritages alongside the project of (post)modernity. In other words, Fourth World development occurs when the formerly colonized transform their consciousness from that of powerless objectified beings to subject-agents who can publicly act and speak in the language of their choice on the basis of their own cultural histories, knowledges, and capacities. Media play a critical role in documenting and publicly asserting their ownership rights to these very things.

Insofar as looking at aboriginal broadcasting in development terms, the material generated from this case study not only reinforces general problems associated with development theory as a result of antiquated conceptual frameworks but also proposes some alternatives that are based on social movement models as described in the works of Arturo Escobar (1994), Alain Touraine (1981), and Alberto Melucci (1989), among others. As the experience of indigenous media in Canada demonstrates, social transformation typically begins with the protest of a people whose national objectives are not met and for whom there are no existing institutionalized processes to address their needs. They organize collectively and push for changes that will meet those needs. In this sense, First Peoples' protest, collective actions, and proffering of media alternatives have been akin to social movements.

In the North, early broadcasters became part of a social movement by directing their energies towards the establishment and expansion of broadcasting and cultural rights. The current visibility of Northern native broadcasters in the South is an indicator – a sign to Southern audiences – of their shifted (and shifting) political place in Canadian society. In other words, there has been a relatively gentle seizure of control over the production, representation, and distribution of First Peoples histories, politics, and cultures. Moreover, in the televisual joining of Canada's North and South, of its east to its west, First Peoples have taken charge of new media venues and are using them in ways that are consistent with their own priorities, cultural orientations, and performative and pedagogical strategies. They have tackled technological and administrative challenges at many levels and have pushed for and gained new mediating structures. Northern and aboriginal broadcasting policies, innovative practices, technological infrastructures, funding programs, a dedicated channel, and a pan-Northern and -Southern public all represent new resources in Canada's communications system(s). First Peoples' versions of history, their knowledges, and their cultural practices are now the preferred content of their own broadcasting undertakings, which are coexistent with those owned and operated by Southern Canadians and Americans. The organizational alignments of Native Communications Societies across the country have provoked social changes and have helped to replace outdated notions of broadcasting with "postdevelopment" terms that are characterized by anticolonial thinking.

Aboriginal media constituency groups have symbolically noted and, in practice, raised important questions about the actual diversity of power relationships in Canada. Their experiences inform us that institutional politics has its limitations and that (in)visible networks of small groups can persuasively engage with federal bureaucrats outside the purview of the general public to challenge, initiate, and change their dominant codes of everyday administrative procedures and logics.

To the Canadian viewing public, APTN represents a public screen upon which the culturally and politically symbolic challenges that First Peoples' societies are laying out for themselves and exhibiting to others are being projected. Emerging into public visibility and audibility through the APTN undertaking, First Peoples television awakens us to the fundamental importance of indigenous issues on the national political agenda.

First Peoples' self-organized media projects, the clustering of their broadcasters into policy lobby groups, and their cross-cultural programming initiatives have transformed them into new social actors who do media politics differently from others in Canada. In many ways and on many instances over the last three decades, First Peoples have used a Tai Chi approach, bypassing completely or tiptoeing lightly past technological and social constraints. Leading the way to a series of infrastructural and policy changes, First Peoples have transformed the Canadian broadcasting system, making it a little less mired in the narrow traditions of its history.

TOWARDS A "CO-DEVELOPMENT" PERSPECTIVE

As Kumar noted (1988–89), what seems to be required to revitalize development communications at this particular historical conjuncture is "a theoretical pluralism where each culture and tradition develops its own theory or theories and practices or strategies in terms of its own philosophy, its resources, its history and experience" (10). If we, no matter what our cultural origins may be, recognize that there is no fixed or terminating point to development and if we acknowledge that we are living in a complex, multicultural, and multiracial world in which we can no longer depend on the stability we once took for granted, then it is clear that we have to rethink the categories of development communications frameworks. Furthermore, if we also acknowledge that internal colonialism vis-à-vis First Peoples and some minority cultural and racial communities exists in "developed" states like the USA and Canada, among others, then we should be prepared to recognize that the West, too, is in a process of constant social flux. It is not frozen in time as a model for others to emulate. Nor are we as citizens of all nationalities politically innocent in our arrangement of power configurations in our societies.

Given this sociocultural and political-economic reality, the ultimate challenge for First Peoples (beyond changing, developing, and increasing awareness of their heritage and active political presence in Canadian society), is – in the words of Gustavo Esteva – "to co-move" and "to intensify the processes of construction of direct democracy." Co-moving does not imply that people move in a predetermined direction. Rather, it is a project that recognizes peoples' agency and both the parallel and the distinct movements a constituency group chooses to follow. "Co-moving," as Esteva asserts, "is a process about which ... indigenous peoples ... have much to say" (Esteva in Escobar 1992, 27–8).

The notion of co-moving could be central in helping scholars and engaged citizens unpack and repair often outmoded, hierarchical, policitally elitist, and impractical views within development thinking and applications thereof. Using co-movement as a core processual concept in studying sociocultural transformation, and coupling it with a more flexible range of dialogical styles and a wider range of representational (voice and image) practices, we can begin to anticipate the possibility of new political and cultural imaginaries – ones that recognize the multiple trajectories of complex and erratic social transformation processes in non-unitary states. New media cultures and systems must take into account the fluid, irregular landscapes of rapid social changes and conflicts, and the border crossings and disjunctures that occur within postmodern, multicultural/multiracial societies due to technological innovations and a different sense of timing. Within the context of globalization, we all need to be more attentive to culturally diverse forms of knowledge, to new styles and paces of participation (the slow Tai Chi vs the abrubt karate styles of intervention) and to local and regional autonomy over the production of a wider range of norms and discourses. APTN is a window through which we can begin to access some of these alternatives being considered by First Peoples. For scholars seeking to "re-vision" the field of development and inter"nation"al communications, the history of First Peoples' television broadcasting in Canada may suggest new conceptual pathways out of the current theoretical impasse.

In emancipating the concept of development from its Eurocentric, neocolonial legacy in order to (re)think power relations, the term co-development comes to mind. As noted in the Introduction to this book, I see co-development as a sophisticated analytic concept because it recognizes the parallel but diverse pathways, discourses, paces, and timelines initiated and followed by various constituency groups, cultural/racial communities, and nations living within multicultural, plurilinguistic, settler states. Co-development can encompass consenting and conflictual constituency groups, as well as allow for their unique timing issues and power relationships as they coexist within a single state and co-move at various rhythms and paces on their way towards social, cultural, political, and economic transformation. It may also be a useful way of framing the relationships between interregional and international communities involved in collaborative projects across national or state borders when two or more collectivities work cooperatively, or in alignment, towards a particular end or project, such as APTN, TV-5, or the North American Free Trade Agreement.

At the very least, First Peoples' experiences with broadcasting can help us to think through the ways in which collaborative and conflicting aspects of co-movement and co-development could be applied to the construction of new social arrangements. A case that illustrates how multiple societies can co-move (first locally, then regionally, and now nationally) towards a common development end of self-determination, First Peoples' broadcasting services have played an equally important role in mediating relationships between, on the one hand, indigenous peoples and, on the other, Canadian cultural institutions and their constituency groups. First Peoples have persisted in constructing a television channel that will, in many ways, remain rooted to their cultural pasts and futures. As a venue for exploring, performing, teaching, and (re)producing multiple cultures, the Aboriginal Peoples Television Network could be seen as a complex mirror structuring the reflections of indigenous nations as they work on changing their place in Canadian society.

First Peoples have become communities-in-motion, capturing their own images and projecting their social, cultural, and political stories and agendas on the screens of Canadian audiences from coast to coast to coast. Over time, broadcasting audiences will inevitably hear their words, see and appreciate their imagery, and – at least to some extent – recognize their special status as a national constituency group. Politically, sufficient recognition is likely to be longer in coming, but one thing is certain: First Peoples broadcasters in Canada are in the process of consolidating their position among mainstream television institions, policy bodies, and audiences, both here and around the world, and this is no small accomplishment. They have given Canadian audiences and institutions the gift of "Something New in the Air"; a national aboriginal channel worthy of both recognition and acclaim as a valuable contribution to ongoing international media developments and dialogues.

Appendix A
Communities Served by Frontier Coverage Packages

Fiscal Year Installed	Location of Transmitter*
1967–68	Yellowknife, Northwest Territories, Lynn Lake, Manitoba Havre-Saint-Pierre,Quebec (French Service)
1968–69	Uranium City, Saskatchewan, Whitehorse, Northwest Territories, Churchill Falls, Newfoundland Saint Anthony, Newfoundland, Watson Lake, Yukon Territory, Cassiar, British Columbia
1969–70	La Ronge, Saskatchewan Fort McMurray, Alberta Fort Nelson, British Columbia Clinton Cheek, Yukon Territory Dawson, Yukon Territory Elsa, Yukon Territory Fort Smith, Northwest Territories Pine Point, Northwest Territories Inuvik, Northwest Territories
1970–71	Churchill Falls, Newfoundland (French service)
1971–72	Frobisher Bay, Northwest Territories Faro, Yukon Territory

*A few transmitters served more than one community.

Appendix B
Specific Recommendations of the Northern Communication Conference, Yellowknife, Northwest Territories, 9–11 September 1970

(Adapted from Northern Communications Conference Record 1970, 5–8.)

1. There is an urgent requirement to provide reliable two-way telephone and teletype services to remote communities in the territories and Northern parts of the provinces. The prime need is for telecommunication facilities to support essential health and emergency services. Priority must be given to establishing telecommunication links between remote communities and centres where hospitals are located, e.g., Frobisher Bay. The Northern residents want good facilities for:

a) intraregional communications;
b) interregional communications;
c) local exchange connections.

This reliable service should be available to permanent communities having populations greater than twenty-five or fifty on a one-day/twenty-four-hour basis and not be subject to outages due to climatic or other natural variations. Reliable telephone and teletype services are also required by territorial and provincial governments and by federal agencies for administrative purposes. A teletype circuit is essential for administration when the community has more than three hundred people. More sophisticated services (medium- and high-speed data) should be provided where demand is indicated by commercial agencies.

The situation generally is that existing point-to-point services are inadequate and that problems are particularly acute in the District of Keewatin, Baffin Island, and the Arctic Coast. It is also widely agreed that high-frequency (HF) radio is inadequate as presently operated.

2. Each community should have a radio program service for education, information, entertainment, and social action purposes. This service might be established by low-

power community-operated radio stations. The broadcast material should be in the native language for part of the time. Full participation and operation by local people is recommended. Community ownership – as distinct from CBC overlap – is mentioned as a possibility although government subsidies would be required. Consideration should also be given to higher-powered AM broadcasting stations to serve complete regions. At present, there are large areas, such as the District of Keewatin, without broadcast services. Relaxation of regulations and technical standards to permit the use or development of low-cost equipment should be encouraged if this does not interfere with public safety and convenience. The stations at Churchill and Inuvik provide a service that could be used as a precedent for other areas.

3. Low-power community broadcast stations should be connected intraregionally, interregionally, and to the national radio CBC network. Northern orientation of programming is essential. Radio network service is presently unavailable in the Central and Eastern Arctic and along the Arctic Coast. The CBC short-wave service is unreliable and subject to long outages due to fading. Steps to improve this service should be taken. Radio coverage should be available to everyone as the essential means of mass communication in the North. The CBC Northern Service should be established in the North (perhaps at Yellowknife) and be given full program control including choice of what it wants from the national network.

4. Nomadic or hunting groups should be provided with low-cost radio units to contact their resident community in emergency or other urgent situations. Special equipment may have to be developed for the purpose and have incorporated a homing device in addition to voice capability. A task force of technologists and users should be formed as soon as possible to pursue this concept. The equipment should be inexpensive, portable, and rugged for Arctic conditions.

5. More extensive use should be made of technology for educational and social development purposes. Services such as videotape recorders (VTR), films, sound cassettes, and records are flexible and economical. Videotape recorders are particularly valuable and should be widely distributed for local use. They can be used effectively for group-interaction discussions and for recording community news and events for subsequent presentation to government legislators and staff. Videotapes can be exchanged between communities for regional dissemination of news and affairs. Regular airlifts of video and audio tapes should be considered. Each community should have trained personnel for the necessary maintenance of equipment. Primary power sources within communities are required. Videotape recorders might be installed in isolated communities as part of a pilot study to aid in establishing program requirements for regular TV service.

6. Live television and Frontier Package Coverage service should be extended to more communities in the North with programming suited to Northern needs. This may mean an additional channel on Anik to ensure that the transmission medium exists for carrying Northern network programming the feasibility of programming originating in the North (possibly Yellowknife) can be developed. It is recognized also that the availability of live television could stimulate industrial initiatives.

Concern is expressed by native people that programming designed for Southern audiences would distract and disturb their culture. It would also widen the generation gap between the older traditional groups and the younger people who have been exposed to the Southern way of life.

7. From the information provided at this conference the proposed satellite will not service the immediate communication needs of the North. It is recommended that conventional methods of communication be expanded to meet these needs.

8. The common carriers should give adequate preventive maintenance service on a routine basis. A long-range program should plan at giving education to Northern operators so that they can become permanent maintenance staff in the North; interest in amateur radio clubs should be fostered.

9. A pool of portable equipment should be made available in every settlement to be leased or loaned to all trappers and others who are leaving the settlement and are going on traplines to permanent camps, oil sites, etc.

10. An inventory should be compiled of radio frequencies in use, systems, equipment, and purpose in Northern Canada so that services can be optimized and duplication eliminated.

11. The postal services in the North are too slow and deliveries proceed by extremely indirect routes. This service is very important to residents and improvements are required.

Appendix C
Profiles of Native Communication Societies Involved in the Northern Native Broadcast Access Program and the Northern Distribution Program — Sponsored by the Department of Canadian Heritage

Source: Department of Canadian Heritage (NNBAP & NDP Evaluation), 23 June 2003. Printed with permission of the Department of Canadian Heritage.

PROFILE OF BROADCAST ORGANIZATIONS

Organization	Aboriginal Multi Media Society of Alberta		
Location Served	Alberta		
Hours per week of radio broadcast	Original 70		Rerun 98
Hours per week of television broadcast	Original N/A		Rerun N/A
Languages of broadcast	English, Cree, Blackfoot, Nakoda Sioux, Chipewyan		
Estimated percentage of programming broadcast in Aboriginal languages	Radio 3%		TV N/A
Number of communities served	41 sites, 100+ communities with Starchoice		
Number of employees	Full-time Staff Total 14		Aboriginal # and % 14 (100%)
NNBAP Funding	Total Estimated Funding $2,707,111	NNBAP Funding $326,855	NNBAP Portion of Total Funding 12.07%

Organization	Inuit Broadcasting Corporation		
Location Served	Nunavut		
Hours per week of radio broadcast	Original N/A		Rerun N/A
Hours per week of television broadcast	Original 3.5		Rerun 2.5
Languages of broadcast	Inuktitut		
Estimated percentage of programming broadcast in Aboriginal languages	Radio N/A		TV 100%
Number of communities served	26		
Number of employees	Full-time Staff Total 36		Aboriginal # and % 33 (91.6%)
NNBAP Funding	Total Estimated Funding $2,531,071	NNBAP Funding $1,389,016	NNBAP Portion of Total Funding 54.88%

Organization	Inuvialuit Communications Society		
Location Served	Inuvialuit Settlement Region: Inuvik, Aklavik, Holman, Sachs Harbour, Tuktoyaktuk, and Paulatuk		
Hours per week of radio broadcast	Original N/A		Rerun N/A
Hours per week of television broadcast	Original 1		Rerun 2
Languages of broadcast	Inuvialuktun, English		
Estimated percentage of programming broadcast in Aboriginal languages	Radio N/A		TV 60%
Number of communities served	6		
Number of employees	Full-time Staff Total 8		Aboriginal # and % 8 (100%)
NNBAP Funding	Total Estimated Funding $740,705	NNBAP Funding $389,705	NNBAP Portion of Total Funding 52.61%

Organization	James Bay Cree Communications Society		
Location Served	James Bay Cree, 12,000-14,000 people		
Hours per week of radio broadcast	Original 22		Rerun 0
Hours per week of television broadcast	Original N/A		Rerun N/A
Languages of broadcast	Cree		
Estimated percentage of programming broadcast in Aboriginal languages	Radio 80%		TV N/A
Number of communities served	officially 9, although reaches other communities via CBC network		
Number of employees	Full-time Staff Total 7		Aboriginal # and % 7 (100%)
NNBAP Funding	Total Estimated Funding $517,200	NNBAP Funding $292,200	NNBAP Portion of Total Funding 56.5%

Organization	Missinipi Broadcasting Corporation		
Location Served	All of Saskatchewan (50+ Northern Communities), in addition to the major cities in the south		
Hours per week of radio broadcast	Original 112		Rerun 56
Hours per week of television broadcast	Original ?		Rerun ?
Languages of broadcast	Cree, Dene, English		
Estimated percentage of programming broadcast in Aboriginal languages	Radio 20%		TV 90%
Number of communities served	50+		
Number of employees	Full-time Staff Total 26		Aboriginal # and % 18 (69.2%)
NNBAP Funding	Total Estimated Funding $1,825,000	NNBAP Funding $326,855	NNBAP Portion of Total Funding 17.9%

Organization	Native Communications Incorporated		
Location Served	Radio broadcasts to 95% of Manitoba via 49 transmitters located from Winnipeg to Churchill		
Hours per week of radio broadcast	Original 159		Rerun 9
Hours per week of television broadcast	Original 6.5		Rerun 0
Languages of broadcast	Cree, Ojibway		
Estimated percentage of programming broadcast in Aboriginal languages	Radio 30%		TV 30%
Number of communities served	largest Aboriginal radio network in Canada, currently broadcasting to 95% of Manitoba		
Number of employees	Full-time Staff Total 17		Aboriginal # and % 11 (64.7%)
NNBAP Funding	Total Estimated Funding $1,391,108	NNBAP Funding $641,108	NNBAP Portion of Total Funding 46.09%

Organization	Native Communication Society of the Northwest Territories		
Location Served	Northwest Territories		
Hours per week of radio broadcast	Original 60		Rerun 108
Hours per week of television broadcast	Original N/A		Rerun N/A
Languages of broadcast	Dogrib, North Slavey, South Slavey, Chipewyan, English		
Estimated percentage of programming broadcast in Aboriginal languages	Radio 75%		TV N/A
Number of communities served	23		
Number of employees	Full-time Staff Total 10		Aboriginal # and % 9 (90%)
NNBAP Funding	Total Estimated Funding $949,355	NNBAP Funding $326,855	NNBAP Portion of Total Funding 34.43%

Organization	Northern Native Broadcasting, Terrace		
Location Served	British Columbia, Canada through Starchoice, the world through www.cfnr.net		
Hours per week of radio broadcast	Original 168		Rerun 0
Hours per week of television broadcast	Original N/A		Rerun N/A
Languages of broadcast	English		
Estimated percentage of programming broadcast in Aboriginal languages	Radio 0%		TV N/A
Number of communities served	55		
Number of employees	Full-time Staff Total 11		Aboriginal # and % 7 (63.6%)
NNBAP Funding	Total Estimated Funding $876,000	NNBAP Funding $326,855	NNBAP Portion of Total Funding 37.31%

Organization	Northern Native Broadcasting		
Location Served	Yukon for radio programming, Canada for television programming		
Hours per week of radio broadcast	Original 168		Rerun 0
Hours per week of television broadcast	Original 1.5		Rerun 1.5
Languages of broadcast	English, Southern Tutchone, Northern Tutchone, Kaska Tlingit, Gwitchin		
Estimated percentage of programming broadcast in Aboriginal languages	Radio 20%		TV 50%
Number of communities served	Not listed		
Number of employees	Full-time Staff Total 27		Aboriginal # and % 18 (66.7%)
NNBAP Funding	Total Estimated Funding $1,293,769	NNBAP Funding $1,005,769	NNBAP Portion of Total Funding 77.74%

Organization	OKalaKatiget Society		
Location Served	Northern Labrador / Lake Melville region Canadian North and South via cable (TV)		
Hours per week of radio broadcast	Original 21		Rerun N/A
Hours per week of television broadcast	Original 13		Rerun 13
Languages of broadcast	Inuttut, English		
Estimated percentage of programming broadcast in Aboriginal languages	Radio 50%		TV 50%
Number of communities served	7		
Number of employees	Full-time Staff Total 13		Aboriginal # and % 12 (92.3%)
NNBAP Funding	Total Estimated Funding $924,705	NNBAP Funding $389,705	NNBAP Portion of Total Funding 42.14%

Organization	Societe de communication Atikamekw-Montagnais		
Location Served	Mauricie, Lac Saint-Jean, Cote-Nord, Base-Cote-Nord, Labrador		
Hours per week of radio broadcast	Original 25		Rerun 10
Hours per week of television broadcast	Original N/A		Rerun N/A
Languages of broadcast	Atikamek, Montagnais		
Estimated percentage of programming broadcast in Aboriginal languages	Radio 0%		TV N/A
Number of communities served	12		
Number of employees	Full-time Staff Total 11		Aboriginal # and % 10 (90.9%)
NNBAP Funding	Total Estimated Funding $0	NNBAP Funding $578,258	NNBAP Portion of Total Funding 0%

Organization	Taqramiut Nipingat Incorporated		
Location Served	Nunavik		
Hours per week of radio broadcast	Original 15		Rerun 0
Hours per week of television broadcast	Original 0.5		Rerun N/A
Languages of broadcast	Inuktitut and captioned in English		
Estimated percentage of programming broadcast in Aboriginal languages	Radio 100%		TV 100%
Number of communities served	15		
Number of employees	Full-time Staff Total 25		Aboriginal # and % 23 (92%)
NNBAP Funding	Total Estimated Funding $1,298,057	NNBAP Funding $907,317	NNBAP Portion of Total Funding 69.9%

Organization	Wawatay Native Communications Society		
Location Served	Northern Ontario, from James / Hudson Bay to Manitoba Border, primarily in the Nishnawbe Aski Nation		
Hours per week of radio broadcast	Original 40		Rerun 5
Hours per week of television broadcast	Original 1		Rerun 1
Languages of broadcast	Cree, Oji Cree, English		
Estimated percentage of programming broadcast In Aboriginal languages	Radio 90%		TV 10%
Number of communities served	39		
Number of employees	Full-time Staff Total 26		Aboriginal # and % 23 (88.5%)
NNBAP Funding	Total Estimated Funding $2,211,769	NNBAP Funding $1,005,769	NNBAP Portion of Total Funding 45.47%

Notes

PROLOGUE

1 The Distant Early Warning (DEW) line consisted of a series of military outpost camps lined up within the Arctic Circle. They were set up in the post-Second World War era and, during the Cold War years, acted as the frontline warning signal for a possible North American nuclear missile invasion by the Soviets.

2 Inuktitut is the language of the Inuit people, formerly known as the Eskimos in Canada and still called by the latter name in Alaska, United States. The term "Inuk," which is its root word, refers to one Inuit person. The term "Eskimo" (which means "eaters of raw meat") was initially used by the Algonquins as an insult to the Inuit and is unacceptable in Canada today. However, because it was the expression universally accepted by non-Inuit during the period preceding the 1970s, I use it now and then throughout the book when referring to this particular historical context.

3 The word "qallunaat" is the plural term for non-Inuit peoples; its singular is "qallunaaq." Although it literally includes all non-Inuit, in its colloquial form it is most frequently used exclusively for "white people," with other terms developed to specify peoples of darker skin colours.

4 The name of the administrative centre of the Baffin Region, Frobisher Bay, was changed in 1987 in recognition of the right of Inuit people to name their own homeland.

5 "First Peoples" refers to all of Canada's indigenous peoples: Amerindian, Métis, Inuit, and Inuvialuktun (Inuit who live in the area of Inuvik). The term "First Nations" refers only to Amerindians, Métis, and mixed blood Amerindians. Although one can never be sure of the most current politically correct term used by aboriginal peoples to refer to themselves, I believe that First Peoples is the most inclusive term and therefore use it most frequently. Often, the word "native" is used to refer to all indigenous peoples, as in Native Communications Societies. So I, like others, use the term "native" as a generic way of describing the

communications organizations created by indigenous peoples for administrative purposes.

6 That said, it is interesting to note just how few academic analyses have been undertaken of First Peoples Television since the Aboriginal Peoples Television Network was licensed by the CRTC. Other than my own work and that of Gail Valaskakis, Valerie Alia, Michael Meadows, Helen Molnar, and Faye Ginsburg, all that is out there are some short articles promoting the network and its programming and some brief references in works that document the international indigenous media movement. I find this curious, and I suspect that researchers have been more interested in making a case for the *existence* of the network, than in the network operation itself. It seems that, once APTN was up and running, researchers lost interest: either shifting their focus to other indigenous media sites, projects, and products that were less developed and more in need of legitimacy within the field of media studies, or to those that were more developed and already making an impact on the international media-sphere, such as feature films like *Atanarjuuat* or *Whale Rider*.

INTRODUCTION

1 A term coined by Cree author George Manual, founding president of the World Council of Indigenous Peoples, "The 4th [*sic*] World is the name given to in-digenous peoples descended from a country's aboriginal population and who today are completely or partly deprived of their own territory and its riches. The peoples of the 4th World have only limited influence or none at all in the nation state [in which they are now encapsulated]. The peoples to whom we refer are the Indians of North and South America, the Inuit (Eskimos), the Sami people [of northern Scandinavia], the Australian aborigines [*sic*], as well as the various indigenous populations of Africa, Asia, and Oceana [*sic*]" (Churchill 1992, 10).

The term "Third World" was first used in 1952 during the Cold War and designated those countries non-aligned with either the United States or the Soviet Union. "First World" refers to the dominant economic powers of the West; "Second World" is used in reference to the Soviet Union and its satellite spheres of influence at the time of the Cold War. Currently, the term "Second World" is being used by some postcolonial critics to designate "settler colonies" such as Australia and Canada to emphasize their difference from colonies of occupation (Ashcroft et al. 1998, 231–2).

2 It is important at this point to clarify my use of the terms "state" and "nation." Drawing on the work of Karl Aun (1980), I refer to a state as "a political system (or community) having three definitive elements: a territory, a body of citizens, and an independent (sovereign) government. State is a political and legal concept as is also citizenship – the nexus between state and individual – a legal term

which implies political loyalty or allegiance" (Aun 1980, 65). In actual operation, as Bob Jessop (1990) emphasizes, "the state is a specific institutional ensemble with multiple boundaries, no institutional fixity and no pre-given formal or substantive unity" (Jessop 1990, 267).

Nation, on the other hand, refers to "an ethno-cultural community (or ethno-cultural system) and is primarily a socio-psychological concept. Communal cohesiveness of a nation can emerge from several objective variables such as common language, religion, 'homeland,' historic experience, mores, myths, and biological origin and is subjectively derived from loyalty, or the feeling of belongingness, to a specific ethno-cultural community. Hence the nexus between the nation and the individual is conscious and/or subconscious self-identification, nationality or ethnicity in an ethno-cultural sense. A nation is not territorially bound nor does it have any legalized political power per se. A nation and a state can, however, coincide, and that is exactly what the notion of nation-state assumes – that nations and states coincide or should coincide" (Jessop 1990, 67).

The problems associated with the use of the term "nation" are complex, and its usage by different cultural communities tends to reflect differing and competing conceptions of society. In the past, both Francophone and Anglophone Canadians have tended to agree that Canada has two founding nations and that First Peoples communities were not to be considered within this category. This can no longer be assumed, as evidence has emerged showing competitive struggle over the meaning and self-referential uses of the term by dominant Anglophone and Francophone elites. In the early 1990s, both the apparent *ownership* of the term "nation" by the two "founding fathers" and the rules governing the antiquated discourses of Canadian nationalism began to be actively challenged by aboriginal peoples. Elijah Harper's refusal to sign the Meech Lake Accord in 1990 and the Oka/Kanehsatake conflict of that same year are but two examples of this phenomenon. Just as many Québécois(es) insist on calling themselves a sovereign nation, so too do the Mohawk Indians. It is interesting to note that during the Oka/Kanehsatake conflict, some of the former became quite upset by the latter's seeming appropriation of *their* term for themselves. (For more details on this, see Roth 1992.)

3 By "media citizenship," I mean recognition of the "national" status of First Peoples, in contradistinction to "special interest" and other constituency groups. National media citizenship for indigenous peoples would entail a nationwide discursive space in the Canadian communications system, in the form of both a separate channel *and* broader access to existing national channels. In other words, it would mean not only having a voice broadcast over conventional channels, but *also* having *control* over their own voices on *their own* channel. The term was originally suggested by Thierry Le Brun in a personal conversation.

4 Those few include Alia 2000; Valaskakis 1976 (unpublished paper), 1979, 1981, 1992a,b; Coldevin 1977; O'Connell 1977; Wilson 1981, 1987; Roth 1983, 1989, 1992, 1999, 2000; Koebberling 1984, 1988; Meadows and Molnar 2001.

5 The work of Faye Ginsburg (1991) and a short publication by Marcia Langton (1993) both grapple with new and recent questions of cross-cultural communications between indigenous and non-indigenous communities in Australia. The case of Imparja refers to the satellite downlink to central Australia owned by Aboriginal people; the other cases they discuss are the very local low-cast pirate stations of the Warlpiri Media Association at Yuendumu and Ernabella Video and TV (EVTV) at Ernabella. The parallel developments between Canadian and Australian indigenous media are pertinent to my arguments in this book. The work of Michael Meadows in Australia also looks at and compares Australian and Canadian aboriginal television development. (For examples, see Meadows 1996a,b,c.) Helen Molnar's work and the writings of Eric Michaels are also invaluable for reading through the lens of Canadian indigenous media. (For further reading, please see: Michaels 1986, 1994a,b; Molnar 1990.)

6 A plurilinguistic society is one in which there is more than one official language. In Canada, to date, there are two official languages – English and French. However, within the Northwest Territories, there are nine official languages – English, French, and seven aboriginal languages.

CHAPTER ONE

1 The terms *development* and *culture* are both multi-discursive in that they are mobilized (often conjuncturally) in a variety of discourses to signify different meanings. In other words, their precise meaning is determined relationally, on the basis of context.

2 In this book, I take the position that First Peoples cultural communities (Indian, Inuit, and Métis) also have the status of nations. As such, when I use the term "transnational" in an indigenous context, I mean relations between and among First Peoples communities of different ethnicities both within and outside of Canada (for example, the James Bay Cree and the Inuit of Northern Canada, Alaska, Greenland, or Siberia).

3 Given the complexity of recent debates, I take the broadest view of the meanings of culture within this analysis. In the context of development, I mean culture in the anthropological sense in that it consists, as Raymond Williams has suggested, of the patterned relationships among elements of a whole way of life, and is expressive of the meanings and values located in the active, lived experiences of individuals and communities (Williams 1961, 57-63). In relation to communications in general, I consider culture to be "composed of seriously

contested codes and representations" (Clifford 1986, 2), some of which are public, visible, and audible, others of which are privately negotiated. Finally, there is something known as "documentary culture," which refers to the "body of intellectual and imaginative works in which, in a detailed way, human thought and experience are ... recorded" (Williams 1961, 62).

4 Like Anne McClintock and Ella Shohat, I prefer the term *neocolonial* to *postcolonial* as the latter "implies premature celebration of the end of colonial domination and fails to take account of the variety of new (and not so new) geopolitical dispensations of power" (McClure and Mufti 1992, 5). The term *neocolonial*, on the other hand, allows for the possibility that in the late twentieth/early twenty-first century, domination may have taken on forms other than overt colonial rule. When, on occasion, I use the term *postcolonial*, I do so only because it is the expression used by the author to whom I am alluding, or by the text to which I am referring.

5 Among others, these include their view of development as: a self-controlled, participatory process which may be reinforced by state- and private-supported mass media; a means by which to develop a "critical consciousness" of a political, social, economic, and cultural nature, incorporating local, regional, and national traditions (Freire 1973); and a basis for the construction and utilization of indigenous cultural channels of communication for self-development goals (Shinar 1987).

It is also important to note that most of these early versions of development excluded the perspectives of women and rural inhabitants. This had the effect of distorting and narrowing publicly accessible views of actual lived conditions in developing regions, making them male-oriented and metropolitan. With regard to the former, notable early exceptions are the ISIS publication on Women in Development (1984), the Canadian International Development Agency's (CIDA) preoccupation with women in development as a result of their participation in International Women's Year (1975) and Decade (1976–85) tributes, the work of Gayatri Spivak on the subaltern (1988), and the work of Jean Franco on counterhegemonic discourses (1988). UNESCO's support of women in development, in addition to generating general interest in this area, has resulted in several conferences (the Simone de Beauvoir Institute's 1987 conference "Women and Development: Alternative Approaches" is one example), a number of projects (among these, The United Nations International Research and Training Institute for the Advancement of Women [INSTRAW]), and some short publications (Beemans, Huq, and Ward each have a short article on women in development in *Media, Democracy and Development*, 1988, edited by Peter Desbarats and Robert Henderson).

As for the metropolitan bias of early development research, Robert Chamber's *Rural Development: Putting the Last First* (1983) offers both a harsh critique of this phenomenon and some methodological alternatives that are worthy of careful examination for practitioners in the field.

6 This model is represented by the works of Walter Rostow (*The Stages in Economic Growth*, 1960), Everett Rogers's early publications (*Diffusion of Innovations*, 1963, and *Modernisation among Peasants: The Impact of Communications*, 1969 [with L. Svenning]), Daniel Lerner (*The Passing of Traditional Society*, 1958), Wilbur Schramm (*Mass Media and National Development*, 1964), Lucian Pye (*Communications and Political Development*, 1963), and Katz and Lazarsfeld (*Personal Influence*, 1955). I have chosen to outline the diffusionist paradigm in some detail because it is a primary reference point against which more holistic models have been evaluated.

7 In most research, "the giving society" is either Europe or the United States. For the purposes of this study, the giving society is equally one tier (or more) of the Canadian governments' administrative departments – be they at the federal, provincial, or territorial level.

8 Walter Rostow's *The Stages of Economic Growth* (1960) is the classic work describing the stages of take-off into capitalist economic structures.

9 The diffusionist model was most popular in the 1960s and early 1970s. In the mid-1970s, it was subjected to vigorous criticism, precipitated by Latin American scholars (Luis Beltran, in particular) and furthered by North Americans whose experience in the field provided them with documentary evidence that, in application, this theory was failing to achieve its promised results. In 1976, Everett Rogers edited a complete issue of *Communication Research* (vol. 3, no. 2, April 1976) on this international critique.

10 The free flow of information (i.e., the extension of the West's information empire) has been said to be the "political translation of this modernization" paradigm (Servaes 1986, 3).

11 Two Canadian examples of the communitarian paradigm are Harold Innis's work on the extension of empire – in particular, his calls for a proper balance between time (duration) and space (territory) binding biases in developing societies (1951a,b); and Gail Valaskakis's writings, which extend and apply the work of Innis to the Canadian North.

12 Among those criticized for ignoring the importance of indigenous cultures are included technocratic development agencies of capitalist persuasion, left-wing milieux and socially committed NGOs (non-governmental organizations) (Verhelst 1990, 156–7).

13 Although there is no broad consensus on exactly what is meant by internal colonialism, there is general agreement among internal colonial theorists that it has the following common features: political domination exercised by one sector of society over other sectors, segregation by residential location, and a hierarchy of different cultures and value systems. Robert J. Hind (1984) elaborates the con-

ditions as follows: "within a single nation state a relationship characteristic of the external relationships between imperialist states and their colonies" (544); "modes of political domination which assume a racial or ethnic and, therefore, a colonial rather than a class form (545); no indigenous institutions (547); and economic subjection, juridical incapacity, social inferiority of one racial or ethnic group within the society (548). For more details and a useful overview of the literature in this area, see Hind's "The Internal Colonial Concept" (1984).

14   Although their work is very interesting, it is not within the realm of this book to elaborate on its specific points. For further details of their work, as well as relevant texts of other less well-known authors in this field, see Nelson and Grossberg (eds), *Marxism and the Interpretation of Culture* (1988); Grossberg, Nelson, and Treichler (eds), *Cultural Studies* (1992); and Fergusun, Gever et al., *Out There: Marginalization and Contemporary Cultures* (1990). As well, the *Journal of Communication Inquiry* (Summer 1986, vol. 1, no. 2) put out a special edition dedicated to the work of Stuart Hall. Also, see Hall's "Signification, Representation, Ideology: Althusser and the Post-Structuralist Debates" (1995), in which he details his self-inscription within a signifying chain which constructs his ideological identity on the basis of the categories of colour, ethnicity, and race.

15   "Inter-cultural" or "cross-cultural" communications refer to a communications event or exchange in which the sender and receiver (whether individuals or groups) originate from at least two distinct cultural backgrounds, each of which operates from within a different set of value orientations. I use these terms interchangeably in this book.

CHAPTER TWO

1   The idea here was that "primitive" cultures on the verge of extinction could be saved by capturing their key rites, rituals, artifacts, practices, and documents and storing them in "safe" places such as museums, where they might be preserved for, and exhibited to, others.

2   Ignoring the advice of native film consultants is not just a thing of the past. A Cree communications colleague of mine was hired to be the cultural consultant for Bruce Beresford's *Black Robe* (1991), which was shot in Quebec. She complained constantly that the director was ignoring the depiction advice that she had been hired to provide and, in the end, begged him not to place her name in the credits – worried that some of the film's distortions would reflect back on her and prove embarrassing. Her request was also ignored.

3   The "Indian Princess" was the subject of an imaginative exhibit called *Princesses Indiennes et Cowgirls: Stéreotypes de la Frontière* put together by Gail Guthrie Valaskakis and Marilyn Burgess (23 May to 21 June 1992) at the Oboro Gallery

in Montreal. It has subsequently been displayed in numerous museums and galleries across Canada and is still "on the road."

4 Another extraordinary case that received a lot of attention in the early 1990s was not that of a First Nations person, but rather a "Congolese pygmy" called Ota Benga, who, from 1904 to 1906, became "Exhibit A in the monkey house at the Bronx Zoo." As Bradford and Blume (1992) explain: "To an era awestruck by anthropology and Social Darwinism, the razer-toothed [sic] pygmy was fair game, prodded by tourists, poked by would-be scientists, and displayed with primates in a cage" (back cover).

5 For excellent and detailed analyses of photographic and film materials on Arctic imagery, see the following two texts: Fienup-Riordan (1995) and King and Lidchi (1998).

6 Pitseolak was exceptional and singularly stands out as the first Inuit photographer. His photographs and life history are published in *People from Our Side* (1975), which he put together with the assistance of Dorothy Eber (oral biographer) and Ann Hanson (translator of Pitseolak's manuscript).

CHAPTER THREE

1 The Board of Broadcast Governors was the regulatory body that preceded the CRTC (Canadian Radio-television Commission), which came into being in 1968. Its name was modified in 1976 to Canadian Radio-television and Telecommunications Commission.

2 Some publications refer to twenty-three remote TV stations; others to twenty-four.

CHAPTER FOUR

1 By this time, native groups had already requested help in learning research methods by which needs could be identified and articulated in a format appropriate to the planning authorities.

2 During discussions regarding the two previous years at Rankin Inlet in 1976, Inuit residents recognized the complexity of this problem and "were not convinced that television should be blamed for all the changes in the community that the anthropologists had noticed" (ITC 1976, 32). Here is one man's explanation for the reduced interest in hunting that he began to notice at around the same time TV was introduced:

> I do not think it is because of television being introduced to the settlement.
> I think it is because of prospectors, and what not, going around in the areas where people want to go caribou hunting or fishing. Maybe the reason why

they do not go out often (to hunt) is because there are helicopters flying so low to scare the caribou or anything away ... I do not think that it is because of television that people are not going out. (ITC 1976, 32)

3 "Real Inuk" refers to a traditional hunter able to demonstrate those skills necessary to survive on the rugged terrain of the Arctic (Brody 1975, chapter 7).

4 Caron's research concluded that "children use a varied number of sources and that television had to be considered as one of the principal ones responsible for their cultural images especially in the case of unfamiliar groups that appeared on television" (Caron 1977, 3).

5 This was also confirmed by my own research and that of others. See Coldevin 1974, 1975, 1976, 1977; Dicks 1975, 1977; Granzberg et al. 1975, 1977, 1979; ITC Communications Study 1975–76; O'Connell 1975, 1976; NQIA 1974; Salisbury et al. 1976; Valaskakis 1975, 1976.

6 Other significant factors included the introduction of non-native religions, the relatively new wage-labour economy, settlement in villages instead of camps, contact with transient work populations from the South, dependency on store-bought foods and other products, and Southern oriented social control agencies.

7 *Animation from Cape Dorset* won special recognition at the Zagreb International Animation Film Festival in 1974.

8 It has never been established clearly why the NFB discouraged political and social topics. One can only speculate that it did not want to be associated with politicking in the North. Nor did it want to be perceived as having influenced the content of Inuit perceptions about the world.

9 Historical background is interesting with regard to these issues. In 1968, the National Film Board (*Challenge for Change*) had agreed to train a First Nations film crew at its headquarters in Montreal. Financially supported by the Company of Young Canadians (a federal government youth program), it represented a certain kind of leadership training that was targeted at a select group of male trainees. The effort was not the success it might have been because (a) trainees were removed from a stable cultural context in which they had the support of community support groups and (b) training took place in an economically unviable environment. In other words, no film jobs were easily made available to these trainees at the Film Board or elsewhere in the South after they had completed the program. Nor were many communications jobs available in native territories, since media was not a financially supported priority in the late 1960s. However, what the project succeeded in doing was organizing a small constituency group who applied newfound filmmaking skills to social and political activism in its home regions. It is interesting to note that many of these trainees went on to become political leaders.

After the dismantling of this project, some NFB personnel who had been involved recognized that any future long-term training for indigenous peoples would have to take place on their home territory. This information, however, was not necessarily shared with the Animation Department. In other words, Koenig's desire to establish workshops in the North and provide incentives such as salaries for trainees was based largely on his own intuitive sense.

10 The NFB rented half of the Inuit Tapirisat's (Eskimo Brotherhood of Canada) building to house the project. Although it was not intended as such, this turned out to be a good political move in that it enabled ITC workers and visitors to explore the workshop space and chart the progress of participants during their spare time. This unexpected interest helped to make filmmaking seem to be a credible undertaking within the community.

11 It was probably for this reason that the Cape Dorset workshop effort was abandoned so abruptly in 1975 in response to an Inuit/non-Inuit personal confrontation in the community.

12 In practice, it was often an outside filmmaker-cum-organizer who initiated projects, instead of local community leaders.

13 Also known as the Eskimo Brotherhood of Canada.

14 Before the implementation of the ACP, 900,000 people (in 260 communities) had never been served by CBC television and 400,000 people did not receive FM radio broadcasts, although they did receive short-wave. After the ACP installations were completed, 99 percent of the total Canadian population received both services in English, or French, or both (CBC 1974b, 3). The remaining underserved communities in the NWT and Yukon would eventually be connected as a result of financial support from the two territorial governments.

15 Igloolik eventually accepted television in 1984 – three years after the Inuit Broadcasting Corporation was formed and on the air. Ironically, although Igloolik was involved as a production centre for IBC, its residents could not receive programming because it was carried on CBC Northern Service (which they had earlier refused).

CHAPTER FIVE

1 The term "policy-ing" comes from Michael Dorland (1991, 266–73).

2 This poem was quoted in Waugh 1984, xv.

3 Although other First Peoples were involved in some of these experiments and projects, Inuit participants were the most organized in terms of how they used the data generated from the outcomes. It is for this reason that I mostly focus on the Inuit case as a representative exemplar. It is important to note, however, that, as the Inuit were developing and arguing their policy strategies with federal bureaucrats, other Native Communications Societies were undertaking parallel

efforts and working in convergence with the Inuit. I stick to the Inuit corpus of materials because I was personally involved with *their* efforts, thereby having the actual on-site experience of working with the people, the materials, the policy proposals, etc.

4 There are still some civil servants and politicians who are not convinced of the special status of First Peoples and treat them as if they *do* fall under the jurisdiction of the Multiculturalism Act. Fortunately, for current aboriginal broadcasters, most have been transferred away from positions where they might have participated in license decisions.

5 The Native Communications Program (NCP) of the Secretary of State, Native Citizens Directorate commenced on 10 December 1973. At this time, the federal government began to provide long-term funding to Native Communication Societies (NCSs) – the organizational bodies designated to take charge of communications for each First Peoples' region across the country – in order to carry out a variety of communication services for the benefit of native peoples. NCP remained in place until it lost 100 percent of its funding in a major budgetary cutback in February 1990. During its existence, funding was provided to twenty-one Native Communications Societies across the country in the North and in the South in order to assist in training, media workshops, audiovisual production, community radio activities, and special projects. When the NCP was cut in 1990, the South was left with no federal subsidization at all for native media activities.

6 More specifically, the NFB proposed to:
- improve upon and increase the number of films for native-language versioning and make more titles available on three-quarter-inch videocassette for easier distribution (NFB 1990, 8);
- encourage technical innovation in video hardware and formats (9);
- make maximum use of CBC Northern Service for regular broadcasting of NFB films (9);
- encourage more sponsored films on Northern subjects using native production centre resources (9) and on subjects suggested by Inuit groups (10);
- encourage standardization of video technology in conjunction with CBC (9);
- continue production support services at no cost (9);
- operate training support programs for Inuit production centres upon request (10).

7 It is disappointing that one of the more interesting experimental aspects of the Inukshuk project – the two-way interactive use of the satellite for community and cultural development purposes – was not considered a viable long-term investment by the government and hence never again received government funding.

8 The Commission went on to outline specifically what it expected Cancom to do:
    a. provide one video and two audio uplinks, in Northern locations suitable to native groups, for native-produced programming;
    b. substitute up to ten hours per week of native-produced television programming, to be distributed at appropriate times, on the satellite channels in the place of Southern-originated programming;
    c. appoint one native representative as a vice-president of the licensee company with direct responsibility to the Board of Directors of the company for the co-ordination and scheduling of native programming;
    d. consult with Native Communications Societies and assist their members to develop their own local productions (CRTC 1981b, 12).

9 At this time, there was still confusion on the part of some at the CRTC as to how native broadcasters should be differentiated from ethnic broadcasters. Clearly, some federal officials had not accepted the native argument for a special status based on ancestral land occupation rights.

10 This package included three US commercial stations and one non-commercial public television station (CRTC 1983, 4).

11 It is interesting to note how these figures were arrived at. A study of minority languages in Europe had determined that broadcasting in a "lesser-used language" – defined as one spoken by less than one million people – for a minimum of forty hours per week at peak times in the case of radio, and twenty to twenty-five hours in the case of television, would assure the preservation of that language (Alcock and O'Brien 1980, 3: 120). The Alcock and O'Brien study was one to which the federal government referred for background information when designing the NBP and NNBAP. Obviously, the Canadian government could not afford the costs involved in such an undertaking and, therefore, reduced the number of hours for native-language broadcasting production support on the assumption that it was better to fund a portion of this amount than nothing at all.

12 "FACTOR, The Foundation to Assist Canadian Talent on Records was founded in 1982 by CHUM Limited, Moffat Communications, and Rogers Broadcasting Limited, in conjunction with the Canadian Independent Record Producers Association (CIRPA) and the Canadian Music Publishers Association (CMPA). Standard Broadcasting merged its Canadian Talent Library (CTL) development fund with FACTOR's in 1985. As a private non-profit organization and an industrial strategy, FACTOR is dedicated to providing assistance toward the growth and development of the Canadian independent recording industry. The foundation administers the contributions of its 16 Sponsoring Broadcasters and 3 of the 6 components of the Department of Canadian Heritage's Sound Recording Development Program. Support is provided through 15 different programs.

The funds not only help Canadian recording artists and songwriters to get their material produced and their videos created, and to tour internationally, but they provide support for Canadian record labels, distributors, producers, engineers, directors – all those facets of the infrastructure which must be in place in order for artists and the Canadian independent recording industry to progress in the international marketplace. What was once an annual budget of $200,000 has grown to over $7 million" (excerpted from www.factor.ca/whatisfactor.html).

13 Completed and submitted in March 1990, the Annotated Bibliography only began getting circulated two years later, when the NNBAP group received a complementary copy from me and realized that it might be a valuable resource to other researchers in the field.

14 The Japanese reparation case involved compensatory funds for those who had been interned in concentration camps during the Second World War. My sources for this comment asked that I please maintain confidentiality about their names.

15 Other legislation includes Section 15, on Equality Rights in the Charter of Rights and Freedoms (1982), the Multiculturalism Act (1988), the Human Rights Act (1976–77), and the Employment Equity Act (1986).

16 While in the Yukon in the summer of 1990, I interviewed a former federal bureaucrat who strongly believed that the decision to cut the budgets was made on the basis of bureaucratic expediency rather than on concerted strategy. He believed that the minister had been compelled to cut a specific amount from his overall program budget. This person suspected that the minister just scanned his directory of sponsored programs and found that, if he cut the two *Native Communications Programs* and the *Women's Program*, it was the simplest way to equal the overall figure that was required to be chopped. So he did this without deliberation. After receiving approximately fourteen thousand protest letters from women's groups and individuals, the Women's Program was re-instated. A similar number of letters did not have the same effect for Native Communications.

CHAPTER SIX

1 The author's name is not identified anywhere in the document. I assume this is because the management wanted it to appear to represent Multilingual Television's position as an organization.

2 "The Inuit Circumpolar Conference (ICC) is the international organization representing approximately 145,000 Inuit living in the Arctic regions of Alaska, Canada, Greenland, and Chukotka, Russia. The principal goals of the ICC are:
   • to strengthen unity among Inuit of the circumpolar region;

- to promote Inuit rights and interests on an international level;
- to develop and encourage long-term policies that safeguard the Arctic environment;
- to seek full and active partnership in the political, economic, and social development of circumpolar regions.

The ICC General Assembly is held every three years, bringing together Inuit from across the Northern circumpolar region. Assembly delegates elect a president and an executive council, and develop policies and resolutions for the coming term. The General Assembly is integral to the organization as it allows for the discussion of common concerns, gives direction to the ICC and strengthens the cultural bonds between all Inuit." (Source: www.randburg.com/gr/inuitcir.html)

CHAPTER SEVEN

1 Due to financial constraints, TVNC was unable to subtitle most programs, but the visuals conveyed a lot of cultural information.

2 Especially notable was its video on the Mission School syndrome, which was informative, moving, and useful as a therapeutic tool for those who had been sent to religious schools in their childhood.

3 Another AIDS ad showed a full-screen domino game being set up with a musical background and no voiceover. As the set of dominoes was fully in place, a deep male voice explained: "Mary slept with Simeonie; Simeonie slept with Sarah; Sarah slept with Jonah. Jonah had AIDS." The visuals then took over as the third to the beginning of the long line of dominoes fell one after the other, like a house of cards. The voice then came on and said: "Be careful who you sleep with. Someone you sleep with can have AIDS. You never know who they slept with before you. When you make love with someone, you make love with everyone they ever slept with. Be careful. Use condoms. Your health and your life are valuable."

4 Please note that these were accurate figures in 1992 and are hard to track due to the mobility of the population.

CHAPTER EIGHT

1 To view a current schedule, visit the APTN home page at www.aptn.ca/Schedule/schedule_html.

2 It used to be possible to view APTN's channel locations within Canada at www.aptn.ca/chplace.html. However, the only way to find this information now is to check local newspaper listings or contact APTN via its Viewer Feedback Page: www.aptn.ca/Feedback/feedback_html.

3 To put this in a larger context, it must be said that, in the late 1990s and early 2000s, TV guides in general struggled to adjust their traditional formats to the rapidly changing and expanding array of television channels.

4 APTN's website describes each program in detail. It also sells bingo cards for *BAMM* (*Bingo and a Movie*).

5 Although what follows does not directly apply to the television sector, this anecdote – written by Fran Williams, the executive director of the OKalaKatiget Society in Labrador – gives us some sense of the popularity of radio among its listeners. One can easily speculate a similar financial commitment to aboriginal-language television.

> The OKalaKatiget Society staff will never forget April 23, 1997, the day our radio console board ceased to function and effectively disrupted our radio programming for an indefinite period. Our reaction was "What are we going to do now? Where will we get money to purchase a new one? Who will install it? After the initial shock to this crisis wore off, we started making plans to get it replaced. The numerous phone calls from the audiences in our communities wanting to know why we were not "on-air" and when programming will resume mobilized us into action. An interview about our problem on the CBC program "On the Go" resulted in some individuals and companies coming to our rescue. Torngait Services Incorporated, a 51% Inuit-owned company wanted to make a donation for the purchase of a new console. Air Labrador offered to fly technicians from the Island portion to Nain at no cost to the Society. The local hotel owner in Nain agreed to provide free accommodation to the technicians. These were the friends we didn't know we had and who came to our assistance when we needed financial help desperately! After an absence of 28 days, our radio programming was restored on May 27th.
>
> The unconditional support and assistance the companies gave us at that particular instance will not be forgotten by the Society, and more importantly, by those who were impacted the most, our audience. (Fran Williams, personal correspondence, 11 November 2003)

6 For more information on the Australian Aboriginal broadcasting situation, see the accumulated works of Michael Meadows, Helen Molnar, Faye Ginsburg, and Eric Michaels, some of which are listed in the bibliography.

7 Much of the Inuit contact and sharing of media information takes place at the Inuit Circumpolar Conference, which began in 1977 and meets bi-annually in one of the eight circumpolar states. The World Wide Web, which carries innumerable listserves and aboriginal media bulletin boards, chatrooms, etc., provides the basic links for other international contacts, out of which many collaborative projects may evolve.

CONCLUSION

1 As noted in chapter 8, there are still six Native Communication Societies in the North that don't yet qualify to produce television programming and are not provided with the funding to do so. This excludes them from participation in the national service of APTN. A more equitable funding distribution formula should be established to correct this unfairness. (See profiles of the Native Communication Societies in appendix C for further information.)

2 What follows is a brief overview of Weaver's examples of old and new paradigm thinking. She derived these from the Penner Report on Indian self-government (Penner 1983) and the Coolican Report (1986), which examined the obstacles to existing policy on comprehensive land claims, but they have relevance in the context of media policy paradigms as well.

   Old paradigm thinking: The relationship between First Nations and the state is a "convergent one where the two political entities are expected to meld into a unitary form."
   New paradigm thinking: "The relationship between the First Nations and the state (Canada) is a permanent organic relationship, one that will prevail into the distant future." This means that there is no concept of "termination" in these relations with the state and that the parallel forces respect each other's autonomy but seek peaceful co-existence.

   Old paradigm thinking: Culture, seen as fixed and either "traditional" or "real," was expected to erode under the forces of acculturation to the point where it would disappear.
   New paradigm thinking: Policy makers see First Nations as sustaining an evolving cultural co-existence with the Euro-Canadian cultural system.

   Old paradigm thinking: Traditional policy making procedures ignored First Nations opinions and initiatives.
   New paradigm thinking: Without removing the executive function and the government's responsibility, the more policies can be shaped to the satisfaction of both parties, the more effective they will be in securing public legitimacy and in addressing the self-defined needs of First Nations communities. This notion supports policy consultation, negotiation, and consent.

   Old paradigm thinking: The furthest that the government would go in terms of the empowerment of the First Nations was to allow them to become involved in advisory bodies. Joint management schemes were out of the question.
   New paradigm thinking: Joint management of resources and power sharing between First Nations and the State are desirable (Weaver 1990, 11–14).

Bibliography

Aboriginal Peoples Television Network. 1999. APTN Fact Sheet. Available at www. aptn.ca/facts.html.

– 1999. APTN Listings. Available at www.aptn.ca/chplace.html.

– 1999. APTN Schedule. Available at www.aptn.ca/schedule.html.

Acton, Lord. 1862. "Nationality." *The Home and Foreign Review* 1 (July 1862): 146–74.

Alcock, Antony and Terence O'Brien. 1980. "Policies to Support Radio and Television Broadcasting in the Lesser Used Languages of the European Community." (Consultative draft.) Northern Ireland: University of Ulster.

Alia, Valerie. 1999. *Un/Covering the North: News, Media, and Aboriginal People.* Vancouver: UBC Press.

– 1994. *Names, Numbers and Northern Policy: Inuit, Project Surname and the Politics of Identity.* Halifax: Fernwood Publishing.

– 1989. "Re-identifying the Inuit: Name Policies in the Canadian North." *Onomastica Canadiana* 71, no. 1 (June): 1-12.

Amin, Samir. 1989. *Eurocentrism.* New York: Monthly Review Press.

Anderson, Alan B. and James S. Frideres. 1981. *Ethnicity in Canada – Theoretical Perspectives.* Toronto: Butterworths.

Anderson, Benedict. 1983. *Imagined Communities: Reflections on the Origin and Spread of Nationalism.* London: Verso.

Ang, Ien. 1985. *Watching Dallas: Soap Opera and the Melodramatic Imagination.* London: Methuen.

Appadurai, Arjun. 1990. "Disjuncture and Difference in the Global Cultural Economy." *Global Culture: Nationalism, Globalization and Modernity*, ed. Mike Featherstone, 295–310. London: Sage Publications.

Appignanesi, Lisa, ed. 1984. *Culture and the State.* London: Institute of Contemporary Arts.

Applebaum, L. and Hébert J. (Department of Communications). 1982. *Federal Cultural Policy Review Committee. Summary of Briefs and Hearings.* Ottawa: Minister of Supply and Services.

Armitage, Peter. 1992a. "Les Premières Nations, les médias et le pouvoir de l'opinion publique." *Anthropologie et Société* 16, no. 3: 77-101.

– 1992b. "First Nations, Media, and the Power of Public Opinion." (Unpublished draft.)

Armour, Leslie. 1981. *The Idea of Canada and the Crisis of Community.* Ottawa: Steel Rail Publishing.

Ashcroft, Bill, Gareth Griffiths, and Helen Tiffin. 1998. *Key Concepts in Post-Colonial Studies.* London: Routledge.

Atwood, Margaret. 1972. *Survival: A Thematic Guide to Canadian Literature.* Toronto: Anansi Press.

Aun, Karl. 1980. "A Critique of the Nation-State." *Unity in Diversity* (The Proceedings of the Interdisciplinary Research Seminar at Wilfrid Laurier University), eds Nicolas A. Nyiri and Toivo Miljan. Waterloo: Wilfrid Laurier University Press.

Baran, Paul A. 1957. *The Political Economy of Growth.* New York: Monthly Review Press.

Baudrillard, Jean. 1973. "Requiem for the Media." *Toward a Critique of the Political Economy of the Sign.* St Louis: Telos Press, 164–84.

Beltran, Luis. 1980. "Farewell to Aristotle: 'Horizontal' Communication." Document prepared for UNESCO: International Commission for the Study of Communication Problems.

– 1976. "National Communication Policies in Latin America: A Glance at the First Steps." Paper presented at the International Conference on Communications Policy and Planning for Development (April 5–10) at East-West Centre, Honolulu.

Bennett, Tony. 1993. "Useful Culture." *Relocating Cultural Studies: Developments in Theory and Research*, eds Valda Blundell, John Shepherd, and Ian Taylor. London: Routledge.

Bennett, Tony, Graham Martin, Colin Mercer, and Janet Woollacott, eds. 1981. *Culture, Ideology and Social Process: A Reader.* London: The Open University Press.

Berger, Peter L., and Thomas Luckmann. 1967. *The Social Construction of Reality: A Treatise in the Sociology of Knowledge.* New York: Anchor Books.

Berkhofer Jr, Robert F. 1979. *The White Man's Indian: Images of the American Indian from Columbus to the Present.* New York: Vintage Publications.

Berrigan, Frances J. 1977. *Access: Some Western Models of Community Media.* Belgium: UNESCO.

Berton, Pierre. 1975. *Hollywood's Canada: The Americanization of Our National Image.* Toronto: McClelland and Stewart.

– 1954. "The Mysterious North." *MacLean's Magazine* (15 November): 11–19.

Bhabha, Homi K. 1994. *The Location of Culture.* London: Routledge.

– 1990. *Nation and Narration.* London: Routledge.

– 1989. "Of Mimicry and Man: The Ambivalence of Colonial Discourse." *October* 28 (Spring).

– 1983. "The Other Question ... Homi K. Bhabha Reconsiders the Stereotype and Colonial Discourse." *Screen* 24 (November/December).

Bird, Roger, ed. 1988. *Documents of Canadian Broadcasting*. Ottawa: Carleton University Press.

Black, Ayanna. 1989. "Recognizing Racism." *Fuse* 12, no. 5 (April/May): 27–36.

Bordo, Jonathan. 1992–93. "Jack Pine – Wilderness Sublime or the Erasure of the Aboriginal Presence from the Landscape." *Journal of Canadian Studies/Revue d'études Canadiennes* 27, no. 4 (Hiver/Winter): 98–128.

Boulay, Robert, J.-P. Lamonde, and G. Larochelle. 1983. *Communications Media Development Plan for the Native Communities*. Ministère des Communications, Gouvernement du Québec.

Bourdieu, Pierre. 1979. "Public Opinion Does Not Exist." *Vol 1: Capitalism, Imperialism*, eds Armand Mattelart and Seth Siegelaub, 124–30. New York: International General.

Bradford, Philips Verner and Harvey Blume. 1992. *Ota Benga: The Pygmy in the Zoo*. New York: Delta Books.

Brody, Hugh. 1987. *Living Arctic: Hunters of the Canadian North*. Toronto: Douglas and McIntyre.

– 1975. *The People's Land: Whites and the Eastern Arctic*. New York: Penguin Books.

Brooks, Stephen. 1989. *Public Policy in Canada: An Introduction*. Toronto: McClelland and Stewart.

Browne, Donald. R. 1996. *Electronic Media and Indigenous Peoples: A Voice of Our Own?* Ames: Iowa State University Press.

Burgess, Robert. 1984. *In the Field: An Introduction to Field Research*. London: George Allen & Unwin.

Canada Law Reports. 1939. "Supreme Court of Canada Decision – Reference Re: Whether Eskimos Are Indians. Rendered 5 April 1939." *Documenting Canada: A History of Modern Canada in Documents*, eds Dave De Brou and Bill Waise, 351–5. Saskatoon: Fifth House Publishers, 1992.

Canadian Association of Broadcasters. 1988. *A Broadcaster's Guide to Canada's Cultural Mosaic (Programming Opportunities and Community Relations)*. Ottawa: CAB.

Canadian Council on Social Development. 1987. *A Guide to the Charter for Equality-Seeking Groups*. Ottawa: Court Challenges Program of the CCSD.

Canadian Human Rights Commission. 1988. *The Right to Be Different – Human Rights in Canada: An Assessment/L'égalité dans la différence – Les droits de la personne au Canada: un bilan*. Ottawa: Minister of Supply and Services.

Caplan, G.L. and F. Sauvageau. 1986. *Report of the Task Force on Broadcasting Policy*. Ottawa: Minister of Supply and Services.

Careless, J.M.S. 1969. "'Limited Identities' in Canada." *The Canadian Historical Review*, no. 191 (March): 1–10.

Carey, James W. 1989. *Communication as Culture: Essays on Media and Society.* Boston: Unwin Hyman.

– 1975. "Canadian Communication Theory: Extensions and Interpretations of Harold Innis." *Studies in Canadian Communications,* eds G.J. Robinson and Donald F. Theall. Montreal: McGill University Program in Communications.

Caron, André. 1977. "The Impact of Television on Inuit Children's Cultural Images." Paper presented at the International Communications Association Conference (June), Berlin.

CBC. 19 October 1998. *Intervention Letter to* CRTC. Ottawa.

– 1980. *Submission to the 10 March* CRTC *Hearing,* "Extension of Service to Northern and Remote Communities: Pay-Television and Canadian Broadcasting."

– 1979. *Radio and Television in the Keewatin District of the Northwest Territories: A Survey of Listening and Viewing Behaviour in Rankin Inlet, Baker Lake and Eskimo Point.* Ottawa: CBC Research Department.

– 1978a. "Background and Historical Mileposts in the Operations of CBC Northern Service." Ottawa: CBC Northern Service.

– 1978b. "The CBC – A Perspective: Submission to the CRTC in Support of Applications for Renewal of Network Licenses." Ottawa: CBC.

– 1974a. "Material in Support of CBC Applications for Renewal of Network Licenses - Northern Service." Ottawa: CRTC Examination Files (18 February).

– 1974b. *ACP Information Meeting Notes* (11 July). Ottawa: CBC.

– 1972a. "Report on the Frontier Package Television Service in the North of Canada." 17 March. Prepared for the Embassy of Denmark. Ottawa: CBC Northern Service.

– 1972b. *CBC's Use of Anik, Canada's Domestic Communications Satellite.* Ottawa: CBC Northern Service.

– 1972c. *CBC: A Brief History and Background.* Ottawa: CBC Information Services.

– 1963–64; 1964–65; 1967–68; 1968–69; 1971–72. *Annual Reports of the Canadian Broadcasting Corporation.* Ottawa: CBC.

CCTA (Canadian Cable Television Association). 12 November 1998. "Intervention Letter to CRTC."

Chambers, Robert. 1983. *Rural Development: Putting the Last First.* New York: Longman.

Chanter, Elaine R. 1990. "Mass Media, Development, and Indigenous People: the Case of Australia." Paper presented to the Annual Convention of the International Communication Association (June), Dublin, Ireland.

Charland, Maurice. "Technological Nationalism." *Canadian Journal of Political and Social Theory – Mediascape: The Postmodern Scene* 10, nos. 1–2 (Winter/Spring): 196–220.

Chiasson, Rod and Rachelle Chiasson. 1977. *Ikarut Silakkut: Bridges-over-the-Air.* Included in Toronto: Multilingual Television Submission to the CRTC (May 24).

Chrétien, Jean. 1968. "The New North." Address delivered to The Vancouver Institute, University of British Columbia (16 November). Ottawa: Department of Indian Affairs and Northern Development.

Churchill, Ward. 1992. "I Am Indigenist: Notes on the Ideology of the Fourth World." *Z Papers* 1, no. 3, (July–September): 8–22.

– and M. Annette Jaimes, eds. 1992. *Fantasies of the Master Race: Literature, Cinema and the Colonization of American Indians*. Monroe: Common Courage Press.

Chwialkowska, Luiza. 23 February 1999. "Coming Soon to Your Living Room." *National Post*, A-3.

Clastres, Pierre. 1988. "On Ethnocide." *Art and Text*, no. 28 (March–May): 51–8.

– 1987. *Society against the State*. New York: Zone Books.

Clifford, James. 1988. *The Predicament of Culture: Twentieth-Century Ethnography, Literature, and Art*. Cambridge: Harvard University Press.

– 1986. "Introduction." *Writing Culture: The Poetics and Politics of Ethnography*, J. Clifford and George E. Marcus. 1986, 2–26. Berkeley: University of California Press.

Coates, Kenneth S. and William R. Morrison, eds. 1989. *Interpreting Canada's North: Selected Readings*. Toronto: Copp Clark Pitman.

Cobb, Chris. 23 February 1999. "Aboriginal TV Goes Canada-Wide." *The Montreal Gazette*: F-5.

Cohen, Anthony P. 1985. *The Symbolic Construction of Community*. London: Tavistock Publications.

Cohen, Phil. 1987. *Racism and Popular Culture: A Cultural Studies Approach (Working Paper, no. 9)*. London: University of London Institute of Education.

Coldevin, Gary O. 1977a. "Anik I and Isolation: Television in the Lives of Canadian Eskimos." *Journal of Communication* 27, no. 4: 145–53.

– 1977b. "Developmental Effects of Television Via Satellite on Canadian Inuit Heads of Households." Research paper, Concordia University (June).

Collins, Richard. 1990. *Culture, Communication and National Identity: The Case of Canadian Television*. Toronto: University of Toronto Press.

Comaroff, John and Jean Comaroff. 1992. *Ethnography and the Historical Imagination*. Boulder: Westview Press.

Condon, John and Fathi Yousef. 1975. *An Introduction to Intercultural Communication*. New York: Bobbs-Merrill Series.

Cook, G.R. 1967. "Canadian Centennial Celebrations." *International Journal* 12 (Autumn).

Council for Yukon Indians. 1988–89. *Cross Cultural Strategies: A Collection of Background Information for Teachers of Indian Students*. Whitehorse: CYI-Curriculum Development Program and Social Programs.

Cowan, Andrew. 1971. *Report* (25 February). Ottawa: CBC Northern Service.

– 1970. "The Social Impact of Broadcasting in the North." Speech prepared for the Conference on Northern Communications (9–11 September), Yellowknife, NWT. Ottawa: CBC Northern Service Information Office.

– 1969. "The Medium and the Message." Address delivered to the Third Northern Resources Conference (10 April), Whitehorse, Yukon Territories. Ottawa: CBC Northern Service Information Office.

CRTC. 1999. *Decision CRTC 99–42* (22 February).

– 1993. "TVNC Presentation." *Public Notice CRTC 1992-13* (1 March).

– 1991. "Television Northern Canada Incorporated." *Decision CRTC 91-826* (28 October).

– 1990a. "Review of Native Broadcasting – A Proposed Policy." *Public Notice CRTC 1990-12* (2 February).

– 1990b. "Native Broadcasting Policy." *Public Notice CRTC 1990–1989* (20 September).

– 1989. "Review of Northern Native Broadcasting: Call for Comments." *Public Notice CRTC 1989-53* (26 May).

– 1985. "A Broadcasting Policy Reflecting Canada's Linguistic and Cultural Diversity." *Public Notice CRTC 1985-139* (4 July).

– 1984. *Public Notice CRTC 1984-310.*

– 1983. *Cancom License Decision 83-126* (27 April).

– 1981a. *Balance in Broadcasting – A Report on a Seminar Held 16–17 January 1981 in Hull, Quebec.* Ottawa: Supply and Services Canada.

– 1981b. *Cancom Decision. CRTC 81-252* (14 April).

– 1980. *The 1980's – A Decade of Diversity: Broadcasting Satellites and Pay-TV. Report of the Committee on Extension of Service to Northern and Remote Communities.* Ottawa: Canadian Government Publishing House.

– 1979. "Renewal of the CBC's Television and Radio Network Licenses." *Decision CRTC 79-320* (April 30).

– 1975. "Application for CBC Northern Television Service in Cambridge Bay and Coppermine, NWT." *Decision CRTC 75-516* (October 28).

– 1974. License Renewal for CKQN FM in Baker Lake, NWT. *Decision CRTC 14-483* (20 December).

– 1973. *Radio Broadcasting in the Yukon and Northwest Territories.* Ottawa: CRTC.

– 1970. "New License Application for an AM Radio Station in Tuktoyaktuk, NWT Operating at 600 kh and 1000 watts of Power Day and Night." *Decision CRTC 70-114* (15 June).

Dahlgren, Peter and Colin Sparks, eds. 1991. *Communication and Citizenship: Journalism and the Public Sphere in the New Media Age.* London: Routledge.

Dahlie, Jorgen and Tissa Fernando, eds. 1981. *Ethnicity, Power and Politics in Canada.* Toronto: Methuen Publications.

De Brou, Dave and Bill Waise, eds. 1992. *Documenting Canada: A History of Modern Canada in Documents*. Saskatoon: Fifth House Publishers.

de Certeau, Michel. 1986. *Heterologies: Discourse on the Other*. Minneapolis: University of Minnesota Press.

de Certeau, Michel. 1984. *The Practice of Everyday Life*. Translated by Steven Rendall. Berkeley: University of California Press.

Department of the Secretary of State of Canada. 1992. *Projections of Canada's Aboriginal Population: 1986–2011*. Ottawa: Native Citizens Directorate.

Desbarats, Peter and Robert Henderson, eds. 1988. *Encounter '87: Media, Democracy and Development*. London: The University of Western Ontario, the Graduate School of Journalism.

Dewey, John. 1927. *The Public and Its Problems*. Athens: Swallow Press.

DIAND (Department of Indian Affairs and Northern Development). 1969. *[The White Paper] Statement of the Government of Canada on Indian Policy 1969*. Ottawa: Queen's Printer.

Dicks, Dennis. 1977. "From Dog Sled to Dial Phone: A Cultural Gap?" *Journal of Communication* 27, no. 4: 120–9.

di Norcia, Vincent. 1984. "Ideas of Canada." *Canadian Journal of Political and Social Theory* 8, no. 3 (Fall): 146–50.

Diubaldo, Richard. 1981. "The Role of the Arctic Islands in the Defense of Canada." *A Century of Canada's Arctic Islands: 1880–1980*, ed. Morris Zaslow, 93–110. Ottawa: Royal Society of Canada.

Dodd, Carley H. 1982. *Dynamics of Intercultural Communication*. Dubuque: William C. Brown Company Publishers.

Dominguez, Virginia. 1987. "Of Other Peoples: Beyond the 'Salvage' Paradigm." *Discussions in Contemporary Culture*, ed. Hal Foster, 1: 131–7. Seattle: Bay Press.

Dorfman A. and A. Mattelart. 1975. *How to Read Donald Duck: Imperialist Ideology in the Disney Comic*. New York: International General Editions.

Dorland, Michael. 1991. "The Discursive Economy of the Emergence of the Canadian Feature Film: Discourses of Dependency and the Governmentalization of a Displaced National Cinema, 1957–1968." Doctoral dissertation, Concordia University.

Dosman, Edgar J. 1972. *Indians: The Urban Dilemma*. Toronto: McClelland and Stewart.

Doxtater, Deborah. 1988. *Fluffs and Feathers: An Exhibit on the Symbols of Indianness – A Resource Guide*. Brantford: Woodland Cultural Centre.

Driscoll, Dan. 1972. "Can We Evaluate Challenge for Change?" *Access: Challenge for Change Newsletter*, no. 10: 22–3.

Dutt, Shyla. 1988. *Canada's Cultural and Racial Diversity – A Challenge for Broadcasters: A Background Paper*. Prepared for The Forum on Multiculturalism and Broadcasting (May).

Dyck, Noel and Waldram, James B. 1993. *Anthropology, Public Policy and Native Peoples in Canada*. Montreal: McGill-Queen's University Press.

Editorial. 1999. "Consumers Should Decide What They Want to Watch." *Vancouver Province*, 2 September, A-36.

Editorial. 1999. "The Native Media." *The Globe and Mail*, 24 February, A-16.

Elberg, Nathan. 1984. "In Search of ... Real Inuit." Unpublished paper presented at Fourth Inuit Studies Conference (November 15–18), Montreal.

Enzensberger, Hans Magnus. 1974. "Constituents of a Theory of the Media." *The Consciousness Industry: On Literature, Politics and the Media*. New York: The Seabury Press.

Escobar, Arturo. 1992. "Imagining a Post-Development Era? Critical Thought, Development and Social Movements." *Social Text* 10, no. 31/32: 20–56.

Explore North. 1999. *The Birth of A P T N Milestones in Television Broadcasting in Northern Canada*. Available at www.explorenorth.com/library/weekly/aao91799.htm

Fabian, Johannes. 1983. *Time and the Other: How Anthropology Makes Its Object*. New York: Columbia University Press.

Featherstone, Mike, ed. 1990. *Global Culture: Nationalism, Globalization and Modernity*. London: Sage Publications.

Feaver, Charles. 1976. "The Politics of the Introduction of Television in the Canadian North: A Study of the Conflict Between National Policies and Needs of Native People in the North." M A thesis, Carleton University, Ottawa.

Fienup-Riordan, Ann. 1995. *Freeze Frame: Alaska Eskimos in the Movies*. Seattle: University of Washington Press.

Fisher, Robin and Kenneth Coates, eds. 1988. *Out of the Background: Readings on Canadian Native History*. Toronto: Copp Clark Pitman.

Fiske, John. 1986. "Television: Polysemy and Popularity." *Critical Studies in Mass Communication* 3, no. 4 (December): 1–18.

Flaherty, Robert. 1980. *Photographer/Filmmaker – The Inuit 1910–1922*. Vancouver: The Vancouver Art Gallery.

Foster, Hal, ed. 1987. *Discussions in Contemporary Culture*, no. 1 Seattle: Bay Press.

Foucault, Michel. 1980. *Power/Knowledge: Selected Interviews and Other Writings 1972–1977*. Brighton: The Harvester Press.

Francis, Daniel. 1992. *The Imaginary Indian: The Image of the Indian in Canadian Culture*. Vancouver: Arsenal Pulp Press.

Franco, Jean. 1988. "Beyond Ethnocentrism: Gender, Power, and the Third-World Intelligentsia." *Marxism and the Interpretation of Culture*, eds Cary Nelson and Larry Grossberg. Chicago: University of Illinois Press.

Frank, André Gunder. 1970. "The Development of Underdevelopment." *Imperialism and Underdevelopment: A Reader*, ed. Robert I. Rhodes. New York: Monthly Review Press.

– 1970. *Latin America: Underdevelopment or Revolution; Essays on the Development of Underdevelopment and the Immediate Enemy.* New York: Monthly Review Press.

– 1967. *Capitalism and Underdevelopment in Latin America; Historical Studies of Chile and Brazil.* New York: Monthly Review Press.

Fraser, Nancy. 1990. "Rethinking the Public Sphere." *Social Text*, no. 25/26: 56–80.

– 1989. *Unruly Practices: Power, Discourse and Gender in Contemporary Social Theory.* Minneapolis: University of Minnesota Press.

Freire, Paulo. 1973. *Education for Critical Consciousness.* New York: The Seabury Press.

Friar, Ralph E. and Natasha A. Friar. 1972. *The Only Good Indian ... The Hollywood Gospel.* New York. Drama Book Specialists/Publishers,

Frideres, James and Rasporich, Anthony, eds. 1990. "Special Issue – First Nations: The Politics of Change and Survival." *Canadian Ethnic Studies/Etudes ethniques au Canada* 22, no. 3.

Frye, Northrop. 1971. *The Bush Garden: Essays on the Canadian Imagination.* Toronto: Anansi Press.

Garnham, Nicholas. 1987. "Concepts of Culture: Public Policy and the Cultural Industries." *Cultural Studies* 1, no. 1 (January): 23–37.

– 1986. "The Media and the Public Sphere." *Communicating Politics: Mass Communications and the Political Process*, eds Peter Golding, Graham Murdock, and Philip Schlesinger. New York: Leicester University Press.

– 1985. "Communication Technology and Policy." *Mass Communication Review Yearbook*, volume 5, eds Michael Gurevitch and Mark R. Levy, 65–74. Beverly Hills: Sage Publications, 1985.

Gedalof, Robin, ed. n.d. *Paper Stays Put: A Collection of Inuit Writing.* Edmonton: Hurtig Publishers.

Geddes, Carol. 1986. *Community Visions – Networking Film and Video in the 80's and Beyond.* Native People (June). Montreal: National Film Board of Canada.

Geertz, Clifford. 1986. "The Uses of Diversity." *Michigan Quarterly Review* (Winter): 105–23.

– 1983. *Local Knowledge: Further Essays in Interpretive Anthropology.* New York: Basic Books Inc.

– 1973. *The Interpretation of Cultures.* New York: Basic Books Inc.

Gerbner, George and Marsha Siefert, eds. 1984. *World Communications: A Handbook.* New York: Longman.

Gibbon, John Murray. 1938. *Canadian Mosaic: The Making of a Northern Nation.* Toronto: McClelland and Stewart.

Ginsburg, Faye. 1993. "Aboriginal Media and the Australian Imaginary." *Public Culture* 5 (Spring): 1–20.

– 1992. "Indigenous Media: Faustian Contract or Global Village?" *Rereading Cultural Anthropology*, ed. George E. Marcus. Durham: Duke University Press.

Golding, Peter, Graham Murdock, and Philip Schlesinger, eds. 1986. *Communicating Politics: Mass Communications and the Political Process*. New York: Leicester University Press.

Gordon, Milton. 1964. *Assimilation in American Life: The Role of Race, Religion, and National Origins*. New York: Oxford University Press.

Gormley, John, (MP and Chairman of Committee). 1988. *A Broadcasting Policy for Canada: A Report of the Standing Committee on Communications and Culture* (June). Ottawa.

Government of Canada. 1991. *Broadcasting Act*, June 4.

– 1988. *Government Response to the Fifteenth Report of the Standing Committee on Communications and Culture: A Broadcasting Policy for Canada*. Ottawa. June.

– 1986. *Living Treaties: Lasting Agreements – Report of the Task Force to Review Comprehensive Claims Policy*. Contributor Murray Coolican. Ottawa: Department of Indian Affairs and Northern Development.

– 1983a. *The Northern Broadcasting Policy – A News Release*. March 10.

– 1983b. *Discussion Paper: Northern Broadcasting*. Ottawa: Minister of Communications, Minister of Indian and Northern Affairs, Secretary of State. February 18.

– 1983c. *Indian Self-Government in Canada: Report of the Special Committee*. Contributor Keith Penner. Ottawa: Published under the authority of the Speaker of the House of Commons by the Queen's Printer for Canada.

– 1982. *Federal Cultural Policy Review Committee. Summary of Briefs and Hearings*. Ottawa: Minister of Supply and Services.

– 1971. Telecommission Study 8 (C): Contributions 1–4. Ottawa: Department of Communications.

– 1969. *Statement of the Government of Canada on Indian Policy – Presented to the First Session of the Twenty-eighth Parliament by the Honourable Jean Chrétien, Minister of Indian Affairs and Northern Development*. Ottawa.

– 1967–68. *Broadcasting Act*, c.25, s.1.

– 1965. *Report of the Committee on Broadcasting – Fowler Committee*. Ottawa: Queen's Printer.

– 1957. *Royal Commission on Broadcasting: Report – Fowler Commission*. Ottawa: Queen's Printer.

– 1876. *Indian Act*.

Grantzberg, Gary. 1982. "Television as Storyteller: the Algonkian Indians of Central Canada." *Journal of Communication* 32, no. 1 (Winter).

Gray, Oliver. 1973. "Minorities and the New Media: Exclusion and Access." *Communications Technology and Social Policy: Understanding the New "Cultural Revolution,"* eds George Gerbner, Larry P. Gross, and William H. Melody. New York: John Wiley and Sons.

Green, Rayna. 1988. "The Tribe Called Wannabee: Playing Indian in America and Europe." *Folklore* 99, no. 1: 30–55.

Grierson, John. "Memo to Michelle – About Decentralizing the Means of Production." *Access*, no. 8 (1972): 4–5.

Grossberg, Lawrence. 1987. "Critical Theory and the Politics of Empirical Research." *Mass Communication Review Yearbook* 6, 86–106. London: Sage Publications.

Guly Christopher. 1991–92. "First Nations Network: Television Northern Canada Links the Natives of the Arctic." *Broadcaster* (December/January).

Habermas, Jurgen. 1979. "The Public Sphere." *Communication and Class Struggle Vol. 1: Capitalism, Imperialism*, eds Armand Mattelart and Seth Siegelaub, 198–201. New York: International General.

– 1970. *Toward a Rational Society: Student Protest, Science, and Politics*. Beacon Press: Boston.

Hall, Stuart. 1992. "Race, Culture, and Communications: Looking Backward and Forward at Cultural Studies." *Rethinking MARXISM* 5, no. 1 (Spring): 10–18.

– 1989. "Cultural Identity and Cinematic Representation." *Framework*, no. 36: 68–81.

– 1985. "Signification, Representation, Ideology: Althusser and the Post-Structuralist Debates." *Critical Studies in Mass Communication* 2, no. 1 (June): 91–114.

– and David Held. 1989. "Citizens and Citizenship." *New Times: The Changing Face of Politics in the 1990s*, eds Stuart Hall and Martin Jacques, 173–90. London: Lawrence & Wishart.

Hamelin, Louis-Edmond. 1984. "Managing Canada's North: Challenges and Opportunities: Rapporteur's Summary and Comments." *Canadian Public Administration/Administration Publique du Canada* 27, no. 2 (Summer): 165–81.

– 1979. *Canadian Nordicity: It's Your North, Too*. Montreal: Harvest House.

Hamelink, Cees J. 1984. *Cultural Autonomy in Global Communication*. Paris: UNESCO.

Hannerz, Ulf. 1989. "Culture Between Center and Periphery: Toward a Macroanthropology." *Ethnos* 54, no. 3–4: 200–16.

Hardt, Hanno, Stig Hadenius, L.S. Harms et al. 1977. "Communication Policy and the Right to Communicate." Paper presented at the International Congress of Communications Sciences (June), West Berlin.

Harms, L.S. and Jim Richstad. 1977. *Evolving Perspectives on the Right to Communicate*. Honolulu: East-West Communication Institute.

Harper, Kenn. 1986. *Give Me My Father's Body: The Life of Minik, the New York Eskimo*. Iqaluit: Blacklead Books.

Hartley, John and Alan McKee. 2001. *The Indigenous Public Sphere: The Reporting and Reception of Indigenous Issues in the Australian Media, 1994–1997*. London: Oxford University Press.

Hauser, Gerard A. 1987. "Features of the Public Sphere." *Critical Studies in Mass Communication* 49: 423–43.

Hénaut, Dorothy Todd. 1971–72. "Powerful Catalyst." *Access*, no. 7, 3–7.

Henderson, Hazel. 1974. "Information and the New Movements for Citizenship Participation." *Annals of the American Academy of Political and Social Sciences*, March.

Herringer, Jay. 1988. "Canadian Satellite Basics: Regulations Confront Northern Native Communities." *Cinema Canada* 153 (June): 19–21.

Hilger, Michael. 1986. *The American Indian in Film*. London: The Scarecrow Press Inc.

Hill, C.W. and G. Valaskakis. 1979. *An Assessment of Project Naalakvik I*. Sugluk: Taqramiut Nipingat Inc.

Hind, Robert J. 1984. "The Internal Colonial Concept." *Society for the Comparative Study of Society and History* 26: 543–68.

Hindley, Patricia, Gail M. Martin, and Jean McNulty. 1977. *The Tangled Net: Basic Issues in Canadian Communications*. Vancouver: J.J. Douglas Ltd.

Hirschman, Albert O. 1982. *Shifting Involvements: Private Interest and Public Action*. Princeton: Princeton University Press.

Hodge, Robert. "Aboriginal Truth and White Media: Eric Michaels Meets the Spirit of Aboriginalism." *Continuum* 3, no. 2: 201–25.

Hodgins, B.V. and Hobbs, M., eds. 1985. *Nastawagan: The Canadian North by Canoe and Snowshoe*. Toronto: Betelgeuse.

Hogarth, David. 1992. "Networks of Record: All-News Television and Public Affairs Coverage in North America." *Canadian Journal of Communication Special Edition – Turbulence in the International Mediascape* 17, no. 4 (Autumn): 479–92.

Honigmann, John J. and I. Honigmann. 1965. Eskimo Townsmen. Ottawa: Canadian Research Centre for Anthropology, St Paul University.

hooks, bell. 1992. "Representing Whiteness in the Black Imagination." *Cultural Studies*, eds Lawrence Grossberg, Cary Nelson, and Paula Treichler, 338–46. New York: Routledge.

Hothi, J. 1980. *Availability of Television in Rural and Remote Areas* (17 April). Ottawa: Department of Communications.

Hudson, Heather. 1985. *The Need for Native Broadcasting in Northern Canada: A Review of Research*. Ottawa: Department of Secretary of State.

– 1977a. "The Role of Radio in Northern Canada." *Journal of Communication* 27, no. 4: 130–9.

– 1977b. *Northern Airwaves: A Study of the CBC Northern Service*. Ottawa: Keewatin Communications Studies Institute.

Hughes Aircraft Ltd. 1972. *Anik Launch Handbook*. Pamphlet. California: Hughes Aircraft Company.

Innis, Harold Adams. 1951a. *Empire and Communications*. Toronto: University of Toronto Press.

– 1951b. *The Bias of Communication*. Toronto: University of Toronto Press.

Inuit Circumpolar Conference. 1992. *Principles and Elements for a Comprehensive Arctic Policy*.

Inuit Tapirisat of Canada. 1981. "ITC Project." *List of Events in Northern Broadcasting*. February.

– 1980. "Conditional Application by ITC on Behalf of the Inuit Broadcasting Corporation (A Proposed Non-Profit Corporation) for a Network Television License to Operate an Inuit Television Service and Intervention Statement Regarding License Applications for Extension of Service to Remote and Underserved Communities." 17 December

– 1977. "Inuit Tapirisat's Final Argument Before the CRTC Regarding Bell Canada's Proposed Rate Increase." *Submission to the CRTC Hearing, 19 April, Hull*.

– 1976. *Inuit Today* 4, no. 9; 5, no. 7. Ottawa: ITC.

Ipellie, Alootook. 1992. "The Colonization of the Arctic." *Indigena: Contemporary Native Perspectives*, eds Gerald McMaster and Lee-Ann Martin. Toronto: Douglas and McIntyre.

– n.d. *The Inukshuk Project*. Pamphlet. Ottawa: ITC.

Jessop, Bob. 1990. *Putting the Capitalist State in Its Place*. Southport: Polity Press.

Jhappan, C. Radha. 1992. "Global Community?: Supranational Strategies of Canada's Aboriginal Peoples." *The Journal of Indigenous Studies/La Revue des Etudes Indigènes* 3, no. 1 (Winter): 59–97.

– 1990. "Indian Symbolic Politics: The Double-Edged Sword of Publicity." *Canadian Ethnic Studies/Etudes Ethniques au Canada* 12, no. 3: 19–39.

Journal of Communication Inquiry – Special Edition on Stuart Hall 10, no. 2 (Summer 1986).

Kaplan, E. Ann. 1989. "Aborigines, Film and Moffatt's 'Night Cries – A Rural Tragedy': An Outsider's Perspectives." *The Olive Pink Society Bulletin* 2: 13–17.

Karim H. Karim. 1993. "Constructions, Deconstructions, and Reconstructions: Competing Canadian Discourses on Ethnocultural Terminology." *Canadian Journal of Communication* 18, no. 2 (Spring): 197–218.

Katz, Elihu. 1987. "Communications Research Since Lazarsfeld." *Public Opinion Quarterly* 51, no. 4, part 2 (Winter): S25–S45.

– 1980. "On Conceptualizing Media Effects." *Studies in Communication* 1: 119–41.

– 1977. "Can Authentic Cultures Survive New Media?" *Journal of Communication* (Spring).

– and Paul F. Lazarsfeld. 1957. *Personal Influence: The Part Played by People in the Flow of Mass Communication*. New York: Free Press.

– and Paul F. Lazarsfeld. 1955. *Personal Influence*. New York: The Free Press.

Kenney, G.I. 1971. *Communications Study: Man in the North Project – Parts I and II*. Montreal: The Arctic Institute of North America.

King, J.C.H. and Henrietta Lidchi. 1998. *Imaging the Arctic*. Seattle: University of Washington Press.

Kingdon, John W. 1984. *Agendas, Alternatives, and Public Policies*. Boston: Little, Brown and Company.

Koebberling, Ursel. 1988. "The Application of Communication Technologies in Canada's Inuit Communities." Doctoral dissertation, Simon Fraser University.

– 1984. "Industrialization, Telecommunication and Broadcasting Development in the Western Arctic: Political-Economic and Socio-cultural Implications for the Inuit." MA thesis, Simon Fraser University.

Kroeber, Theodora. 1987. *Ishi in Two Worlds: A Biography of the Last Wild Indian in North America*. London: The Cresset Library.

Kroker, Arthur. 1984. *Technology and the Canadian Mind: Innis/McLuhan/Grant*. Montreal: New World Perspectives.

Kulchyski, Peter. 1993. "Anthropology in the Service of the State: Diamond Jenness and Canadian Indian Policy." *Journal of Canadian Studies/Revue d'études Canadiennes* 28, no. 2 (Summer): 21–50.

– 1989. "The Postmodern and the Paleolithic: Notes on Technology and Native Community in the Far North." *Canadian Journal of Political and Social Theory* 30, no. 3: 49–62.

Kumar, Keval J., 1988/89. "The Passing of Development Communication?" *Communication Research Trends* 9, no. 3: 10–11.

Kymlicka, Will and Wayne Norman. 1994. "Return of the Citizen: A Survey of Recent Work on Citizenship Theory." *Ethics* 104, no. 2 (January): 352–81.

Laba, Martin. 1988. "Popular Culture as Local Culture: Regions, Limits and Canadianism." *Communication Canada: Issues in Broadcasting and New Technologies*, eds R. Lorimer and D. Wilson, 82–101. Toronto: Kagan and Woo Limited.

Langton, Marcia. 1993. *"Well, I heard it on the radio and I saw it on the television ...": An Essay for the Australian Film Commission on the Politics and Aesthetics of Filmmaking by and about Aboriginal People and Things*. North Sydney: Australian Film Commission.

Lazar, Barry and Ross Perigoe. 1989. "Visible Minorities and Native Canadians in National Television News Programs." A Content Analysis Conducted in August and September, 1989. Montreal: Study Commissioned by the CBC.

Leong, Wai-Teng. 1989. "The Culture of the State: National Tourism and the State Manufacture of Cultures." *Communication For and Against Democracy*, eds M. Raboy and Peter A. Bruck. Montreal: Black Rose Books.

Lerner, Daniel. 1958. *The Passing of Traditional Society*. Glencoe: Free Press.

Lichtenberg, Judith, ed. 1990. *Democracy and the Mass Media*. Cambridge: Cambridge University Press.

Loftus, D.S. 1973. "Communications in the Canadian North." *Polar Record* 16, no. 104: 675–82.

Lougheed and Associates. 1986. *Report on the Native Communications Program and the Northern Native Broadcast Access Program*. Ottawa: Secretary of State.

Lorimer, Rowland M. and Donald C. Wilson, eds. 1988. *Communication Canada: Issues in Broadcasting and New Technologies*. Toronto: Kagan and Woo Limited.

MacBride, Sean. 1980. *Many Voices, One World*. Paris: Unipub.

MacKenzie, Scott. 1994. "Mad Priests and the Mimetic Faculty: Ethnographic Film, Post-Colonialism, and the (new) World Order." *Ciné Action: Radical Film Criticism and Theory*, no. 33: 12–22.

MacPherson Lorne W. and Wil Campbell. 1993. "A Proposal To Research and Implement the Creation of a Canadian Aboriginal Film and Video Production Fund and A Canadian Film and Video Delivery System as an economic Development Strategy." Unpublished Proposal.

Mahon, Rianne. 1977. "Canadian Public Policy: The Unequal Structure of Representation." *The Canadian State: Political Economy and Political Power*, ed. Leo Panitch. Toronto: University of Toronto Press.

Mancini, Paolo. 1991. "The Public Sphere and the Use of News in a 'Coalition' system of Government." *Communication and Citizenship: Journalism and the Public Sphere in the New Media Age*, eds Peter Dahlgren and Colin Sparks, 137–54. London: Routledge.

Mander, Gerry. 1991. "Television (a): Satellites and the Cloning of Cultures: The Case of the Dene Indians." *In the Absence of the Sacred: The Failure of Technology & the Survival of the Indian Nations*. San Francisco: Sierra Club Books.

Manual, George and Michael Posluns. 1974. *The Fourth World: An Indian Reality*. Don Mills: Collier-Macmillan Canada, Ltd.

Mattelart, Armand. 1983. *Transnationals and the Third World: The Struggle for Culture*. Massachusetts: Bergin & Garvey Publishers, Inc.

– et al. 1984. *International Image Markets: In Search of an Alternative Perspective*. London: Comedia Publishing Group.

– and Jean-Marie Piemme. 1979. "New Technologies, Decentralisation and Public Service." *Communication and Class Struggle, Volume 1: Capitalism, Imperialism*, eds A. Mattelart and S. Siegelaub. New York: International General.

Mayes, Robert G. 1972. *Mass Communication and Eskimo Adaptation in the Canadian Arctic*. M A thesis, McGill University Department of Geography.

McClintock, Anne. 1992. "The Angel of Progress: Pitfalls of the Term 'Post-Colonialism.'" *Social Text* 10, no. 31/32: 84–98.

McClure, John and Amir Mufti. 1992. "Introduction." *Social Text* 10, no. 31/32: 3–7.

McClymont, Ian. 1988. "Laurier and Arctic Sovereignty." *The Archivist* (September–October): 10–12.

McMaster, Gerald and Lee-Ann Martin, eds. 1992. *Indigena: Contemporary Native Perspectives*. Toronto: Douglas and McIntyre.

McNulty, Jean. 1988. "Technology and Nation-Building in Canadian Broadcasting." *Communication Canada: Issues in Broadcasting and New Technologies*, eds R. Lorimer and D. Wilson. Toronto: Kagan and Woo Limited: 176-98.

McPhail, Thomas L. 1987. *Electronic Colonialism: The Future of International Broadcasting and Communication*. Newbury Park: Sage Publication.

Meadows, Michael. 1996a. "Indigenous cultural diversity: Television Northern Canada." *Culture and Policy* 7, no. 1: 25–44.

– 1996b. "Making cultural connections: Indigenous media in Australia and Canada." *Australian-Canadian Studies Journal* 14, nos 1–2: 103–17.

– 1996c. "Reclaiming the public sphere: Indigenous journalism in Australia and Canada." *Australian Studies in Journalism*, no. 5: 61–81.

– 1994. "Reclaiming A Cultural Identity: Indigenous Media Production in Australia and Canada." *Continuum: The Australian Journal of Media and Culture* 8, no. 2.

– 1993a. "Voice blo mipla all ilan man: Torres Strait Islanders' struggle for television access." *Public Voices, Private Interests: Australia's Media*, eds J. Craik, J. James Bailey, and A. Moran. Allen & Unwin.

– 1993b. "Indigenous Media Responses to Racism." Paper delivered to Post Colonial Formations Conference (July 7–10), Griffith University, Nathan.

Melody, William H., Liora R. Salter, and Paul Heyer, eds. 1981. *Culture, Communication and Dependency: The Tradition of H.A. Innis*. New Jersey: Ablex Publishing Corporation.

Melucci, Alberto. 1989. *Nomads of the Present*. Philadelphia: Temple University Press.

Memmi, Albert. 1968. *Dominated Man – Notes Towards a Portrait*. Boston: Beacon Press.

– 1965. *The Colonizer and the Colonized*. Boston: Beacon Press.

Michaels, Eric. 1994a. *Bad Aboriginal Art: Tradition, Media, and Technological Horizons*. Minneapolis: University of Minnesota Press.

– 1994b. "Reclaiming A Cultural Identity: Indigenous Media Production in Australia and Canada." *Continuum: The Australian Journal of Media and Culture* 8, no. 2.

– 1986. *The Aboriginal Invention of Television in Central Australia: 1982–1986*. Canberra: Australian Institute of Aboriginal Studies.

Minh-ha, Trinh T. 1989. *Woman, Native, Other: Writing Postcoloniality and Feminism*. Bloomington: Indiana

Ministère des communications, Québec. 1985. *Présentation du Ministère des communications du Québec lors de l'audience publique du Conseil de la radiodiffusion et des télécommunications canadiennes sur l'examen de la radio communautaire*, April.

Mitchell, David, ed. 2000. *Canadian Journal of Communication* 25, no. 1 (Winter).

Molnar, Helen. 1990. "The Broadcasting for Remote Areas Community Scheme: Small vs Big Media." *Media Information Australia*, no. 58: 147–54.
– and Michael Meadows. 2001. *Songlines and Satellites: Indigenous Communication in Australia, the South Pacific and Canada.* Sydney: Pluto Press.
Morris, Jim. 1985. *Community Radio in Native Communities.* Ottawa: Secretary of State.
Morris, Peter. 1978. *Embattled Shadows: A History of Canadian Cinema – 1895–1939.* Montreal: McGill-Queen's University Press.
Multilingual Television, Ontario (Channel 47). 1985. *Response of Multilingual Television to CRTC Public Notice 1985–67 on Northern Native Broadcasting.* 24 May.
Murray, Catherine A. 1983. *Managing Diversity: Federal-Provincial Collaboration and the Committee on Extension of Services to Northern and Remote Communities.* Kingston: Queen's University.
National Aboriginal Communications Society (NACS). n.d. *Retrospective: Twenty Years of Aboriginal Communications in Canada.*
National Film Board of Canada. 1992. "Studio One Newsletter." (September). Edmonton: NFB.
– 1990. *Our Home and Native Land: A Film and Video Resource Guide for Aboriginal Canadians.* Winnipeg: NFB.
– 1979. *Outpost Library Film Catalogue.* NFB: Quebec Region.
Nelson, C. and L. Grossberg, eds. 1988. *Marxism and the Interpretation of Culture.* New York: Routledge.
Nisbet, Robert A. 1953. *The Quest for Community: A Study in the Ethics of Order and Freedom.* New York: Oxford University Press.
Northern Native Broadcasting, Yukon. 19 October 1998. *An Intervention of Conditional Support of Application 199804068 to the CRTC.* Whitehorse, Yukon.
– 1990. *Nedaa: Your Eye on the Yukon – Video Catalogue.* Whitehorse: NNBY.
– 1984. "Northern Native Broadcasting Audience Survey." Whitehorse: April.
Northern Quebec Inuit Association. 1974. *The Northerners.* Quebec: NQIA.
Nutaaq Média Inc. 1993. *Press Release.* 4 August.
Nyiri, Nicolas A. and Toivo Miljan, eds. 1980. *Unity in Diversity.* Waterloo: Wilfred Laurier University Press.
O'Brien, Rita Cruise. 1977. "Professionalism in Broadcasting in Developing Countries." *Journal of Communication* (Spring).
O'Connell, Sheldon. 1977. "Television and the Canadian Eskimo: The Human Perspective." *Journal of Communication* 27, no. 4: 140-4.
– 1974. "Television Impact on Eskimo People of Canada." MA thesis, Concordia University Department of Educational Technology.
O'Regan, Tom and Philip Batty. 1993. "An Aboriginal Television Culture: Issues, Strategies, Politics." *Australian Television Culture.* Sydney: Allen and Unwin.

Paine, Robert. 1977. *The White Arctic: Anthropological Essays on Tutelage and Ethnicity.* Institute of Social and Economic Research monograph, no. 7. St John's: Memorial University of Newfoundland.

– ed. 1971. *Patrons and Brokers in the Eastern Arctic.* Newfoundland Social and Economic Papers, no. 2. St John's: Memorial University of Newfoundland, Institute of Social and Economic Research.

Peers, Frank W. 1979. *The Public Eye: Television and the Politics of Canadian Broadcasting 1952–1968.* Toronto: University of Toronto Press.

PEN. 1991. "'Silencing Native Voices': International Law and the 1990/1991 Federal Budget's Restriction of Aboriginal Cultural Development." *A Report Prepared by the International Human Rights Programme (January).* Toronto: University of Toronto and The Canadian Centre, International PEN.

Pitseolak, Peter and Dorothy Eber. 1975. *People from Our Side.* Edmonton: Hurtig Publishers.

Pratt, Brian and Jo Boyden. 1985. *The Field Directors' Handbook: An OXFAM Manual for Development Workers.* Oxford: Oxford University Press.

Pross, A. Paul. 1986. *Group Politics and Public Policy.* Toronto: Oxford University Press.

Pye, Lucian W. 1963. *Communications and Political Development.* Princeton: Princeton University Press.

Raboy, Marc. 1990a. *Missed Opportunities: The Story of Canada's Broadcasting Policy.* Montreal: McGill-Queen's University Press.

– 1990b. "From Cultural Diversity to Social Equality: The Democratic Trials of Canadian Broadcasting." *Studies of Broadcasting* (Japan Broadcasting Corporation), no. 26: 7–41.

– 1987. "No Canadianization without Democratization: The Contradictions of National Policy-Making in the Shadow of the American Empire." Paper presented at CCA (May), Montreal.

Raudsepp, Enn. 1985. "Emergent Media: The Native Press in Canada." *Canadian Journal of Communication* 11, no. 2: 193–209.

Reid, A.A.L. 1978. "New Telecommunications Services and Their Social Implications." *Telecommunications in the 1980's and After,* eds B.I. Edelson and R.C. Davis. London: United Press Cambridge.

Reitz, Jeffrey G. 1980. *The Survival of Ethnic Groups.* Toronto: McGraw-Hill Ryerson Ltd.

Riggins, Stephen Harold. 1992. "The Media Imperative: Ethnic Minority Survival in the Age of Mass Communication." *Ethnic Minority Media: An International Perspective,* ed. Stephen Harold Riggins. London: Sage Publications.

Rogers, Everett M., ed. 1976. Communication and Development-Critical Perspectives. *Communication Research* 3, no. 2 (April).

- 1962. *Diffusion of Innovations.* New York: The Free Press.
- and D. Lawrence Kincaid. 1981. *Communication Networks: Toward a New Paradigm for Research.* New York: The Free Press.
- (with L. Svenning). 1969. *Modernisation among Peasants: The Impact of Communications.* New York: Rinehart and Winston.
Roncagliolo, Rafael. 1991. "Notes on 'The Alternative.'" *Video the Changing World,* eds Nancy Thede and Alain Ambrosi. Montreal: Black Rose Books.
Root, Deborah. 1993. "The Anxious LIBERAL: Natives and Non-Natives in Recent Movies." *Ciné Action,* no. 32 (Fall): 43–9.
Rostow, Walter. 1960. *The Stages of Economic Growth.* Cambridge: Cambridge University Press.
Roth, Lorna. 2000. "The Crossing of Borders and the Building of Bridges: Steps in the Construction of the Aboriginal Peoples Television Network in Canada." *Special Issue on Canadian Communications. Gazette International Journal of Communication Studies* 62, nos. 3–4: 251–69. London: Sage Publications.
- 1999. "How Comfortably Does the Internet Sit on Canada's Tundra? Reflections on Public Access to the Information Highway in the North." *Cyberidentities: Canadian & European Presence in Cyberspace,* ed. Leen d'Haenens, 83–97. Ottawa: University of Ottawa Press.
- 1998. "Television Broadcasting North of 60." *Images of Canadianness: Visions on Canada's Politics, Culture, Economics,* ed. Leen d'Haenens, 147–66. Ottawa: University of Ottawa Press – International Canadian Studies Series.
- 1994. *Northern Voices and Mediating Structures: The Emergence and Development of First Peoples' Television Broadcasting in the Canadian North.* Ph.D. dissertation. Montreal: Concordia University.
- 1992. "Media and the Commodification of Crisis." *Media, Crisis and Democracy: Mass Communication and the Disruption of Social Order,* eds Marc Raboy and Bernard Dagenais. London: Sage Publications.
- 1991. "The CBC Northern Service and the Federal Electoral Process: Problems and Strategies for Improvement." *Election Broadcasting in Canada,* ed. Fred Fletcher, vol. 21 of the Research Studies, Royal Commission on Electoral Reform and Party Financing. Toronto: Dundurn Press.
- 1990. *Summaries of Key Documents and Annotated Bibliography of Native Communications Research in Canada.* Ottawa: Department of Communications.
- 1983a. "The Role of Communication Projects and Inuit Participation in the Formation of a Communication Policy for the North." MA thesis, McGill University.
- 1983b. "Inuit Media Projects and Northern Communications Policy." Monograph on Northern Native Communications. Montreal, Concordia University.
- and Gail Valaskakis. 1989. "Aboriginal Broadcasting in Canada: A Case Study in Democratization." *Communication for and against Democracy,* eds Marc Raboy and Peter A. Bruck. Montreal: Black Rose Books.

Rotha, Paul (Jay Ruby, ed.) 1983. *Robert J. Flaherty: A Biography*. Philadephia: University of Pennsylvania Press.

Rothstein, Abraham. 1988. "The Use and Misuse of Economics in Cultural Policy." *Communication Canada: Issues in Broadcasting and New Technologies*, eds R. Lorimer and D. Wilson, 140–56. Toronto: Kagan and Woo Limited.

Rowlandson, John. 1988. *Aboriginal Community Radio in Canada: A Report on the National Native Community Radio Survey – Aboriginal Communications and Broadcast Program*. Commissioned by the Secretary of State. November.

Roxborough, Ian. 1983. *Theories of Underdevelopment*. Hong Kong: The MacMillan Press.

Sachs, Wolfgang, ed. 1992. *The Development Dictionary: A Guide to Knowledge as Power*. London: Zed Books.

Said, Edward W. 1979. *Orientalism*. New York: Vintage Books.

Salter, Liora. 1988. "Reconceptualizing Public Broadcasting." *Communication Canada: Issues in Broadcasting and New Technologies*, eds R. Lorimer and D. Wilson, 232–48. Toronto: Kagan and Woo Limited.

– 1981. "Public and Mass Media in Canada: Dialectics in Innis' Communication Analysis." *Culture, Communication and Dependency: The Tradition of H.A. Innis*, eds W.H. Melody et al. Norwood: Ablex.

– 1980. "Two Directions on a One-Way Street: Old and New Approaches to Media Analysis in Two Decades." *Studies in Communications* 1: 85–117.

Samovar, L. and R. Porter. 1976. *Intercultural Communication: A Reader*. California: Wadsworth Publishing Co., Inc.

Schiller, Herbert I. 1989. *Culture Inc.: The Corporate Takeover of Public Expression*. New York: Oxford University Press.

– 1978. *Communication and Cultural Domination*. White Plains: M.E. Sharpe Inc.

– 1969. *Mass Communications and American Empire*. Boston: Beacon Press.

Schramm, Wilbur. 1964. *Mass Media and National Development*. Paris: UNESCO.

Seaton, Elizabeth and Gail Valaskakis. 1984. *New Technologies and Native People in Northern Canada: An Annotated Bibliography of Communications Projects and Research*. Ottawa: UNESCO.

Servaes, Jan. 1990. "One World, Multiple Cultures: Participatory Research for Development Communication." Paper presented at ICA Conference (June), Dublin.

– 1986. "Communication and Development Paradigms: An Overview." *Media Asia* 13, no. 3.

Shields, Rob. 1991. "The True North Strong and Free." *Places on the Margin: Alternative Geographies of Modernity*. London: Routledge.

Shinar, Dov. 1996. "'Re-membering' and 'Dis-membering' Europe: A Cultural Strategy for Studying the Role of Communication in the Transformation of Collective Identities." *Globalization, Communication and Transnational Civil Society*, eds Sandra Brahman and Annabelle Sreberny-Mohammadi. Hampton Press.

– 1987. *Palestinian Voices: Communication and Nation Building in the West Bank.* Boulder: Lynne Rienner Publishers.

Shkilnyk, Anastasia M. 1985. *Canada's Aboriginal Languages: An Overview of Current Activities in Language Retention.* Ottawa: Secretary of State. October.

Shohat, Ella 1992. "Notes on the 'Post-Colonial.'" *Social Text* 10, no. 31/32: 99–113.

– and Robert Stam. 1994. *Unthinking Eurocentrism: Multiculturalism and the Media.* New York: Routledge.

Simeon, Richard. 1976. "Studying Public Policy." *Canadian Journal of Political Science/Revue Canadienne de Science Politique* 9, no. 4 (December): 548–80.

Smith, Anthony D. 1990. "Towards a Global Culture?" *Global Culture: Nationalism, Globalization and Modernity,* ed. Mike Featherstone, 171–92. London: Sage Publications.

Smith, Dorothy E. 1990. *The Conceptual Practices of Power: A Feminist Sociology of Knowledge.* Toronto: University of Toronto Press.

Smith, Greg and Associates. 1988. "Review of Native Broadcasting." A Study Commissioned by the CRTC. Ottawa: CRTC.

Smythe, Dallas W. 1981. *Dependency Road: Communications, Capitalism, Consciousness, and Canada.* Ablex: New Jersey.

Spitulnik, Debra. 1993. "Anthropology and Mass Media." *Annual Review of Anthropology* 22.

Spivak, Gayatri Chakravorty. 1988. "Can the Subaltern Speak?" *Marxism and the Interpretation of Culture,* eds Cary Nelson and Larry Grossberg. Chicago: University of Illinois Press.

Squires, Judith, ed. 1992. *New Formations: Special Edition on Hybridity,* no. 18 (Winter).

Stach, Erwin. 1970. "Communications in the North." *Canadian Communications Law Review* 2 (December): 145–76.

Stam, Robert. 1993. "From Stereotype to Discourse: Some Methodological Reflexions on Racism in the Media." *Ciné Action,* no. 32 (Fall): 10–29.

Statistics Canada. 1996. *First Peoples Population Data from the Census.* Ottawa

– 1992. *Catalogue 93-301 – A National Overview: Population and Dwelling Counts.* Ottawa, Minister of Industry, Science and Technology.

– 1991. *Aboriginal Origin Responses for Canada, Provinces and Territories, 1991 – 20% Sample Data.* Ottawa: Statistics Canada.

Stedman, Raymond William. 1982. *Shadows of the Indian: Stereotypes in American Culture.* Norman: University of Oklahoma Press.

Stiles, J. Mark & Associates. 1985. *Towards Employment Equity: A Native Recruitment and Training Strategy for CBC Northern Service.* Ottawa: CBC Northern Service.

Stiles, J. Mark and J. Lachance. 1988. *History and Present Status of Community Radio in Quebec.* Government of Ontario, Ministry of Culture and Communications.

Stiles, Mark and William Litwack. 1988. *Native Broadcasting in the North of Canada*. Ottawa: Canadian Commission for UNESCO-Report 54.

Stymeist, David H. 1975. *Ethnics and Indians: Social Relations in a Northwestern Ontario Town*. Toronto: Peter Martin Associates Ltd.

Tehranian, Majid. 1982. "Development Theory and Messianic Ideologies: Dependency, Communication and Democracy in the Third World." Paper presented at the International Association for Mass Communication Research (September 6–10), Paris.

– 1977. "Communications and National Development: Reflections on Theories and Policies." *Communications Policy for National Development: A Comparative Perspective*, eds Majid Teheranian, Farhad Hakimzadeh, and Marcello L. Vidale. London: Routledge & Kegan Paul.

Telesat Canada. 1980a. *Let's Get Together*. Pamphlet. Ottawa: Telesat Canada.

– 1980b. "Extension of Service to Northern and Remote Communities: Pay-Television and Canadian Broadcasting." Submission to the CRTC Hearing. 18 February.

– 1976. "Telesat Canada – The First Six Years: September, 1969–December, 1975." Ottawa: Telesat Information Department.

Television Northern Canada. March 1999. *North Link – TVNC Newsletter*. Ottawa.

– 30 October 1998. Replies to Interventions submitted with respect to an application by TVNC Inc. for a national aboriginal television network – Application #199804068. TVNC Letter to the CRTC. Ottawa.

– March 1998. *North Link – TVNC Newsletter*. Ottawa.

– 1 March 1993. *Response to CRTC Public Notice 1992-13*.

– 1992. *The Dawn of a New Era*. Publicity Pamphlet.

– 1987. *Television Northern Canada: A Proposal for a Shared Distribution Service in Northern Canada* (June).

Thede, Nancy and Alain Ambrosi, eds. *Video the Changing World*. Montreal: Black Rose Books.

Thomas, Lorraine. 1992. *Television Northern Canada: Audience Analysis and Scheduling Recommendations* (June 1).

Thorvaldson, Patricia. 1976. "The NFB Film Workshops." *Pot Pourri* (NFB newsletter), Spring: 2–8.

Ting-Toomey, Stella and Felipe Korzenny, eds. 1991. *Cross-Cultural Interpersonal Communication* (International and Intercultural Communication Annual 15). Newbury Park: Sage Publications, Inc.

Tomlinson, John. 1991. *Cultural Imperialism: A Critical Introduction*. Baltimore: The Johns Hopkins University Press.

Touraine, Alain 1981. *The Voice and the Eye*. Cambridge: Cambridge University Press.

Tremblay, Gaetan. 1990. "Communication and Cultural Identity." Paper presented at the International Communication Association Annual Conference (June), Dublin, Ireland.

Tuchman, Barbara W. 1981. *Practicing History: Selected Essays*. New York: Alfred A. Knopf.

Turner, Terence. 1992. "Defiant Images: The Kayappo Appropriation of Video." *Anthropology Today* 8, no. 6 (December): 5–16.

UNESCO. 1983. *Introduction to Intercultural Studies*. Paris: UNESCO.

– 1972. "A Guide to Satellite Communication." *Reports and Paper on Mass Communication*, no. 66. Paris: UNESCO Press.

Valaskakis, Gail. 1995. "The Role, Development and Future of Aboriginal Communications." Paper prepared for The Royal Commission on Aboriginal Peoples. Ottawa: Government of Canada.

– 1992a. "Broadcasting and Native Northerners." *Seeing Ourselves: Media Power and Policy in Canada*, eds Helen Holmes and David Taras, Toronto: Harcourt Brace Jovanovich Canada Inc.

– 1992b. "Communication, Culture, and Technology: Satellites and Northern Native Broadcasting in Canada." *Ethnic Minority Media: An International Perspective*, ed. Stephen Harold Riggins. London: Sage Publications.

– 1988. "Television and Cultural Integration: Implications for Native Communities in the Canadian North." *Communication Canada: Issues in Broadcasting and New Technologies*, eds R. Lorimer and D. Wilson, 124–38. Toronto: Kagan and Woo Limited.

– 1987. "Technology and Culture: Northern Native Broadcasting in Canada." Paper presented at Society for Applied Anthropology (April 8–12), Oaxaca, Mexico.

– 1981. "The Other Side of Empire: Contact and Communication in southern Baffin Island." *Culture, Communication and Dependency: The Tradition of H.A. Innis*, eds William H. Melody, Liora R. Salter, and Paul Heyer, 209–23. Norwood: Ablex Publishing Corporation.

– 1979. "A Communicational Analysis of Interaction Patterns: Southern Baffin Eastern Arctic." Doctoral dissertation, McGill University.

– 1976. "Media and Acculturation Patterns: Implications for Northern Native Communities." Unpublished paper.

– and Thomas Wilson. 1985. *The Inuit Broadcasting Corporation: A Survey of Viewing Behaviour and Audience Preferences Among the Inuit of Seven Communities in the Baffin and Keewatin Regions of the Northwest Territories*. Montreal: Concordia University.

–, Thomas Wilson, and Ron Robbins. 1981. *Evaluation of The Inukshuk Project*. Ottawa: Inuit Tapirisat of Canada.

Vallee, Frank G. 1967. *Kabloona and Eskimo in the Central Keewatin*. Ottawa: Canadian Research Centre for Anthropology, St Paul University.

Vancouver Art Gallery. 1980. *Robert Flaherty: Photographer/ Filmmaker. The Inuit 1910–1922*. Catalogue. Vancouver: The Vancouver Art Gallery.

Verhelst, Thierry G. 1990. *No Life without Roots: Culture and Development*. London: Zed Books.

Verner Bradford, Phillips and Harvey Blume. 1992. *Ota Benga: The Pygmy in the Zoo.* New York: Dell Publishing.

Walker, Morley. 4 September 1999. "Aboriginal TV Deserves Better Spot on Dial." *Winnipeg Free Press*: B-7.

Wallerstein, Immanuel, ed. 1975. *World Inequality: Origins and Perspectives on the World System.* Trans. Ferry de Kerckhove and Immanuel Wallerstein. Montreal: Black Rose Books.

Wartenberg, Thomas E. 1992. "Situated Social Power." *Rethinking Power*, ed. Thomas E. Wartenberg. Albany: State University of New York Press.

Waugh, Thomas, ed. 1984. *"Show Us Life": Toward a History and Aesthetics of the Committed Documentary.* Metuchen: Scarecrow Press.

Weaver, Sally. 1990. "A New Paradigm in Canadian Indian Policy for the 1990s." *Canadian Ethnic Studies/Etudes Ethniques au Canada* 22, no. 3: 8–18.

Weir, E. Austin. 1965. *The Struggle for National Broadcasting in Canada.* Toronto: McClelland and Stewart.

West, Cornel. 1993. "The New Cultural Politics of Difference." *The Cultural Studies Reader*, ed. Simon During. London: Routledge.

WETV. 12 November 1998. *Intervention Transcript from CRTC Hearing of Application 199804068 to the CRTC.*

Whitaker, Ben, ed. 1984. *Minorities: A Question of Human Rights?* Oxford: Pergamon Press.

Whiteduck Resources Inc. and Consilium. 2003. *Northern Native Broadcast Access Program (NNBAP) & Northern Distribution Program (NDP) Evaluation.* Final report. Prepared for Government of Canada, Department of Canadian Heritage.

Wilkinson, Kealy & Associates. 1988. *Community Radio in Ontario: A Dynamic Resource, An Uncertain Future.* Ontario: Ministry of Culture and Communications.

Williams, Frederick, Ronald E. Rice and Everett M. Rogers. 1988. *Research Methods and the New Media.* New York: The Free Press.

Williams, Raymond. 1977. *Marxism and Literature.* Oxford: Oxford University Press.

– 1961. *The Long Revolution.* Harmondsworth: Penguin Books Ltd.

Wilson, Clint C. II and Félix Gutiérrez. 1985. *Minorities and Media: Diversity and the End of Mass Communication.* Beverly Hills: Sage Publications.

Wilson, Thomas C. 1987. Ten Years of Satellite Television in the Eastern Arctic: Cultural Implications for the Diffusion of Educational Technology. Doctoral dissertation, Concordia University.

– 1981. "The Role of Television in the Eastern Arctic: An Educational Perspective." MA thesis, Concordia University.

Worth, Sol and John Adair. 1975. *Through Navajo Eyes: An Exploration in Film Communication and Anthropology.* Bloomington: Indiana University Press.

Yancey, William L., E.P. Ericksen, and R.N. Juliani. 1976. "Emergent Ethnicity: A Review and Reformulation." *American Sociological Review* 41, no. 3 (June): 391–402.

Young, Iris Marion. 1990. *Justice and the Politics of Difference*. Princeton: Princeton University Press.

Young, Oran R. 1992. *Arctic Politics: Conflict and Cooperation in the Circumpolar North*. Hanover: University Press of New England.

Young, Yun Kim, ed. 1986. *International and Intercultural Communication Annual* 10. Beverly Hills: Sage Publications Inc.

FILMS CITED

Blais, Gilles, under the ethnographic direction of Dr Asen Balikci. 1963–65. *Netsilik Eskimo*. NFB.

Tom Giles. 1972. *Journey through Rosebud*.

Bruce Beresford. 1991. *Black Robe*.

Flaherty, Robert. 1922. *Nanook of the North*. Revillon Frères.

Kaufman, Phillip. 1974. *The White Dawn*.

McKennirey, Michael and George Pearson. 1971. *People of the Seal – Eskimo Summer and Eskimo Winter*. NFB.

Michael, Mosha. 1975. *Natsik Hunting*.

Raymont, Peter. 1990. *Between Two Worlds*. NFB and Investigative Films Production.

– 1981. *Magic in the Sky*. NFB and Investigative Films Production.

– 1974. *Sikusilarmiut*. NFB.

– (Executive Producer) 1974. *Animation from Cape Dorset*. NFB.

Nicholas Ray. 1959. *Savage Innocents*.

Wilkinson, Doug. 1952. *Land of the Long Day*. NFB.

List of People Interviewed

Empirical research and observations for this book are based on interviews with the following people, though not all are quoted directly. Where names are cited more than once, it is because they worked for both of the organizations where I did interviewing at different times over the years.

ABORIGINAL PEOPLES TELEVISION NETWORK
Jim Compton
Dan David
Jennifer David
Jerry Giberson
Abe Tagaluk
Pat Tourigny

CBC AUDIENCE RESEARCH (OTTAWA)
Suzanne Reed
Phil Savage

CBC NEWSWORLD
Mike Harris
Maria Mironowicz
Cerry Wright

CBC, YUKON
Jim Boyd

CRTC
Pat Tourigny

INDEPENDENT SCHOLARS AND NORTHERN ACTIVISTS
Valerie Alia
Shannon Avison
Tom Axtell
Ron Blumer
Lyndsay Green
Nicole Matiation
Gail Valaskakis
Tom Wilson

INTERNATIONAL CIRCUMPOLAR CONFERENCE, OTTAWA
Corinne Gray

INUIT BROADCASTING INCORPORATED
Debbie Brisebois
Rosemarie Kuptana
Terry Rudden

JAMES BAY CREE COMMUNICATIONS SOCIETY
George Oblin
Diane Reid

NATIONAL FILM BOARD OF CANADA
Lyle Cruickshank, Media Research Department
Wolf Koenig, executive producer, Animation Studio
Gordon Martin, Media Research Department
Peter Raymont, executive producer

NNBY AUDIENCE VIEWERS/RESIDENTS
Shirley Adamson (Council for Yukon Indians)
Shawna B.
Carol Geddes
Louise Profeit-Leblanc
Jan Staple

NORTHERN NATIVE BROADCAST ACCESS PROGRAM
Robert Boulay
Art King
Terry Rudden
Florence Woolner

NORTHERN NATIVE BROADCASTING, YUKON
Mary Battaya
Rosemary Blair-Smith
Brenda Chambers
Bob Charlie
Frank Fry
Sam H.
George Henry
Joanne Henry
Ken Kane
Brian Levi
Charles Linklater
Gordon Loverin
Gloria Steels
Marion Telep
Lantry Vaughn

NUTAAQ MÉDIA INC.
George Hargrave

NWT GOVERNMENT (DEPARTMENT OF CULTURE AND COMMUNICATIONS)
Peter Crass
Dave Porter

OKALAKATIGET NATIVE COMMUNICATIONS SOCIETY
Fran Williams

TELEVISION NORTHERN CANADA
Jerry Giberson
Lorraine Thomas
Ken Todd

"WHY NOT?" PRODUCTIONS, TORONTO
Barbara Bardy
Jody Button

WORLD ASSOCIATION OF COMMUNITY RADIO BROADCASTERS (AMARC)
Bruce Girard

YUKON GOVERNMENT
Jeff Huston
Sylvia Neschokat
Rob Robbins
John Spicer

YUKON HUMAN RIGHTS COMMISSION
Reggie Newkirk

Index